EVALUATING SPORT AND ACTIVE LEISURE FOR YOUNG PEOPLE

Editors:

Kevin Hylton
Anne Flintoff
Jonathan Long

LSA

LSA Publication No. 88

Evaluating Sport and Active Leisure for Young People

First published in 2005 by
Leisure Studies Association
The Chelsea School
University of Brighton
Eastbourne BN20 7SP (UK)

A catalogue record for this book
is available from the British Library.

ISBN: 0 906337 99 2

Layout, cover and typesetting by Myrene L. McFee

Cover photograph:
Grateful thanks are expressed to Marcus Österberg
for permission to adapt his original photograph.

Printed in the UK by
Antony Rowe Ltd, Eastbourne

Contents

Editors' Introduction v

About the Contributors xii

I   Young People Today! Getting to Know Young People 1

Implications of Sen's Capability Approach for Research
    into Sport, Social Exclusion and Young People
        Naofumi Suzuki 3

Reflections on Researching the Ability of Sports Interventions
    to Reduce Youth Crime — The Hope of Scientific Realism
        Geoff Nichols 23

Evaluating Sports-based Inclusion Projects: Methodological
    Imperatives To Empower Marginalised Young People
        Jacquelyn Allen Collinson, Scott Fleming,
        John Hockey and Andy Pitchford 45

Impoverished Leisure Experiences: How Can Active Leisure
    Programmes Make a Difference?
        Fiona McCormack 61

II   Evaluating Policy and Practice 73

Evaluating Programme Impacts: Champion Coaching on
    Merseyside – pathways to opportunities?
        Barbara Bell 75

The Impact of School Sport Co-ordinators in Dundee:
    A Case Study
        Grant Small and Christine Nash 93

Outdoor Activities and the Development of Young People
    in Birmingham, UK
        Dave Hardy and Duncan Martin 109

Active Lifestyle, Physical Recreation and Health Outcomes
    of Youth in Two Contrasting Nova Scotian Communities
        Glyn Bissix, Darren Kruisselbrink, Liesel Carlsson,
        Peter MacIntyre and Tracey Hatcher 141

Young People, Physical Activity and Physical Fitness:
    A case study of Chinese and Portuguese Children
        Guoyong Wang, Beatriz Pereira and Jorge Mota 157

Beyond Picasso: Bringing Contemporary Modern Art
    into Schools and to Young People
        Doug Sandle 175

Other volumes from LSA Publications 203

Cover art:
Grateful thanks are expressed to Marcus Österberg
for permission to adapt his original photograph.

Evaluating Sport and Active Leisure for Young People

Benjamin Disraeli is reputed to have remarked that 'youth is a blunder'. Certainly media representations of young people's leisure lifestyles seem to dwell on the negative: obesity and mobile phones, truancy and trouble. Yet at the same time, although the populations of 'Western' capitalist societies are 'greying', advertisers 'sell youth' (even in advertising pensions) to make products attractive. Youth is further complicated for young people by parents who are loathe to relinquish the appellation 'young' and the trappings of youth. Perhaps we need to be alert to Bourdieu's (1993) reminder (following Hollingshead, 1949) that 'youth' is socially constructed. Like any classification it is a means of exerting power.

In the face of these kinds of opposition there is a need for leisure scholars to examine alternatives, addressing difference and commonality. Providing a forum for such considerations, the *Active Leisure and Young People* conference of the Leisure Studies Association, held at Leeds Metropolitan University in July 2004, identified several major themes including Policy and Provision; Engagement and Participation; Alienation and Subculture; Health, Risk and Environment; and Consumption. While many may have a narrow conception of what is entailed in 'active leisure' the conference themes encouraged a more expansive definition. For us, active leisure may certainly include physical activity in the shape of sport and physical education, but also embraces active involvement in the arts, tourism or outdoor activity.

The conference facilitated debate that not only examined the problems of youth, but also reviewed their positive contributions: not least through the voices of Leeds youngsters in the shape of the Leeds Young People's Parliament and the rapping of Leeds Young Authors.

From the papers offered we have produced three volumes. The companion publications focus on papers concerned with theory, policy and participation issues (Flintoff, Long and Hylton 2005); and review youth cultures, legislation and risk taking behaviour, the social construction of sexualised youth identities, and health issues and recreation for youth (Bramham and Caudwell, 2005). The papers in this volume focus on methodological issues and the evaluation of initiatives designed to engage young people in active leisure.

When consideration of young people enters leisure policy it seems most commonly to be because, in line with the observations at the start of this introduction, some aspect of them or their behaviour is perceived as a problem. While these concerns have to be addressed, several of the papers at the conference sought to highlight the 'positives'. These positives may occur not just in the practice of active leisure but also in the evaluation and understanding of the related experiences.

Prompted by the interest of the New Labour government in 'evidence based policy', there has been a substantial increase in the number of attempts to evaluate policy interventions in the UK (though a similar trend also seems evident in many other countries). More papers this year were derived from evaluation studies conducted on behalf of individual projects or the funding agencies. This has stimulated a renewed interest in methodological issues among leisure researchers — an interest reflected in the papers in this volume. Perhaps it was prompted by the focus on young people, but a stronger interest in ethical issues was also apparent.

The demands of conducting research with young people, the challenge of assessing success, and accountability to external bodies all encourage methodological review. However, research masquerading as consultation or evaluation might be a mask to avoid challenging the existing power base. For all the protestations about needing to understand not just what works but how and why, the strictures of evaluation are not necessarily the best route to understanding. These are studies conducted in the highly charged political world of competition for resources, where advocates are anxious for data, evidence and arguments to counter the 'big hitters' of, for example, the medical world, armed with their randomised control trials. Less than ideal they may be, but over long years people researching leisure have learned to live in the shadow of other more privileged policy areas.

The contributors to this volume were aware of the problems evaluation research has in producing unambiguous findings. Even if the structure of the evaluation research can be agreed, disputes over what should be measured often arise. But this sort of problem arises at all sorts of different levels: as Glyn Bissix suggested in his presentation, might it not be more appropriate to try to measure 'Gross National Quality of Life' instead of 'Gross National Product'?

Geddes and Rust (2001: p. 42) describe young people as having a 'local democracy deficit' due to their general disengagement, along with others in society, with their civic responsibilities. The Government's plans to get young people involved in the design, provision and evaluation of policies that affect them and services which they use is likely to tackle many of the issues identified by the National Youth Agency (2001), the Joseph Rowntree Foundation (2000) and other youth policy critics. These are issues that the Minister for Young People, John Denham (CYPU 2001) plans to focus on as one of the Government's major objectives. The CYPU (2001) offers evidence that including young people in the decisions that affect them accrues the type of benefits that can only help to satisfy the demands of young people.

Evaluation studies tend to be associated with a very instrumentalist view of leisure, tied to functionalist definitions. Leisure is valued for what it can achieve in satisfying other social policy goals, particularly associated with crime, health and education. Policymakers can be seen to be in search of interventions to 'plug the gaps'. There is, for example, a current vogue for 'social inclusion' being delivered through personal development opportunities created through these activities. A key role for researchers in these circumstances is not just to evaluate, but to inform policymakers' capacity to understand and relate to young people. However, we are mindful of arguments of social control advanced by writers like Bourdieu (1993: p. 125) and long recognised by leisure scholars:

> ... the English public schools saw sport as a means of filling in time, an economical way of occupying the adolescents ... When the pupils are on the sports field, they are easy to supervise, they are engaged in healthy activity, and they are venting their violence on each other rather than destroying the buildings or shouting down their teachers.

The papers here, and in the companion volumes, suggest a need to critique the hegemony of what is 'on offer'. The foundations of many policies and practices seem flawed, assuming everybody 'buys into' particular definitions of sport, physical education, the arts, tourism or outdoor activity. As these papers show, there are more alternatives. Even in evaluation studies it is at least as important to examine the processes and not just the products of these leisure activities. Even then, there is a danger that the research will reinforce established conceptions that offer opportunities to those already included rather than to the excluded. Any consideration of research methods and approaches to evaluation needs to be alert to diversity and difference in contemporary society.

Faced with the confusion between assessing social inclusion *in* sport (increasing participation among excluded groups) and social inclusion *through* sport (insofar as sport is thought to improve health, reduce crime, etc.), **Naofumi Suzuki** advocates Sen's (2000) 'capability' approach. This first paper in the volume focuses on capabilities to achieve the set of functions that represent a person's wellbeing. Following this line, societies become more inclusive the more capabilities they can provide. Hence the more freedom of choice there is in leisure, the more inclusive the society is. This means assessing whether an action increases alternatives for people and reduces constraints on their capabilities. But it is also important to examine who is benefiting. However, Suzuki believes the question should not be about the ability of a policy/project to deliver benefits, but its effectiveness in increasing the capability to benefit. He suggests that this implies a shift from measuring the outcomes to exploring the mechanisms necessary to produce those outcomes.

In the second paper, **Geoff Nichols**' response to the problems of matching the 'gold standard' of randomised control trials when evaluating the contribution of sport is to turn to scientific realism. Nichols argues that this emphasises not just whether a project is successful, but why it has been so. He uses his research on two initiatives designed to use sport to reduce young people's involvement in crime in order to demonstrate how this can be done. This requires researchers and professionals to be precise in specifying the underlying theories of change they are working with. However, as he recognises, he is still left with the problem of deciding when the evidence that has been gathered is sufficient to support, or require a change in, the relationships proposed by the theory of change that has been developed. He does not want research to be a separate exercise, and suggests that policymakers are central in determining the validity of the evidence available.

Jacquelyn Collinson *et al.* take this a step further in enthusiastically promoting the use of participatory evaluation in which the various stakeholders are not just providers of data but are centrally involved in the research process. Quite apart from overcoming some of the ethical problems of doing evaluations 'on' people, it also lessens the methodological challenge that suggests it is impossible to understand the experience without 'having' the experience. As academic researchers cannot be young people, this collaborative approach incorporates young people and allows the effectiveness of the initiative to be assessed from the inside. The goal for the authors is not just understanding, but to change things for the better via action.

Fiona McCormack advocates the use of life history profiles, not just as a research tool but as an aid to leisure counseling. She found that not only are they ideal for identifying the relationship between life events and participation in leisure activity, but the life history chart provides a starting-point for the process of leisure education. This, McCormack argues, can help participants make connections to other life events such as truanting, moving home or school exclusion, so that they can re-evaluate previous assessments that participation stopped because of personal inability or dislike for the activity.

Barbara Bell considers what could be seen as the 'Holy Grail' of sports development for practitioners and policymakers. Bell considers the challenge set out by the Wolfenden Report (1960) that emphasised the gap between young people, school and the community. She goes on to evaluate the success of the Champion Coaching initiative in Merseyside and consequently to challenge sports development professionals to generate better quality data if they intend to make progress amongst social groups that have been difficult to include. Schools are viewed here as sites of intense contradiction, for at the same time as having a captive youth market the quality of provision in schools is constrained by the availability of trained and experienced staff, reliable and robust data, exit routes into community groups/clubs and finally, a clear understanding of 'what works'for young people.

Dave Hardy is confident that he has a good comprehension of 'what works' for young people as he urges outdoor adventure practitioners to start from what young people *want* to know. That is, a clear view of the everyday setting of young people is likely to mitigate participant recreancy from insensitively devised programmes. Hardy seeks to shift the discourse of 'treatment of at-risk' young people to one that understands further their ecological settings and experiences. Changes in behaviour are then more likely to include a range of techniques that consider the 'whole person' rather than 'course members'.

This leaning away from a positivist paradigm is one advocated by **Grant Small and Christine Nash** in their analysis of School Sport Coordinators in Scotland. They are keen to emphasise the need to accept that although we can encourage many to participate in active sport and leisure there are still many who have limitations. Their use of a *Sport Commitment* model considers psychological processes that can limit or enhance the ability of young people to start and maintain regular activity. Young people are clearly viewed as heterogeneous here and as a result the outcome of such a study should lead to more informed policy developments for young people and their active sport and leisure. In addition, Small and Nash outline the policy tensions implicit within the Dundee school sport system and the local-national conflicts around policies, funding and structures. The authors' insights into these very real organisational problems illuminate the fragmentation of active sport and leisure development in the UK that has been a constant source of rancour amongst those charged with implementing national policies at a local level; such discord and fragmentation continues to widen the gap raised by Wolfenden raised all those years ago.

Doug Sandle identifies a range of initiatives directed towards arts education for young people within and beyond school [cf. the sports initiatives referred to by Small and Nash, this volume, and Binks & Snape in the companion volume (Flintoff *et al.*, 2005)]. Evaluating the perceptions of young people studying art at school, aged 14 and 15, he is unsure whether to be pleased or alarmed that 43% had visited an art gallery/exhibition (57% had not!). Reading his data we are once again reminded of the gender distinctions evident in education. On the basis of his evidence Sandle is optimistic that there is a culture of change that will allow young people to benefit from the individual, social and cultural development that can come from engaging with modern art, but cautions that creative practice should not be neglected because of a preoccupation with cultural consumption.

Glyn Bissix *et al.* consider how lifestyle differences in rural and urban populations of Canada contribute to active leisure and self-perceptions of well-being. Common conceptions of rural and urban environments emphasise the qualities of the rural over the urban especially in relation to community safety and identification, and the (dis)advantages of services and facilities/ transport being at a premium. The significance of studies like this is that they challenge stereotypes of 'imagined communities' and force policymakers to look more rigorously at the demography and ecology of rural and urban settings in relation to active sport and leisure.

Finally, **Guo Yong Wang** considers a study that policymakers on a global scale are concentrating on. Wang offers insight into active leisure as his comparative study in Portugal and China juxtaposes PE and extra-curricular participation amongst school children. If the hyperbole in academic and

policy arenas is to be believed, we are in the middle of an obesity epidemic
that threatens our health and well-being. Wong presents data that suggests
that although physical educators and policymakers do have grounds for
concern their implementation structures are less robust than the rhetoric,
and need to catch up.

References

Bourdieu, P. (1993; first published in French, 1984) *Sociology in question*. London,
    Sage.
Bramham, P. and Caudwell, J. (eds) (2005) *Sport, active leisure and youth cultures*
    (LSA Publications No. 86). Eastbourne: Leisure Studies Association.
Children and Young Person's Unit (CYPU) (2001) Government's Response
    to the UK Youth Parliament's 2001 Manifesto, Annex A, http://
    www.cypu.gov.uk/corporate/downloads/manifestoresponse.doc
Flintoff, A., Long, J. & Hylton, K. (eds) (2005) *Youth sport and active leisure:
    Theory, policy and practice* (LSA Publication No. 87). Eastbourne: Leisure
    Studies Association.
Geddes, M. and Rust, M. (2001) 'Catching them young? Local initiatives to
    involve young people in local government democracy', *Youth and Policy*,
    No. 69: pp. 42–61.
Hollingshead, A. (1949) *Elmtown's youth: The impact of social classes on adolescents*.
    New York: John Wiley & Sons.
JRF (2000) *Social care in rural areas: Developing an agenda for research, policy
    and practice*. York: Joseph Rowntree Foundation.
NYA Working Group (2001) *Young people as citizens now: Towards more inclusive
    and coherent policies for young people*. Leicester: Youth Work Press.
Sen, A. (1992) *Inequality re-examined*. Oxford: Clarendon Press.
Wolfenden Committee (1960) *Sport and the community*. London: CCPR.

Kevin Hylton, Anne Flintoff and Jonathan Long
Leeds Metropolitan University
February 2005

About the Contributors

Jacquelyn Allen Collinson worked at the Universities of Lancaster and the West of England, prior to joining the University of Gloucestershire, where she currently works as a Research Fellow in the School of Sport and Leisure. Recent publications include work on doctoral education; occupational and leisure identities; the sociology and phenomenology of the sporting body; ethnomethodological analysis of physical activity; and most recently a collaborative autoethnographic study examining the impact of sporting injuries upon the identities of middle/long-distance runners.

Barbara Bell is currently lecturing in sport and leisure management at Edge Hill College. Previously she was the Field Leader for Sports Studies at Warrington Collegiate Institute and had worked in the management of community sport and recreation for ten years. Her main research interests are in Youth Sport policy and the development of evaluation methods, particularly where they involve the development of personal and or social capital. Her recently completed PhD was on the impacts of the Champion Coaching Scheme and current projects include an evaluation of the Euro 2005 Womens' Football Championships on local sport and the legacy of the event.

Glyn Bissix is professor and acting director of the School of Recreation Management and Kinesiology, Acadia University. He recently co-authored the text: Integrated Resource and Environmental Management: the human dimension with Alan Ewert, Indiana University, USA and Doug Baker, Queensland University of Technology, Australia published by CABI. His teaching and research focuses on outdoor recreation and the environment as well as community health and lifestyle issues. Other current publications are concerned with forest recreation and the political economy of multi-agency ecosystem management. Recent consultation assignments include Rapid Management Assessment of Protected Areas in Belize, Central America, Nature Based Tourism in Labrador, and the Genuine Progress Index.

Liesel Carlsson is a recent graduate of Acadia University where she completed a degree in Nutrition with Honours (BSNH). Within the field of nutrition, her main interests lie in community based programming, culture, food and the interactions there within. Her thesis research focused on culturally influenced factors such as diet and lifestyle, and their relationship with osteoporosis awareness, health beliefs and practices among the Korean immigrant population in Halifax, Nova Scotia. This work was published in the Journal of Immigrant Health. Currently she works as a research assistant for Drs. Bissix and MacIntyre on the Genuine Progress Index community health surveys, producing reports on topics such as youth smoking, employment and health, and physical activity and health.

Scott Fleming is with the School of Sport and Leisure at the University of Gloucestershire, and is the current Chair of the Leisure Studies Association. He has conducted research concerned with 'race' and ethnicity, sport and leisure cultures, and corporate governance. He is co-editor of *Ethics, Sport and Leisure: Crises and Critiques* (with Alan Tomlinson, 1997), and also of LSA volumes entitled *Policy and Politics in Sport, Physical Education and Leisure* (with Margaret Talbot and Alan Tomlinson, 1995); *Masculinities: Leisure Identities, Cultures and Consumption* (with John Horne, 2000); and *New Leisure Environments: Media, Technology and Sport* (with Ian Jones, 2002).

Anne Flintoff is Reader in Physical Education and Education Development in the Carnegie Faculty of Sport and Education at Leeds Metropolitan University. She is part of the Gender, Race and Equity Research Group and teaches on undergraduate and post graduate pathways in the sociology of PE and sport. Her major research interests include gender and physical education; contemporary youth sport policy; young people and active lifestyles; PE teacher education; gender and education; feminist theory and sport. She has published widely in PE and sport studies, and is a member of the Editorial Board of *Physical Education and Sport Pedagogy*.

Dave Hardy is Senior Lecturer in the Centre for Outdoor and Environmental Education at Liverpool John Moores University where he teaches on undergraduate and postgraduate programmes. He is a technical advisor under the terms of the Adventure Activity Licensing Authority. His research interests include: the role of outdoor and adventure activities in the development of young people and the use of experiential strategies in teaching in higher education. His publications include the practice and teaching of adventure sports, rationalization and risk in mountaineering and the evaluation of outdoor programmes.

Tracey Hatcher is a research assistant working on the Glace Bay, Kings County GPI project. Tracey has a Bachelor of Arts from the Cape Breton University with honors in Psychology. Her thesis analyzed the role of zero sum beliefs in an economically depressed area on attitudes toward immigration. Tracey plans to enter a masters program specializing in School Psychology.

John Hockey is a Research Fellow in the School of Education, University of Gloucestershire. He has carried out sociological research on doctoral education, occupations and sport, using both ethnographic and autoethnographic approaches . His current research focuses upon the phenomenology of sport and leisure experiences and the mundane knowledge held by participants.

Kevin Hylton is a Senior Lecturer in the Carnegie Faculty of Sport and Education at Leeds Metropolitan University. He teaches sociology and community studies on the Sport and Recreation Development BA (Hons) and is the course leader for the MA in Sport, Leisure and Equity. Kevin conducts research and consultancies for the Carnegie Research Institute especially in the areas of 'race' and racism in sport. Kevin is co-editor of *Sports Development: Policy, Process and Practice*, London, Routledge.

Darren Kruisselbrink is an assistant professor in the School of Recreation Management and Kinesiology at Acadia University. Among his research interests are the psychological factors that influence and are influenced by physical activity. He has recently published an article on the effects of social context on physique anxiety in the Journal of Sport & Exercise Psychology. Emphasis on community health and lifestyle issues are central themes in the delivery of courses related to the psychology of physical activity, and perceptual motor development. He is the director of the popular Acadia Kinderskills motor development program, which pairs students with preschool children to foster neuro-motor and social development through play. His interest in improving health and well-being has also recently led him to collaborate with local orthopaedic surgeons to examine the role mental imagery may play in rehabilitation from total knee replacement.

Jonathan Long was previously Research Director at the Centre for Leisure Research and the Tourism and Recreation Research Unit. Now a professor in the Carnegie Research Institute, he continues to conduct projects for external clients. Recent research has included various works on social inclusion and the benefits of sport and the arts and a suite of projects on racism in sport. He is currently working on the national evaluation of the Local Exercise Action Pilots. Jonathan has been a member of LSA since 1976; a former member of the Executive, Newsletter Editor and conference organiser. He was also on the editorial board of *Leisure Studies* (the Journal of the Leisure Studies Association) for 15 years, at various times acting as editor and book reviews editor.

Duncan Martin is Senior Lecturer in Outdoor and Environmental Education and programme manager for the MA in Outdoor Education at Liverpool John Moores University where he teaches on undergraduate and postgraduate programmes. His main research interests are: outdoor programme evaluation, and environmental education. He has evaluated local, national and international outdoor programmes and although the focus of this work is generally qualitative, he has moved to a more eclectic approach to the use of evaluation frameworks. He is heavily involved in research in Earth Education through his PhD. and through the Institute for Earth Education. Consequently, his publications reflect this broad research interest.

Fiona McCormack originally worked in adventure activity programmes targeted at young people from deprived communities who were commonly at risk of offending. Having completed the MSc. in Recreation Management at Loughborough University (1989–90) she moved to a staff training role in the leisure and tourism industry in Europe. She embarked on a lecturing career in higher education in 1993, joining Buckinghamshire Chilterns University College. As part of a PhD at Loughborough University she conducted two medium term evaluations of sports related projects which targeted young people at risk. Both were qualitative studies of the relationship between leisure patterns, offending and interventions that seek to use recreation to reduce offending. She is currently lecturing in the areas of Youth and Community Sports Development and Outdoor Education and Adventure Recreation.

Jorge Mota is a full professor and director in the Research Centre in Physical Activity and Leisure, University of Porto, Portugal. His main research areas are leisure physical activity and health, obesity research and etc. (E-mail: jmota@fcdef.up.pt)Key publications include Mota, J., Santos, P., Guerra, S., Ribeiro, J.C., Duarte, J.A. & Sallis, J.F. (2002) 'Validation of a Physical Activity Self-Report Questionnaire in a Portuguese Pediatric Population', *Pediatric Exercise Science* 14 (3): pp. 269–276; Mota, J. & Esculcas, C.(2002) 'Leisure-time physical activity behavior: structured and unstructured choices according to sex, age, and level of physical activity', *International Journal of Behavioral Medecine* 9 (2): pp. 111–121; Mota, J., Guerra, S., Ribeiro, J.C., Pinto, A., Leandro, C. & Duarte, J.A. (2002) 'The association of maturation, sex and body fat in cardiorespiratory fitness'. *American Journal of Human Biology* 14 (6): pp. 707–712.

Peter MacIntyre is a professor of psychology at the Cape Breton University in Sydney, Nova Scotia, Canada. Peter completed his PhD. at the University of Western Ontario in 1992 and went on to a two-year post doctoral fellowship at the University of Ottawa. He has held numerous research grants and published over 50 articles and chapters on topics including communication, second language learning, and stereotyping. Peter's community-based research, in association with GPI Atlantic and other partners, has focused on the integration of research on health, employment, volunteerism, core values, and other facets of community life.

Christine Nash, currently programme tutor for BSc (Hons) Sport Coaching and Development at University of Abertay Dundee. Research interests include coach education and the development of expertise in sport. Current research has involved reflective practice in coaching and comparative football studies.

Geoff Nichols is a lecturer in the Leisure Management Division of Sheffield University Management School. He has published widely on the relationship between sports programmes and a reduction in youth crime, and has recently completing a PhD on this topic. His other major research interest is volunteers in sport.

Beatriz Pereira is an associate professor and vice president in the Institute of Child Studies, University of Minho, Portugal. Her main resarch areas are playground, bullying, children's leisure physical activity, and health. (E-mail: beatriz@iec.uminho.pt) Key publications include: Pereira, B. (2004) 'Bullying in Schools in the North of Portugal: What we know about children' in Rhonda L. Clements and Leah Fiorentino The Child's Right to Play: A global Approach. Rhonda Clements and Leah Fiorentino (Editors). Praeger, pp. 145–152; Pereira, B., Mendonéa, D., Neto, C., Valente, L. & Smith, P. K. (2004) 'Bullying in Portuguese schools', *School Psychology International* 25 (2): pp. 207–222; Pereira, B. (2004)' Children's Playground Accessibility in the North of Portugal', *World Leisure Journal* 46 (1): pp. 38-45.

Andy Pitchford was formerly a Sports Development Officer in the London Borough of Bromley, and has an MA Leisure Management from the University of Sheffield and a PhD from the University of Gloucestershire. He has an academic background in sociology and politics, and teaches on social science, management and vocational modules on a variety of programmes and courses. His research interests relate to the sociology of work and leisure, careers in higher education, community sports development and association football. His recent work includes a five-year project funded by the Football Association, looking at child protection in football.

Doug Sandle is a chartered psychologist and Reader in Visual Studies at The Leeds School of Contemporary Art and Graphic Design, Leeds Metropolitan University. He was founding Chair of Axis, the national information service for contemporary visual art, has research interests in visual art and culture and is a founding partner of the public art consultancy, RKL. He has contributed chapters on aspects of visual culture to other books including one on public art to the LSA volume, *Leisure, Media and Visual Culture: Representations and Contestations* (2004, LSA Publication No. 84). In past times, Doug has been a published poet and a broadcast playwright.

Grant Small is currently a Graduate Assistant in the Division of Sport and Leisure at the University of Abertay Dundee. Current research interests include qualifications and professional practice within the leisure industry and the loco parentis role of elite level sports coaches.

Naofumi Suzuki is currently a PhD student at the Department of Urban Studies, University of Glasgow. His PhD research looks at the role of sport in the regeneration of deprived urban neighbourhoods, with a particular focus on the processes through which sport-related youth services prompt social inclusion.

GuoYong Wang was an associate Professor in Shanghai's University and had 14 years experience of teaching physical education in University in China. Dr. Wang got his Ph.D. degree in Institute of Child Studies, University of Minho, Portugal, His doctoral research is on children's physical activity and health: Effects of school aerobic exercise on children's health-related physical fitness. Key publications are: Wang, G.Y., Pereira, B. & Mota, J. (2004) 'Indoor physical education measured by heart rate monitor: A case study in Portugal', *Journal of Sports Medicine and Physical Fitness* (44); Wang, G.Y., Pereira, B. & Mota, J.(2003) 'Reinforce health-related education early in school: Results of a randomized trial in Portugal', *Journal of Physical Education & Recreation (Hong Kong)*Vol. 9, No. 2; Wang, G.Y., Shen, Y. & Cai, Y.M. (2001) *Handbook of Fitness and Aerobics* (in Chinese), Shanghai Financial University Publishing Company.

I

YOUNG PEOPLE TODAY!
GETTING TO KNOW
YOUNG PEOPLE

IMPLICATIONS OF SEN'S CAPABILITY APPROACH FOR RESEARCH INTO SPORT, SOCIAL EXCLUSION AND YOUNG PEOPLE

A methodological consideration on evaluation of sport-related programmes targeted at young people in deprived urban neighbourhoods

Naofumi Suzuki

Department of Urban Studies, University of Glasgow

Introduction

'Social exclusion' is at the heart of the current urban regeneration policy in the United Kingdom (UK). While the traditional focus was on economic regeneration, since the 1990s it has shifted to more social and community issues, and New Labour regards social exclusion as the central issue in their National Strategy for Neighbourhood Renewal (Social Exclusion Unit (SEU), 1998, 2001). The concept came into the discourse of sport policy when the report to the Social Exclusion Unit by the Policy Action Team 10 (PAT 10) clearly stated that arts and sport could contribute to neighbourhood renewal by improving communities' performance in health, crime, employment and education (Department for Culture, Media and Sport [DCMS], 1999). Subsequently the sport councils have designated 'tackling social exclusion' as one of their main policy objectives (Sport England, 1999, 2001; sportscotland, 2003b, c). Meanwhile, some new streams of funding have become available for community-level sporting programmes. This new trend is characterised by its connection to mainstream regeneration initiatives: sport organisations being part of the strategic partners in the'joined-up' approach to area-based urban regeneration (SEU, 1998). Examples of such new initiatives include Sport Action Zones in England and the New Opportunities Fund at UK level. In Scotland, the National Lottery Fund is distributed by sportscotland to a number of sport-related programmes through the Social Inclusion Partnerships (sportscotland, 2003a).

Of the various recipients of funding, young people tend to be a far more popular target group than any other age group. This tendency could be attributed to several factors. On the one hand, young people are one of the main issues in the government strategy of tackling social exclusion (SEU, 2000). Young people in deprived urban neighbourhoods are regarded as being at risk from a wide range of problems, such as underachievement in education and employment as well as criminal and anti-social behaviour. Moreover, targeting young people may be both economically and morally right considering the potential that could be realised if they are given appropriate support and resources. On the other hand, sport, as well as arts and other forms of leisure, is thought to be what young people are most interested in and therefore an effective tool to 'hook' them. Furthermore, sport has long been believed to have positive effects on such problems as low self-esteem and delinquency, which are supposed to be the underlying factors in the above problems.

Indeed, it is a worthwhile investment if the expected benefits of sport participation to young people and communities are truly realised. However, proper monitoring and assessment are often lacking due to technical difficulties and lack of resources (Coalter *et al.*, 2000). As a result, many programmes attribute their 'success' to the increased number of participants that they have engaged, assuming implicitly that participation automatically entails benefits. In short, what matters most in the policy and practice of sport and social exclusion is that the participation of sport is uncritically appreciated in the name of social inclusion without clear evidence of its positive outcomes to the participants as well as to communities. The underlying reasons for this view are partly that participation in sport itself is thought to be so valuable, and partly that positive outcomes flowing from it are automatically presumed. This is not necessarily true.

Recently, however, more systematic evaluation research of sport-related regeneration programmes has started to be collected (e.g., Collins *et al.*, 1999; Institute of Leisure and Amenity Management, 1999; Brackenridge *et al.*, 2000; Coalter *et al.*, 2000; Coalter, 2001, 2002; DCMS, 2001; McPherson *et al.*, 2001; Long *et al.*, 2002; Collins and Kay, 2003; Bailey, 2003; Ibbetson *et al.*, 2003; and Snape *et al.*, 2003). Roughly speaking, most of the research can be classified into one of two types: one is concerned with unequal participation in sports, and the other is concerned with the individual and collective benefits of sport participation. Coalter (2002) formulates this distinction as *sporting* inclusion and *social* inclusion. Although both approaches could be fruitful and may be necessary, the existing literature does not seem to satisfy the potential of introducing the concept of social exclusion into the research in sport and young people. Firstly, the 'sporting inclusion' perspective tends to assume, rather simplistically, that inequality in sport participation means social exclusion and, therefore, that promoting the participation of less involved groups is regarded as 'social' inclusion (Coalter, 2000). However, this view overlooks the fact that participation in sports is primarily a matter of choice and that, equally, everybody is entitled *not* to participate. On the other hand, the latter group of studies, the 'social inclusion *through* sport' perspective, is basically similar to the traditional discussion regarding the social benefits of sports and it fails to offer additional theoretical advancement, which could be prompted by introducing the idea of social exclusion. Most of the research tries to assess the outcome of sport-related programmes in terms of the policy indicators: health, education, employment and crime. Of course, these attempts at empirical evaluation are worthwhile practices, and it is not intended, here, to criticise them. On the contrary, it is meant to suggest a possible way of developing research.

The primary aim of this paper is to develop a proper strategy to evaluate community regeneration programmes using sport. More specifically, the focus is on social inclusion through sport. However, the 'sporting inclusion' perspective is also relevant since, in the context of sport policy, the term 'social exclusion/inclusion' always denotes both meanings. Thus, the purpose of this paper is twofold. Firstly it tries to clarify the distinction between social inclusion *in* and *through* sport approaches. Then it proposes evaluation strategies appropriate for each of them. In pursuit of these objects, Amartya Sen's capability approach plays the key role. The next section reviews the nature of the emerging literature of sport and social exclusion, and the confusion involved, in more detail. Then, the relevance of Sen's capability approach to sport and social exclusion is examined. Finally, this paper will demonstrate that the notion of capability can not only resolve the confusion between social inclusion in and through sport, but also offers significant implications for research methodologies.

Sport and social exclusion: theoretical confusion and practical problems

As briefly explained above, when social exclusion is discussed in the context of sport, there are two basic themes. One is concerned with unequal participation in sports, often of disadvantaged social groups, such as women, the poor, unemployed and disabled people, and minority ethnic groups, all of them being regarded as the 'socially excluded'. The central concern of this perspective is how to involve under-participating — often disadvantaged — groups into sporting activities. Its common approach is to regard unequal participation in certain activities as the evidence of social exclusion, and try to identify the constraints that prohibit the involvement of under-participating groups. Examples include inequalities with regard to gender (Kay, 2003), minority ethnic groups (Scott Porter Research and Marketing Ltd., 2001a), disability (Scott Porter Research and Marketing Ltd., 2001b), and income poverty (Collins, 2003).

The other theme regards the benefits that are expected to accrue to individuals and communities through participation in sporting activities, which leads to the alleviation of social exclusion in a wider sense. This type of research assesses the ability of sport to contribute to combating social exclusion, mainly in terms of the policy indicators presented by the PAT 10 report. That is to say, the typical research questions would be: "how healthy do people become by doing sports and physical activities?"; "to what extent does sport reduce crime and anti-social behaviour?"; "does sport create employment?"; "does sport participation have positive influences on educational performance?" and so on. Examples of this type of research include Coalter *et al.* (2000), Long *et al.* (2002), and Bailey (2003), *inter alia*.

These two approaches are principally different perspectives, in that the former pursues social inclusion *in* sport, and the latter *through* sport. Coalter (2002) calls them *sporting inclusion* (i.e. the development of sport in communities) and *social inclusion* (i.e. the development of communities through sport) perspectives respectively. In fact, both themes are not particularly new in the realm of sport policy. They were already quite popular in discussions about sport development before the emergence of the term 'social exclusion' (e.g., Pack and Glyptis, 1989; Department of the Environment, 1989; Lyons, 1990; Robins, 1990; Coalter and Allison, 1996; Utting, 1996; Bovaird *et al.*, 1997; Metcalfe, 1998; Arthur and Finch, 1999; Taylor *et al.*, 1999; and Houlihan and White, 2002). However, the new fashionable concept has not simply fuelled these areas of research in terms of quantity, owing to the fact that it connects sport to the mainstream social policy. On the contrary, the new literature seems to involve some confusion and ambiguity, due to the fact that the inherently different perspectives are compounded under the banner of social exclusion.

One source of confusion is the shared attitude observed in the sporting inclusion perspective, which sees simply promoting inclusion of under-participating groups into sporting activities as 'social' inclusion. One rationale of this view is that participation in sports is part of 'social citizenship rights', the denial of which are seen as social exclusion (Lister, 1990). Coalter (2000) observes that this tendency is generally seen in leisure studies under what he calls the 'normative citizenship paradigm', where opportunities for leisure are seen as social citizenship rights, which should be provided by the public sector, and inequality in participation is blamed for being inequitable (Coalter, 1998). He criticises the way that this paradigm has accepted the term in that it seems "to regard 'social exclusion' simply as a synonym for inequality and to take the simple absence of certain groups from public sector leisure facilities as evidence of 'exclusion'" (Coalter, 2000: p. 174). He argues that regarding inequality in outcome as social exclusion and, thus, increased participation by under-participating groups as social inclusion is too simplistic given the complex nature of the concept.

Moreover, as far as sport is concerned, there is another rationale to justify increased participation of the 'socially excluded' as 'social' inclusion. It is the very fact that sport is believed to produce a range of benefits to individuals and communities, which contribute to tackling social exclusion. Taking the example of gender inequality, Kay (2003: p. 105) argues that promoting women's participation matters because "women individually can derive as significant benefits from participation in sport as can men. [...] Women who are involved in sport report positive changes in self-esteem and sense of 'self', and increased physical power and well-being". However, the evidence of such benefits is often anecdotal, while systematic investigations are lacking (Long *et al.*, 2002).

Therefore, it is partly the task of the second approach, which deals with 'social inclusion *through* sport', to resolve the confusion between sporting and social inclusion. However, it has not succeeded in providing conclusive evidence. Much evaluation research has tried to measure, whether quantitative or qualitative, the extent of the outcome produced by sport-related programmes in terms of the indicators considered as elements of social exclusion, but conclusions are often inconsistent (Coalter *et al.*, 2000; Long *et al.*, 2002). In addition, the lack of positive observable evidence in terms of the expected benefits is sometimes compensated by the appreciation of the value of participation *per se*, saying, for example, that "the children had enjoyed the events" or that "they still had fond and happy memories of the events" (Long *et al.*, 2002, p. 60). Here is a logical deadlock: whereas sporting inclusion is appreciated because of its expected positive benefits, the lack of evidence of social inclusion is disregarded due to the intrinsic value of sport.

Furthermore, in some cases, various elements are addressed at once, despite the substantial difference in the mechanisms involved and the research methods to be used. For example, assessment of the impact on participants' physical health is a subject of physiology, while the question of whether social cohesion of the community is enhanced is highly sociological. Each would require enormous effort by experts in the area, even if approached separately. In short, it would be much more beneficial to research respectively unless such synthesis in the name of social exclusion provides any theoretical addition. If this were not the case, the use of the term would just put more burdens on the shoulders of researchers, who could produce more fruitful research if they did not use it.

To sum up, there is significant conceptual ambiguity regarding sport and social exclusion, causing intricacy between sporting and social inclusion, where each perspective supports its value by using that of the other, while observable evidence is missing. In addition, the existing evaluation research has not yet achieved methodological sophistication with which the unproductive cul-de-sac is to be broken through. The following argument thus attempts to resolve these problems. To do this it is necessary to examine whether sporting inclusion can be seen as social inclusion. This can be done by tackling each of the two rationales that underpin the proposition: (a) sport participation is, in itself, valuable, and (b) sport participation is valuable because it provides indirect benefits to the socially excluded. Amartya Sen's capability approach and his understanding of social exclusion provide useful insights for this purpose.

Social exclusion and Sen's capability perspective

The relevance of Sen's capability perspective to the issues around sport and social exclusion is twofold. Firstly, while the concept of social exclusion is so complex that it allows various interpretations, Sen's view on social exclusion offers a definite and practical understanding, with which the distinction between social inclusion *in* and *through* sport can be clearly defined. Second, the notion of capability itself provides considerable methodological implications for the evaluation of both types of interventions.

Sen (2000) argues that social exclusion is sometimes overused without considering its connection to more traditional and wider literature of poverty research. Indeed, theoretical confusion regarding social exclusion is not a phenomenon only within the area of sport, but is generally observed throughout the literature. Some say that it is a concept which is socially constructed by different combinations of economic, social and political processes (Somerville, 1998), and the only thing that can be agreed about the term is the fact that there cannot be any universally agreeable definition of social exclusion (Atkinson, 1998).

It is broadly agreed that the term 'social exclusion' originated in France in the 1970s, indicating a range of disadvantaged groups of people who were not protected under the social insurance system (Lenoir, 1974). Thereafter it gained popularity, first at European policy level, and then at national level in the UK, while at the same time the list of the 'socially excluded' kept expanding (Parkinson, 1998; Burchardt *et al.*, 2002). Although the value underlying the creation of the term is the French Republican collectivist tradition where social solidarity is championed, its increasing recognition and replacement for the more conventional term 'poverty' in policy discourse required poverty researchers in the UK to conceptualise the new term in relation to the old one despite their inherited preference for liberal individualism and social mobility (Silver, 1994; Berghman, 1995; Room, 1995). Consequently, their effort inevitably led to a comprehensive formulation of the term, as Walker (1997: p. 8) summarises:

> ...regarding *poverty* as a lack of the material resources, especially income, necessary to participate in British society and *social exclusion* as a more comprehensive formulation which refers to the dynamic process of being shut out, fully or partially, from any of the social, economic, political and cultural systems which determine the social integration of a person in society. Social exclusion may, therefore, be seen as the denial (or non-realisation) of the civil, political and social rights of citizenship.

Indeed, this definition is comprehensive enough that it would encompass most of the meanings actually in use. As Sen (2000: p. 2) describes, however:

> ... the impression of an indiscriminate listing of problems under the broad heading of 'social exclusion' and of a lack of discipline in selection, combined with the energy and excitement with which the concept has been advocated for adoption by its energetic adherents, has had the effect of putting off some of the experts on poverty and deprivation.

Sen himself does not deny the usefulness of the concept of social exclusion. Rather, he maintains that it is important "to see what it has added and why the addition may well be important. [...] In terms of the usefulness of the idea, we have to scrutinise and examine critically what new insight — if any — is provided by the approach of social exclusion" (p.2). For Sen, the importance of the social exclusion literature is in its emphasis on relational features of capability deprivation. In his view, the recognition of relational features of poverty can be traced back to Aristotle, but the social exclusion literature is useful because it gives a central role to them.

Sen's notion of capability, though, is quite distinctive to other approaches to poverty research. While traditional approaches see poverty as shortage of income, material resources or commodities, he regards it as deprivation of the *capabilities* to achieve *functionings*. Functionings represent the 'beings and doings' that directly consist of a person's well-being. Capability is, then, defined as "all the alternative combinations of functionings a person can choose to have" (Sen, 1992, p. 40). In other words, it is "a set of vectors of functionings, reflecting the person's freedom to choose from possible livings" (p. 40). For Sen, capability is valued not only because it instrumentally enables higher achievement, but also because the ability to choose freely is, in itself, intrinsically important to a person's well-being. Thus, poverty is conceived as deprivation of the freedom to pursue various objectives in living, and its evaluation, Sen argues, should not be based solely on the functionings actually achieved, but also the capabilities to function.

He defends the superiority of the capability approach to other traditional ones that are based on such variables as primary goods, resources, real income and utility. It is, firstly, because functionings belong to the constitutive elements of well-being, while primary goods, resources and real income "are all concerned with the instruments of achieving well-being and other objectives, and can be seen also as the means to freedom" (p. 42). Secondly, he rejects utilitarianism, which focuses on personal mental metric of desire and fulfilment in assessing a person's well-being. This is because, under the condition where inequalities and deprivations are perpetuated and intensified, a deprived person tries to avoid being always aggrieved and take pleasure in small achievements by cutting down personal desires to modest and 'realistic' proportions, and so he or she might not appear to be so badly off in terms of their mental state.

Based on this conception of poverty, Sen (2000) redefines social exclusion as the denial of access to social relations that are relevant to deprivation in terms of capability. He continues, then, that social relations may have both *constitutive* and *instrumental* importance to capability deprivation. They are constitutively relevant if being excluded from them is seen as a loss on its own, whereas instrumentally important social relations lead to serious deprivations in other aspects of life, although being deprived of them is not, in itself, terrible. Thus, social exclusion is defined as exclusion from such relations, whereas social inclusion is seen as being connected to them.

The above argument suggests that, in speaking of sport and social exclusion, it is important to ask if social relations gained from participation in sport are either constitutively or instrumentally relevant to capability deprivation. If participation in sport is, in itself, an essential part of living, non-participation is a constitutive element of capability poverty and so sporting inclusion can be regarded as social inclusion. On the other hand, if a person can improve his or her capability in living because of his or her participation in sports, failure to participate has an instrumental effect on the person's capability. If this is the case, inclusion in sporting activities can also be seen as social inclusion. Thus, the two conditions under which sporting inclusion can be social inclusion are now redefined as: sport participation is either (a) constitutively, or (b) instrumentally important to people's well-being. The following two sections examine whether these conditions can be true and, if so, what evaluation strategies are suitable.

Sporting inclusion as constitutive element of well-being

According to Sen's definition, in order for increased participation in sports to be social inclusion, it must contribute to improvement of people's capabilities either *constitutively* or *instrumentally*. The first discussion is whether sport participation can be a *constitutively* important element of people's living and, if so, how programmes aimed to encourage under-participating people to take part in sports can be evaluated as social inclusion programmes. Social relations are of constitutive importance to capability deprivation when the denial of participation is, in itself, thought to damage the person's living seriously. Thus, the question here is whether participating in sports is such a substantial *functioning* that directly constitutes a person's well-being.

One might argue that participation in sport is fundamentally important since it is a fundamental human right. For example, the United Nations Educational, Scientific and Cultural Organisation (UNESCO) (1978) declares that "every human being has a fundamental right of access to physical education and sport" (p. 31). Thus, it might not be wrong to say sport participation is one of the 'social citizenship rights', the denial of which is seen as equivalent to social exclusion. Nevertheless, it does not necessarily mean that absence of certain groups of people from particular sporting activities is evidence of social exclusion, because what is thought to be fundamental is not participation *per se*, but the *right of access* to the opportunities to play sports. The problem here is simply a methodological matter: what constitutes evidence of the denial of the right?

The distinction between actual achievement and capability to achieve is useful in order to understand the difference fully. The number of participants provides information about actual achievement, whereas capability means the freedom to choose participation. If a person chooses not to participate, even though he or she is able to participate if he or she wishes, this person is not deprived of the capability to pursue participation. In other words, his or her right is not impinged, as far as his or her capability is assured. A person who does not play football might simply prefer to go to the cinema. Barry (2002: p. 19) puts forward another example:

> Imagine two people who graduate with a qualification in law of exactly equal quality. If one opts for a high-pressure career while the other prefers a job that leaves a lot of time for playing golf and gardening, it is not unfair according to the principle of justice as equal opportunity.

Thus, an assessment based solely on information about actual achievement fails to take into account the hidden proportion of voluntary exclusion and may erroneously estimate the degree of inequality. By contrast, an assessment based on capability is more suitable, considering the widely shared view that participation in sport is a matter of choice (Coalter *et al.*, 2000).

As Sen (1992) holds, however, one of the difficulties with the capability approach is the fact that capabilities are basically unobservable, and so it requires many presumptions in order to estimate the proportion of voluntary exclusion in sport participation. Thus, some supplementary data is necessary in addition to that of actual participation, so that one can judge what percentage of actual non-participation is as a result of voluntary choice. However, it must be noted that apparently 'voluntary' exclusion is often caused by capability failure (Burchardt *et al.*, 1999; Barry, 2002). For example, an experience of discrimination often ends up with the unwillingness of the person to take part. Therefore, simply to exclude those who are unwilling to participate from analysis would be insufficient, since they might not have capability to participate. The ideal approach would be the one that can address the structural constraints as well, which is obviously not a straightforward practice. Despite such difficulties, though, the capability approach has significant potential in the assessment of social exclusion *in* sport.

While the argument above is about the rights of access to sports in general, it may be possible that, under certain circumstances, participation in a particular kind of sport is regarded as a constitutive element of well-being. For example, in a society where football is so dominant that a large majority of the members see it as important, being deprived of capability to take part in it may be a serious capability failure. Under such circumstances, initiatives for the development of the sport may be justifiable from the viewpoint of social inclusion. Of course, assessment of such projects should also be based on capability, not the actual participation.

This case, however, raises another issue concerning social exclusion: how to include the 'excluded'. Many writers suggest that 'inclusion' often means integration into the dominant culture (Silver, 1994; Levitas, 1996). Although some defend it from the viewpoint of social solidarity (Barry, 2002), and others reject it in appreciation of pluralism or post-modernism (Jordan, 1996), as far as the capability perspective is concerned, integration into the dominant culture may not be the best way of social inclusion. For example, immigrants from developing countries to a developed one would initially experience social exclusion due to the difference of lifestyle, but would be able to acquire higher achievement by adapting themselves to the dominant culture. This certainly means improvement in well-being because they have acquired a higher level of functioning, but at the same time a loss in capability to some extent as they have lost the freedom to pursue their original lifestyle. Of course, their migration itself reflects their choice to change their lifestyle to some extent in pursuit of better functionings. However, if they were able to maintain certain aspects of life after moving, the constraints of migration would be less. Hence, the more capabilities a society can provide, the more inclusive it would be.

The same logic is applicable to the context of sport. Under the circumstances where a particular sport is dominant, the freedom to choose other activities may tend to be restricted. Imagine members of a certain social group are under-participating in football due to some social constraints (for example, racial discrimination or income poverty). Their capability to pursue participation in football is improved by removing such constraints. However, some of them would not choose to participate in it, if they are not interested in it, simply because of their own preference. Therefore, their improved capability does not add to their improved well-being as achievement. Thus, promoting participation of under-participating groups in a dominant sport is not a sufficient way to include them when the interests of the dominant and the marginalised population are significantly different.

Again, it should be remembered that participation in sport is basically a matter of choice. It is impossible to agree on a commonly applicable preference ranking in terms of sport. It cannot be decided that participation in football represents higher achievement than participation in basketball. Moreover, even non-participation could be as good an option for one person as participation in football is for another. In fact, it is apparent that many people prefer non-sporting leisure activities, and it is not a problem as far as the constitutive importance of sport is concerned. In short, each sport, as well as non-sport, activity should be equally weighted in the space of leisure activities as a functioning constituting a person's well-being. A society where only one kind of sport is available, no matter how many people can enjoy that sport, works exclusively to those who do not want to play it. On the other hand, if people can choose one sport from many possible options including other sports as well as non-sporting activities, the society allows diverse ways of achieving the functioning of enjoying leisure time. In other words, the more freedom of choice in the leisure space, the more inclusive the society is, since it allows its members to have variety of interests.

Therefore, another strategy for the evaluation of a sport-based intervention is to assess its contribution to the improvement of the capability of those who are limited in their capability in the leisure sphere. There are two criteria. One is to what extent it increases the number of alternatives from which people can choose their leisure activities. 'Alternatives' mean not only the number of kinds of activities, but also variety in locations, frequencies or degrees of difficulty, all of which would enlarge opportunities of participation. The other criterion is to what extent it reduces the constraints that have hindered participation of those experiencing capability deprivation in terms of leisure. In most cases, introducing a sport-related programme will increase someone's capability. But the assessment has to include the nature of the people whose capability is and is not increased by such an intervention. For example, if a football coaching programme for young people has mainly attracted relatively affluent people, it is either providing an inappropriate alternative that does not interest the poorer population, or it is failing to diminish the factors prohibiting them from participation. The next step to take differs in each case.

Social inclusion through sport: instrumental relevance

The discussion above has seen the evaluation strategy when sport participation is purely seen as constitutively important. However, sporting inclusion is also justified because of its instrumental relevance. Even in saying 'funda-mental rights', one might refer to instrumental importance to support it. It is the task of the 'social inclusion through sport' perspective to look at whether sport participation *instrumentally* improves capabilities to achieve important functionings in a person's living other than participation *per se*.

Even if participation in sport, in itself, is not considered as constitutively relevant to a person's living, if it leads to widening of people's capabilities in other important spheres of life, such participation is instrumentally relevant to (the alleviation of) capability deprivation. For example, if the person who dislikes football is discriminated against in employment owing to his non-participation, it is instrumental social exclusion. By contrast, a local football club may constitute an important part of the social network that provides its members with employment opportunities, social support and so on. On such occasions, involvement in the club can be seen as social inclusion, since its membership is a means to achieve important functionings.

If such connections can be established, a mere increase in participation can be justified from the viewpoint of social inclusion. Examples of intervention using sport instrumentally include health promotion through physical education and an educational support programme provided for under-achieving pupils by professional football clubs (for example, Sharp *et al.*, 2003). It is important, though, that in such cases, the above discussion regarding the constitutive relevance of sport should not be combined in the assessment. It should be based on the evidence of the intended benefits.

Therefore, the evaluation of regeneration programmes aiming for social inclusion through sport is to assess whether they are social relations through which people's capabilities are broadened. The capability approach implies two things for the evaluation strategy of this perspective. First, the outcomes to assess are not only the actual achievements but also the capability to achieve them. In other words, one should look at whether a sport-related programme has enlarged the freedom to pursue better well-being in terms of the evaluative spaces such as health, education, employment, crime and so on. However, this would not resolve the most serious problem regarding this area of research: the inconsistency in the results. Moreover, since measuring capability involves more technical difficulties than only dealing with actual achievement, such a strategy might find itself to be even less productive.

Rather than a simple shift of focus from actual achievement, the notion of capability provides a more important implication. The capability approach considers that a person is better-off when he or she can achieve the same functionings in various ways. That is, if sport is the only way to achieve functionings, a person's capability is not that large. Recall the discussion about the imposition of a dominant sport. If only a dominant sport is used as a tool to attract young people, those who are not interested in it are likely to be excluded from that programme. Therefore, it is not important to establish correlation between sport participation and the expected outcomes. It is apparent that mere participation in sport does not always assure the expected benefits. As Coalter *et al.* (2000) maintain, sport participation is not a sufficient but, at most, a necessary condition to achieve important functionings. In fact, it might not be even a necessary condition from the viewpoint of the capability approach, which appreciates the existence of many alternatives in achieving a certain functioning.

Therefore, what is more important is to explore the mechanisms to produce outcomes, than to measure the outcomes themselves. The most common strategy for evaluation of sport-related regeneration programmes is outcome measurement in terms of policy indicators. But an overwhelming focus on establishing the evidence in terms of outcome preserves the weakness of experimental or quasi-experimental approaches to evaluation, which render "the research findings arbitrary and inconsistent" (Pawson and Tilley, 1997: p. 54). As Coalter *et al.* (2000) hold, sport varies in terms of its properties and so does the nature of the expected benefits. Various mechanisms are involved in the process of the benefits to be generated. Some programmes are aimed at benefiting the participants directly through personal development, whereas others aim to produce benefits to the community as a whole through increased social cohesion. Thus, each of these mechanisms should be approached separately. The goal of such evaluation research is not to assess the extent of the benefits the programmes produce, but to develop models representing the mechanisms, which are transferable to the future development of programmes.

Conclusion: towards the synthesis of the two approaches

No matter what objectives are officially stated, every sport-related intervention has the potential to improve people's well-being, both constitutively and instrumentally. Sporting inclusion programmes, which primarily pursue social inclusion in sport, can, at the same time, accrue wider benefits to the participants and communities, whereas those aiming for social inclusion in a wider sense could add to the capability in leisure for the people living in these communities. In this sense, it is justifiable to use the evidence relating to both aspects in evaluating either type of programme. Indeed, some argue for the strategies for programme evaluation not limiting the analysis in terms of officially stated goals, but involving other theoretically possible ones, in order for evaluation research to contribute more fruitfully to social scientific knowledge (Chen and Rossi, 1980).

However, it must be remembered that the methodologies of approaching these two aspects fundamentally differ from each other. Constitutive relevance of a sport-related programme should be assessed in terms of its contribution to improved capability in the leisure sphere. On the other hand, the assessment of instrumental contribution is to examine whether it has succeeded in creating the mechanism to generate benefits leading to improved capabilities. For example, in evaluating a programme using football as a tool to attract young people to an educational programme, one can move onto the constitutive aspect after concluding that it has failed instrumentally to produce educational benefits. However, simply referring to the enjoyment of the participants is, obviously, not enough. It may be a good element of the programme, but it is certainly insufficient as evidence of success in social inclusion. Presumably this kind of programme tends to use the most popular sport to attract as many young people as possible, and the fact that it is the most popular suggests that young people who like it have relatively many opportunities to enjoy their leisure time in comparison to those who are interested in less popular leisure activities. Thus, it might have failed to cater for the more socially excluded in terms of leisure, despite the enjoyment reported by the participants.

To conclude this paper, if enjoying leisure activities is one of the important functions consisting of well-being and, given that this is probably true especially for young people, perhaps it is right to synthesise the two aspects in the evaluation of sport-related social inclusion programmes targeted at young people. However, they are concerned with different time scales: one measures the impact on the present life of young people, while the other is about their capability in the future. The latter certainly involves more technical difficulties. Nonetheless, one of the important rationales for targeting young people in urban regeneration is their potential to make a difference in the future. The very fact that many sport-related programmes are funded for that purpose, shows that it is an urgent requirement for researchers to produce evidence in this area. It is not, though, to establish a correlation between sport participation and the expected benefits, but to reveal the mechanisms between them and to propose models that are transferable to future programmes.

References

Arthur, S. and Finch, H. (1999) *Physical activity in our lives: Qualitative research among disabled people*. London: Health Education Authority.

Atkinson, A. B. (1998) 'Social exclusion, poverty and unemployment', in A. B. Atkinson and J. Hills (eds) *Exclusion, employment and opportunity* (CASE paper no. 4). London: Centre for Analysis of Social Exclusion, London School of Economics.

Bailey (2003) Evaluating the relationship between physical education, sport and social inclusion [online]. Available from: http://education.cant.ac.uk/Centre-for-Educational-Research/profiles/Richard-Bailey.htm [Accessed 5 July 2004].

Barry, B. (2002) 'Social exclusion, social isolation, and the distribution of income', in J. Hills, J. Le Grand and D. Piachaud (eds) *Understanding social exclusion*. Oxford: Oxford University Press, pp. 13–29.

Berghman, J. (1995) 'Social exclusion in Europe: Policy context and analytical framework', in G. Room (ed) *Beyond the threshold: The measurement and analysis of social exclusion*. Bristol: The Policy Press, pp. 10–28.

Bovaird, T., Nichols, G. and Taylor, P. (1997) *Approaches to estimating the wider economic and social benefits resulting from sports participation*. Birmingham: Aston Business School Research Institute.

Brackenridge, C., Howe, D. and Jordan, F. (eds) (2000) *Just leisure: Equity, social exclusion and identity* (LSA Publication No. 72). Eastbourne: Leisure Studies Association.

Burchardt, T., Le Grand, J. and Piachaud, D. (1999) 'Social exclusion in Britain 1991–1995', *Social Policy and Administration* Vol. 33, No. 3: 227–244.

—— (2002) 'Introduction', in J. Hills, J. Le Grand and D. Piachaud (eds) *Understanding social exclusion*. Oxford: Oxford University Press, pp. 1–12.

Chen, H. T. and Rossi, P. H. (1980) 'The multi-goal, theory-driven approach to evaluation: A model linking basic and applied social science', *Social Forces* Vol. 59, No. 1: 106–122.

Coalter, F. (1998) 'Leisure studies, leisure policy and social citizenship: the failure of welfare or the limits of welfare?', *Leisure Studies* Vol. 17, No. 1: pp. 21–36.

—— (2000) 'Public and commercial leisure provision: active citizens and passive consumers?', *Leisure Studies* Vol. 19, No. 3: pp. 163–181.

——— (2001) *Realising the potential: The case for cultural services: the case for sport*. London: Local Government Association.

——— (2002) *Sport and community development: a manual* (sportscotland research report No. 86). Edinburgh: sportscotland.

Coalter, F. and Allison, M. (1996) *Sport and community development* (Scottish Sport Council Research Digest No. 42). Edinburgh: Scottish Sport Council.

Coalter, F., Allison, M. and Taylor, J. (2000) *The role of sport in regenerating deprived areas*. Edinburgh: Scottish Executive Central Research Unit.

Collins, M. F. (2003) 'Poverty: The core of exclusion', in M. F. Collins and T. Kay *Sport and social exclusion*. London: Routledge, pp. 34-59.

Collins, M. F., Henry, I. P., Hoolihan, B. and Buller, J. (1999) *Research report: Sport and social exclusion* (a report to the Department of Culture, Media and Sport). Loughborough: Institute of Sport and Leisure Policy, Loughborough University.

Collins, M. F. and Kay, T. (2003) *Sport and social exclusion*. London: Routledge.

Department for Culture, Media and Sport (1999) *Policy Action Team 10: Report on social exclusion*. London: HMSO.

——— (2001) *Building on PAT 10: progress report on social inclusion*. London: DCMS.

Department of the Environment (1989) *Building on ability: Sport for people with disabilities*. London: HMSO.

Houlihan, B. and White, A. (2002) *The politics of sports development: Development of sport or development through sport?* London: Routledge.

Ibbetson, A., Watson, B. and Ferguson, M. (eds) (2003) *Sport, leisure and social inclusion: Potential, participation and possibilities* (LSA Publication No. 82). Eastbourne: Leisure Studies Association.

Institute of Leisure and Amenity Management (1999) *The contribution of the arts and sport to neighbourhood renewal and reducing social exclusion*. Reading: Institute of Leisure and Amenity Management.

Jordan, B. (1996) *A theory of poverty and social exclusion*. Cambridge: Polity Press.

Kay, T. (2003) 'Gender, sport and social exclusion', in M. F. Collins and T. Kay (eds) *Sport and social exclusion*. London: Routledge, pp. 97–112.

Lenoir, R. (1974) *Les exclus*. Paris: Seuil.

Levitas, R. (1996) 'The concept of social exclusion and the new Durkheimian hegemony', *Critical Social Policy* Vol. 16: pp. 5–20.

Lister, R. (1990) *The exclusive society: Citizenship and the poor.* London: Child Poverty Action Group.

Long, J., Welch, M., Bramham, P., Butterfield, J., Hylton, K. and Lloyd, E. (2002) *Count me in: The dimensions of social inclusion through culture and sport.* Leeds: Leeds Metropolitan University.

Lyons, A. (1990) *Asian women and sport.* London: Sports Council.

McPherson, G. and Reid, G. (eds) (2001) *Leisure and social inclusion: New challenges for policy and provision* (LSA Publication No. 73). Eastbourne: Leisure Studies Association.

Metcalfe, M. (1998) The central route to urban regeneration: a nice try? in *Sport in the city: Conference proceedings volume 2.* Sheffield 2–4 July 1998, pp. 369–389.

Pack, C. and Glyptis, S. (1985) *Developing sport and leisure.* London: HMSO.

Parkinson, M. (1998) *Combating social exclusion: Lessons from area-based programmes in Europe.* Bristol: The Policy Press.

Pawson, R. and Tilley, N. (1997) *Realistic Evaluation.* London: Sage.

Robins, D. (1990) *Sport as prevention: The role of sport in crime prevention programmes aimed at young people* (occasional paper No. 12). Oxford: Centre for Criminological Research, University of Oxford.

Room, G. (1995) 'Poverty and social exclusion: The new European agenda for policy and research', in G. Room (ed) *Beyond the threshold: The measurement and analysis of social exclusion.* Bristol: The Policy Press, pp. 1–9.

Scott Porter Research and Marketing Ltd. (2001a) *Sport and ethnic minority communities: Aiming at social inclusion* (sportscotland Research Report No. 78). Edinburgh: sportscotland.

——— (2001b) *Sport and people with a disability: Aiming at social inclusion* (sportscotland Research Report No. 77). Edinburgh: sportscotland.

Sen, A. (1992) *Inequality re-examined.* Oxford: Clarendon Press.

——— (2000) *Social exclusion: Concept, application, and scrutiny* (Social development papers No. 1). Manila: Asian Development Bank.

Sharp, C., Blackmore, J., Kendall, L., Greene, K., Keys, W., Macauley, A., Schagen, I. and Yeshanew, T. (2003) *Playing for success: An evaluation of the fourth year* (Research report No. 402). London: Department for Education and Skills.

Silver, H. (1994) 'Social exclusion and social solidarity: Three paradigms', *International Labour Review* Vol. 133, No. 5/6: pp. 531–78.

Snape, R., Thwaites, E. and Ferguson, M. (eds) (2003) *Access and inclusion in leisure and tourism* (LSA Publication No. 81). Eastbourne: Leisure Studies Association.

Social Exclusion Unit (1998) *Bringing Britain together: A national strategy for neighbourhood renewal*. London: HMSO.

——— (2000) *Report of Policy Action Team 12: Young people*. London: HMSO.

——— (2001) *A new commitment to neighbourhood renewal: National strategy action plan*. London: HMSO.

Somerville, P. (1998) 'Explanation of social exclusion: Where does housing fit in?', *Housing Studies* Vol. 13, No. 6: 761–780.

Sport England (1999) *The value of sport*. London: Sport England.

——— (2001) *Sport and regeneration*. London: Sport England.

sportscotland (2003a) *Lottery fund strategy review: Consultation document*. Edinburgh: sportscotland.

——— (2003b) *Sport 21 2003–2007: The national strategy for sport*. Edinburgh: sportscotland.

——— (2003c) *Sports policy — social inclusion* [online]. Edinburgh: sportscotland. Available from: http://www.sportscotland.org.uk/contents/sportspolicy/socialinclusion.htm [Accessed 8 July 2003].

Taylor, P., Crow I., Irvine, D. and Nichols, G. (1999) *Demanding physical activity programmes for young offenders under probation supervision*. London: Home Office.

UNESCO (1978) *International charter of physical education and sport*. Paris: UNESCO.

Utting, D. (1996) *Reducing criminality among young people: A sample of relevant programmes in the United Kingdom*. London: Home Office Research and Statistics Directorate.

Walker, A. (1997) 'Introduction: The strategy of inequality', in A. Walker and C. Walker (eds) *Britain divided: The growth of social exclusion in the 1980s and 1990s*. London: Child Poverty Action Group, pp. 1–13.

REFLECTIONS ON RESEARCHING THE ABILITY OF SPORTS INTERVENTIONS TO REDUCE YOUTH CRIME — THE HOPE OF SCIENTIFIC REALISM

Geoff Nichols
University of Sheffield

Introduction

This paper returns to issues raised in an earlier one (Nichols, 2001a): the extent to which scientific realism offers an alternative methodological approach to 'proving' a causal relationship between policy interventions and outcomes. In contrast to the classical experimental tradition, scientific realism appeared to offer a methodologically rigorous approach to evaluating programmes with relatively small numbers of participants, and in which inherent problems limit the ability to attain the 'gold standard' of validity within the classical tradition. It has the additional advantage of explaining *why*, as well as *whether*, a programme had a particular impact. The approach of scientific realism offers the possibility that small scale research, systematically conducted, can contribute to the bigger picture, as long as one accepts the validity of a range of research methods. However, questions were also raised about the definition of validity and concepts within the scientific realist approach.

This paper returns to these issues by reviewing research subsequently conducted into two sports-related programmes designed to reduce youth crime. The efficacy of such programmes has been a contested debating point for some years; as noted in the Department of Culture Media and Sport (DCMS) strategy review (2002). This reflects a more general concern over the ability to establish any causal relationship between programmes which use leisure as a medium, and desired policy objectives, for example, programmes aimed to reduce social exclusion (Long, *et al.*, 2002; Collins with Kay, 2003) or increase health.

After describing the philosophical foundations of scientific realism, contrasted with those of a more positivist approach to criminology, the paper applies scientific realism to evaluations of two programmes, which both use sport as a medium, and aim to reduce youth crime. These show how scientific realism can build on theory to explore relationships between contexts, mechanisms and outcomes (CMO configurations), but also that it is still not clear at what point evidence is sufficient to prove or disprove the existence of such a configuration. This leads to a discussion of how views of the 'validity' of such evidence will still reflect the value judgements of academics, policy makers and practitioners.

Scientific realism

Within criminology the methodological approach of scientific realism advocated by Pawson and Tilley (1997), has gained prominence as a reaction to positivism, although the debate between academics has been lively and acrimonious (see Crow, 2000, for a commentary). This paper focuses on Pawson and Tilley's application of scientific realism, both because it has been used in evaluation of crime reduction programmes, and because it is explicitly developed in their publications. Pawson and Tilley's application of Bhaskar's (1975) critical realism to the evaluation of crime reduction programmes can be seen as a criticism of the predominance of 'classic experimental research' in criminology, in particular, a criticism that this positivistic approach implies deterministic causation: the programme seems to have caused a change — but it does not take sufficient account of agency. Tilley (2000: p. 110) has also acknowledged a personal academic agenda:

> In my particular case, realistic evaluation has provided a way of dealing with two sources of contemporary unease: about that aspect of postmodernism which casts doubt on the possibility of objective knowledge; and about that aspect of modernism that promises universal unconditional truths. Realistic evaluation ... seems to me to steer a course between the Scylla of relativism and the Charybdis of absolutism.

Pawson and Tilley's epistemological position is that "it is not programmes that work, but the generative mechanisms that they release by way of providing reasons and resources to change behaviour" (Pawson and Tilley, 1997: p. 79). This is termed 'generative causality'. Causality has to be understood as a combination of human agency and its reaction to new opportunities and resources. Rather than a programme having an impact on a participant — the successionist causality assumed by quasi-experimentation — it is necessary to understand the interaction between the programme and the participant; that is, between structure and agency. Thus scientific realism is concerned not only with what has happened as a result of the intervention, in this case, sports based programmes to reduce youth crime, but also why the programme has this effect.

The ontological position of scientific realism is that (following Bhaskar, 1975), the social world has to be understood at different levels. Human activity has to be understood at a different level of nature from that studied by biology or physics (Collier, 1998). Social reality itself is stratified (Pawson and Tilley, 1997: p. 64), and different social actors will perceive their own situations, opportunities and resources in different ways. So one needs to understand the social world as perceived by the programme participant, including their view of the programme, which is 'embedded' in their particular level of social reality.

The mechanism of the programme (the way in which a sports programme affects youth crime) is contingent on a particular context. Some programmes will work with some participants, in some contexts, but not in others. The combination of mechanism and context tells us why a programme has a particular impact; however we still need to know how often or how much a programme causes a particular effect, and in what circumstances. Pawson and Tilley use a context, mechanism, regularity configuration as the starting point for research (Figure 1).

Figure 1   A context, mechanism, regularity / outcome configuration (CMR/O)

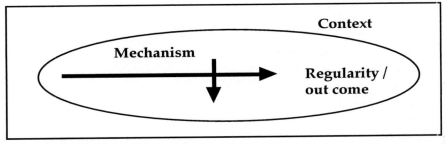

Source: Pawson and Tilley (1997)

A further distinguishing feature of scientific realism's ontology is the assumption that, as in positivism, "there is an external reality to which scientists direct their attention" (Bryman, 2001: p. 13), but unlike positivism, the "scientist's conceptualization is simply one way of knowing that reality". Bryman quotes Bhaskar, the philosopher who founded this approach (1975: p. 250): "science then is the systematic attempt to express in thought the structures and ways of acting of things that exist and act independently of thought".

Bhaskar's position is that the researcher can move towards a more complete understanding of an external reality, but, as in the natural sciences, we are dealing with probabilities. We will never be able to say with absolute certainty that 'a causes b': we can say that understanding is moving towards reality, but we must recognize that reality, which exists independently of our knowledge, always has unexplored depths (Collier, 1998). In other words, "we know we can't know everything, but we do know we are moving in the right direction because we have a systematic approach to knowledge generation".

So far we have noted that scientific realism can be advocated on philosophical grounds (of epistemology and ontology); and this is what distinguishes it from a case study approach (Yin, 1994; Tashakkori and Teddlie, 1998). However, like a case study approach, it seeks to answer questions of 'how' and 'why', while in addition asking 'what' has happened. It can also be advocated on the basis of a preference to steer a middle course between the extreme determinism of positivism combined with objectivism and the complete social relativism of postmodernism, which arises from the recognition that social scientists "always present a specific view of social reality, rather than one that can be regarded as definitive" (Bryman, 2001: p. 18).

However, a further reason for rejecting positivism and objectivism might be more pragmatic: this position implies the need for the classic experimental design, as represented in Figure 2, and this 'gold standard' of evaluation just cannot be achieved. Pawson and Tilley (1997: p. 8) discuss in general terms the 'heroic failure' of this model: how it is impossible to keep all the variables in a social situation constant, and how it is impossible to replicate exactly any one 'experiment'.

Figure 2 illustrates that 'classic experimental research' starts with two identical groups. One group is given the treatment, and one group is not. Research is looking for measurable outcomes of a programme in the experimental group, and comparing them to the control group who have

Figure 2   The classic experimental design

	Pre-test	Treatment	Post-test
Experimental group	O1	X	O2
Control group	O1		O2

(source Pawson and Tilley, 1997: 5)

not experienced the same programme. If the group subjected to the treatment changes and the control group does not, it is deduced that the treatment caused the change. If numbers in the two groups are large enough, it can be ascertained whether the evidence of a causal relationship is statistically significant. Causation between the programme and intermediate effects, or the final outcome, is inferred from the repeated succession of similar effects after similar programmes.

Relating this to the problems of evaluating the type of programmes we are discussing, it is not surprising that both academics and programme managers attempting to evaluate their own practice have struggled to achieve a control group, 'before and after' measures', and a large enough sample size to produce statistically significant results. This is especially so when one considers the characteristics of many crime reduction programmes with young people: open access, open ended, the difficulties of applying quantitative measures that will be acceptable to the participants and programme leaders (Nichols, 2001b; 2001c). Similarly, it is no wonder that in reporting on a recent review of projects designed to reduce social exclusion, Long *et al.* (2002) noted that "during the course of our study we received several requests for help in conducting research that project managers felt was beyond their capabilities" (p. 86), and "some of the anticipated outcomes do not readily lend themselves to establishing causal relationships and evaluation is further complicated by the bounds of the project" (p. 82).

Discussing evaluation in his manual for sport and community development, Coalter (2002) uses Bovaird *et al.*'s (1997) model of the relationship between sport and social and economic outcomes as a starting point for examining 'hypothetical chains' of indirect links between sports participation and outcomes. As part of this model he suggests that increased time spent playing sport might lead to increased interaction with others, in turn to an increased stake in social relations, and then to reductions in anti-social behaviour, both directly, and via an increase in self-esteem. It appears that

Coalter is advocating examining each of the 24 causal links in the model individually, however he acknowledges the "complexity of the inter-relationships between the various factors and the problems of measuring all the various connections" (2002: p. 24). This illustrates Pawson and Tilley's point that, in the same way as it is impossible to hold all the variables constant, (see Figure 2), apart from the two one wishes to examine a relationship between, it is also difficult to isolate just one of the causal relationships in Coalter's complex mesh. This immediately becomes a more significant problem when one moves from asking if a programme has had a particular effect to examining the processes that have led to that, which are represented by the causal links in Coalter's matrix.

So, can scientific realism offer an alternative and achievable approach to producing evidence of effectiveness?

Applying scientific realism to researching sports programmes' impact on youth crime — the Splash programme

The East-town Splash programme was a sports-based activity programme, offered in the school summer holidays, run by a local authority, and having an objective of crime reduction. In these respects it was typical of many such programmes (Nichols and Booth, 1999) apart from its continuity over several years. This continuity had allowed it to build up the trust and support of parents and participants. The programme had many of the characteristics, noted above, which made evaluation using the 'classic experimental design' impractical. The programme was 'open access' and it was run at several sites over five weeks, during week days. Participants could attend at any time, there was no defined entry point to the sites, there was no register of attendance and it was not practical to take one. Thus it was impossible to identify an 'experimental group' or match a control group. It was not possible to devise a 'before and after' measure as one could not define what the period of attendance was, or the experience of the programme (the 'treatment' in Figure 2) that one was measuring changes in relation to. Even had this been possible it was not possible to devise a practical research instrument acceptable to both participants and leaders.

A characteristic of scientific realism is that hypothesised CMO config-urations are built up from theory. It was hypothesised that the mechanism by which the Splash programme would reduce crime was through simple diversion from boredom in the school summer holidays with limited alternative opportunities for activity. It is not the purpose of this paper to give full details of the methods and results, which are reported elsewhere (Nichols, 2003). In brief, the methods included: questionnaires of participants over 2 years, questionnaires of parents over two years, brief interviews with 63 participants, focus group interviews of participants, and interviews of programme leaders. In addition, as a requirement of funding by the Youth Justice Board (a central government department), data were collated to compare recorded crime between August 2001 and August 2002 for the 8 Splash areas which received additional funding from Youth Justice in 2002. August was used as this was the month in which the impact would have been expected to be most significant.

Most of the results supported the proposition of a diversion mechanism. In 2001, responding to a closed question, 56% of parents thought a major benefit for their children was 'to relieve boredom / something to do in the holidays'; 12% 'to keep out of trouble'; and 14% to 'keep them off the streets'. Sixty one percent of parents felt Splash reduced crime while it was on. Thirty of the participants interviewed in 2002 reported that Splash reduced crime either at exactly the same time as it was on, or generally over the period of its provision. The major problem for them in the holidays was boredom. Participants reported:

> "I think it just like helps people get out more, the only reason they did stuff what's bad 'cos they did not have else owt to do. And that's like last resort — it's like they wanted attention and did something wrong, and then they got it, so they got chased."
>
> " … get out of the house when bored."
>
> "It was 'boring at home."
>
> "When you are at school it's, yea, it's the holidays, but after a while you get bored, but when they have been doing Splash, there is something to do in the 6 week holidays, it may only be for a week, or two, but it's something to do."

Thirteen participants from those interviewed in 2002 made remarks which implied that they themselves had been prevented from getting in trouble. For example, a participant reported:

> "We used to go out twocing [taking without owner's consent] cars and bricking windows [throwing bricks through windows]. Other

kids would ask us if we wanted to do it. Splash prevents us getting involved."

On one particular site there was strong evidence that offenders were attending the sessions:

"It would be better 'if more kids who were not young offenders came. That has put off some of my friends."

"Yea, I think it does [reduce crime]. Before this summer a series of cars were set on fire here and since then it's been better, there has not been one."

But, on the other hand:

"It does not reduce crime because older kids, when doing crime and that, don't do it till late".

Over the whole sample of 63 interviewed participants only twelve respondents did not think that Splash reduced crime. However, this was not supported by the comparison of local recorded 'youth incidents' between August 2001 and 2002, as shown in Table 1. Youth crime is 'other youth related incidents', in contrast to 'all crime', which includes all crime recorded in the Home Office categories.

Table 1 allows a comparison of the areas in which Splash operations were expanded in 2002, with the trend for East-town overall. The East-town total shows an overall crime increase of 7%, while across the 8 areas including the Splash sites the increase was 16%. Overall this shows that in 5 out of 8 areas, youth related incidents have increased by a higher percentage than the East-town total. Thus the recorded crime statistics do not support a diversion effect.

There may be ways of reconciling the two sets of results. Splash may have a positive effect, but this is outweighed by other factors. The incident data is collected in police 'base command units' (BCU) and the Splash site may be in any geographical position in one of these units (on the edge or in the middle) and so one might expect its impact to vary.

From the perspective of scientific realism the most convincing evidence of the effectiveness of Splash in reducing crime would be a combination of a reduction in the crime figures (the outcome, or regularity of the CMO/R con-

Table 1   Changes in recorded crime between August 2001 and
August 2002 for the 8 Splash areas which received
additional funding from Youth Justice in 2002

Area in which Splash sites were situated	Youth incidents 2001	Youth incidents 2002	% change
Site 1	77	81	+5
Site 2	117	120	+2
Site 3	79	135	+70
Site 4	81	89	+10
Site 5	111	162	+46
Site 6	92	116	+26
Site 7	114	142	+24
Site 8	124	78	-63
Total sites 1–8	795	923	+16
East-town total	2335	2494	+7

Source: Eastshire Police

figuration) and evidence of the process by which Splash had contributed to this, as provided by the other data sources. As it stands, the evidence raises other questions. Does Splash just displace crime to other sites or times of day? Does displacement only take effect when Splash is run on a site where crime takes place? Can a reduction of crime on any one site be as much the result of the presence of the Splash leaders and sessions as it is of the direct involvement in Splash of those who might otherwise offend? This is consistent with Pawson and Tilley's view that scientific realism should "seek(s) cumulation by identifying, more and more minutely, the conjunction of sets of mechanisms and contexts that will bring about a desired outcome" (1998: p. 82).

Thus greater understanding of the situation leads to further hypotheses, in the way that scientific realism progresses towards a more complete understanding of an external reality. But the problem remains: at what point does one reject the hypothetical CMO configuration rather than just modifying it?; and conversely, at what point is evidence adequate to support it? If one had all the research evidence above, except the comparative youth incident data, would one have been justified in accepting the CMO configuration? How incongruent does the evidence need to be with the theory for one to reject it? In the 'classic experimental design' the standard of proof is set by tests of statistical significance; but what standard is applied to scientific realism?

Applying scientific realism to researching sports programmes' impact on youth crime — the Sportaction programme

This second example discusses a programme in which data could only be collected in detail on two participants, who were some of the very few who had significant contact with the programme. In contrast to Splash, the Sportaction programme was targeted on young people who already had a serious record of offending, which work with other agencies or programmes had failed to address. In the context of the UK Youth Justice System, these young people only had to commit one more serious offence to be sent to a detention centre. As with Splash, the programme was open-ended, in that participants could attend for as long as they wanted. However, in contrast, work with each participant was intensive, on a one-to-one basis, with a sports leader. This involved initial participation in sporting activities and building up a relation of trust with the sports leader, before progressing to roles of responsibility in sports leadership situations; for example; helping to lead sessions with younger children. There was also an emphasis on training, helping participants to gain sports coaching qualifications. In the long term there was the possibility that this could lead to paid employment with the Sportaction programme. The one-to-one work meant that the 'programme' only had common elements of sports participation and leadership, but could be adapted infinitely to meet the needs of individual participants and take advantage of opportunities.

During the period of study, 21 young people were referred to the programme but only 4 completed more than 20 hours contact. Of these, one had moved to another programme and one had been sent to a detention centre, leaving only two, Adam and Marvin, who could be researched in detail. Several had moved from the area, showed insufficient interest to attend, or just could not be contacted. To a point this reflected the type of young person being targeted and the multiple problems they faced, but it also reflected a poor referral process — common difficulties in this type of programme.

Although contact with this programme was much greater than for Splash, possibly 3 or 4 hours a week per participant, the main mechanism by which the programme might reduce crime was hypothesised to be long-term pro-social personal development. A model of this process was developed from a synthesis of models from criminology (Farrington, 2000; Catalano and Hawkins, 1996), UK Youth Work (Huskins, 1998) and adventure education (Nichols, 2000; 2004). In short, this involved developing participants' self-esteem, locus of control and social skills in parallel, and directed by pro-social values. This would be achieved through a progressive juxtaposition of participants' developing capabilities with new challenges. For example, as a participant became more skilled in a sport and developed sport leadership skills, he or she might be encouraged to take a leadership role in sessions for younger participants. This process required long-term contact with the programme, the sports leader to take a mentoring role, and a new set of pro-social peers. Sportaction was initially chosen for study because it appeared that the conditions for this process were in place. One would expect the nature of the programme to be particularly suited for a study of 'generative causality' as one could track how participants changed perceptions of their own capabilities enabled them to take advantage of new opportunities.

Although only two participants were available for study, the intensive nature of the work allowed for in-depth case studies to be made. These used programme records (a detailed record was made of each session with each participant by the sports leader), interviews with sports leaders, interviews with the participants, and in one case an interview with the participant's mother. It was not possible to gain access to police records of offending. These might have shown a change in the rate of offending, or times of offending, in relation to involvement in the programme. However, any statistical analysis would have been meaningless. Again, one can see the impossibility of applying the 'classical experimental design'.

In brief, as this is not the main focus of this paper, results were strongly supportive of the hypothesised mechanism of pro-social development for both Adam and Marvin. They had attended voluntarily for 121 and 85 hours respectively, which represented a considerable commitment over the period of involvement. Sportaction became a major influence in their lives, as both were excluded from school, and nether had a commitment to any other organisation or activity. Adam had previously attended a boxing gym for several years but had lapsed membership. Both had developed new skills, demonstrated them in voluntary sports leadership, and taken a series of sports coaching qualifications. The mentor relationship with the sports leader was very significant to them. Adam aspired to part-time employment with Sportaction over the summer when they ran more sessions. Marvin had applied for a full-time college course in sports studies.

The case studies did enable a refinement of the theoretical model of the mechanism. Adam already had very high self-esteem. The need to maintain this, combined with his boxing skills, and his peers' knowledge that he had these skills and was therefore a useful person to have on one's side in a violent argument, continued to lead him into fights. He realized that he needed to control himself more, and the sports leader attributed the situations which led to conflict as arising from a particular peer. In accordance with Emler's (2001) review of the concept of self-esteem it was clear that too much of this attribute could have as negative an impact as too little. At the same time, the importance of peers was confirmed.

Thus far the two case studies supported the hypothesised CMO configuration: the mechanism of pro-social development, in the context of the very difficult circumstances of these two participants, had led to outcomes of voluntary sports leadership, commitment to further training, and potentially paid employment. However, close to the end of the study Adam knocked out a police officer's teeth when the officer came to arrest him in connection with an offence he claimed not to have committed and which the sports leader thought he was very likely not to have been involved in. This lack of self-control, combined with boxing ability and self-confidence, led to Adam being sent to a detention centre. Between Adam being charged and sent to the detention centre, Sportaction decided that they could not offer him any of the employment he was looking forward to, as not only had he hit a police officer, but the police themselves had a leadership role in the programme.

The eventual outcome for Adam was negative. The programme had not prevented him re-offending. But again, at what point does one reject the hypothesis of the CMO configuration? The programme had achieved other positive outcomes. If Adam had not committed this offence, and been detained, would the evidence to this point have confirmed the CMO configuration? Secondly, at what point does one just modify rather than reject the CMO configuration? The case study of Adam showed that changes in self-esteem needed to be built more subtly into the model. But how far can one change the model before accepting that one has a new CMO configuration? Thirdly, and this point is illustrated particularly by this case, one could argue that as only 4 of the 21 young people referred to the programme went on to have significant contact with it, the programme was a failure. On the other hand, one could argue that the very nature of the young people referred, and the inadequacy of the referral agency, meant that the outcomes achieved represented success. If one only considers the two participants, Adam and Marvin, who had significant contact and could be researched, how can one define a positive outcome, and thus make some evaluation of the programme?

Discussion — what can scientific realism add, and what are its limitations?

Methodological issues

Drawing on these examples above, firstly, it can be argued on philosophical grounds that scientific realism is a more 'realistic' way of understanding the world. The recognition that in crime reduction programmes we need to understand a changing interaction between participant and programme certainly accords with the author's experience of two programmes working with more serious, long-term offenders (Nichols, 1999a; 1999b). In both these instances one could see the way that participants developed through experience of the programme and consequently perceived a new set of opportunities as within their capability. This was replicated in the studies of the two Sportaction participants above. This qualitative understanding could not have been achieved by a positivist approach, although it could have been by a traditional case study which focused on 'how' and 'why' the programme had an impact. In this respect scientific realism overcomes a deficiency of the positivistic approach, acknowledged by its advocates (Farrington, 1996), that it does not help us understand the process by which factors interrelate and "any theory of the development of offending is inevitably speculative in the present state of knowledge" (p. 105).

As in the classic experimental design, scientific realism starts by developing theory and then collecting data to test it. In this sense it is deductive. It will ensure an articulation with previous theory development if it uses academic theory to contribute to the hypothesised CMO configurations. However, when Pawson (2003: p. 483) states that "by starting with the program theory one understands immediately just how many and varied are the processes that may lead to an intervention's success or failure", it is not clear if this theory is just derived from those people involved in the programme. Of course, this does not preclude articulation with previous academic theory post-research.

As in a case study approach, a combination of methods is used: credence is given to both quantitative and qualitative data, in contrast to the rather extreme dismissal of interviewees' expressions of their reasoning as invalid (Farrington, 1998: p. 207). The Sportaction example showed how understanding of a CMO configuration can be modified as a result of research. In this case a more subtle understanding was gained of the role of self-esteem: for some participants a moderated level of self-esteem was more important than an enhanced one.

However, a problem remains of the criteria used to decide when to modify the initial hypothesised relationship. This is related to a criticism acknowledged by Tilley (2000: p. 109) that this approach "drives the researcher towards useless detail". Tilley counters this by saying that one has to raise the details of individual cases back up to 'middle level' CMO configurations. But this still leaves the problem of deciding the point at which the configuration is not supported by the observations.

Further, both the examples show the difficulty of deciding at what point the CMO configuration should be abandoned, rather than just modified. In the Splash example, most of the evidence pointed to crime being reduced by the programme relieving boredom, but the local youth incident data did not support this. At this point, does one abandon the hypothesised CMO configuration completely, or start to examine refinements suggested above? Interestingly, in this example it was initially hypothesised that the mechanism of personal growth directed by pro-social values (as in Sportaction) would be important because the continuity of the programme over several years (and other factors) made this possible. However, in the initial year of study it became clear that the mechanism of diversion was much more important. But how can we define 'became clear'? How much evidence is needed to refute a CMO configuration?

An attraction of the scientific realist approach might be that it enables valid research to be conducted in situations where the requirements of the classic experimental design could not be met. But at some point scientific realism requires measurement of outcomes in CMO configurations. [In some descriptions of the approach Pawson and Tilley (1997) use the term 'regularities' instead.] If we are not to use the criteria of statistical significance to attribute *proof,* at what point do we say that the outcomes are sufficient to support the hypothesised position? This is not clear in the examples given by Pawson and Tilley (1997: pp. 88–99) which report changes, but not how much change is required to support the configuration. Further, how do we deal with the situation where we have only two participants, in however much depth they have been researched, and where one is reconvicted and the other is not? If there are just insufficient participants to achieve a statistical test of a relationship, can one still apply a scientific realist approach, but accept that other methods will need to be sufficient?

A difficulty, identified in a previous paper (Nichols, 2001a), is how a context/mechanism/outcome configuration is defined. This has already been touched on in considering when a mechanism or an outcome is sufficiently different from the predicted one to invalidate the initial model. However, a further point is that the examples above show two different levels of CMO complexity. The CMO configuration in the Splash case is the most simple. In contrast, the mechanism of pro-social development, hypothesised to underlie the Sportaction programme, itself involved an interaction of several other relationships (changes in self-esteem, skills / competencies, locus of control, the influence of pro-social value systems of sports leaders and peers, etc). Does one try to examine these relationships together, or break down the mechanism into separate components; and if one breaks it down, how minutely does one do this? Pawson's advice (2003: p. 484) is to begin by mapping out the potential conjectures and influences that might have shaped the programme under investigation:

> ... Remember that chains of influence are infinitely long, so stop ... when you figure that the particular component of programme theory that has been unearthed has relatively little bearing on overall outcomes ... and when you feel the terror of commencing research with an inadequate budget and an inexperienced research team.

However, how does one know, before one has conducted the research, which programme components will have a significant bearing on outcomes? Surely, again, this decision can only be made with reference to previous theory.

A bundle of inter-related relationships between factors is recognised in Coalter's model (2002), although the part of this which deals with a relationship between sport and crime has been expanded again in the theoretical model used to inform the research into Sportaction, above. But incorporating this complexity is at the cost of blunting the precision of the research in examining any one of the component relationships. The Sportaction example was fortunate as the nature of the data available on the two participants allowed a depth of understanding of the process of the programme — the 'how' and 'why' questions. But, conversely, it did not allow examination of changes in offending rates, or any other change, over a large number of participants. So, at what level of detail should a CMO configuration be hypothesised? Again, Pawson and Tilley (1997: pp. 88–113) give some examples. In describing a programme to reduce crime on housing estates, one context is "traditionally managed low-quality housing on a hard-to-let estate with subterranean criminal subculture and some difficult families' housing". But it is not clear how we decide which elements of any one context are crucial contingent factors, and perhaps it is the permutation of them that is crucial, rather than each acting independently.

Paradigm wars and value judgments

Perhaps, once we start thinking of the progression of knowledge, in scientific realist terms, as moving towards reality — a reality which exists independently of our knowledge and always has unexplored depths to it (Collier, 1998) — it is easier to think of understanding progressing from one CMO configuration to another. But how do we know the progression of knowledge is going in the *right* direction, towards greater understanding of an external reality? This is related to the potential criticism from an extreme constructivist / interpretivist position that "the very questions that Pawson and Tilley ask are framed within their own (view of) social reality and this is why they are important to them" (Nichols, 2001a: p. 77); we may not all share the same definition of 'right direction'.

Crow (2000: p. 123) has argued that, in the context of criminology, we are witnessing a clash between two 'paradigms', in a Kuhnian sense of the word (Kuhn, 1970a, 1970b). Kuhn used this word to describe the activity of 'normal science' in which theory represents a framework "within which scientists do their day-to-day work of refining observation and measurements, and constructing a detailed and precise representation of the physical world" (O'Hear, 1989: p. 65). A paradigm is replaced when a critical number of observations are found to be unexplainable within it (Kuhn gives the example of Newtonian science being replaced by Einstein's relativity). However, the shift to a new paradigm is dependent on more than its superior explanatory power. It is also dependent on "the social effect of authority in the scientific community: the way publication and preferment, and research money will be distributed by those at the top of the community and in accordance with their favoured paradigm" (O'Hear, 1989: p. 72). Or as Kuhn put it, "whatever scientific progress may be, we must account for it by examining the nature of the scientific group, discovering what it values, what it tolerates, and what it disdains" (Lakatos and Musgrave, 1970; back page).

The clash between scientific realism and positivism in criminology is not Kuhnian, in that followers of the old paradigm will eventually be able to accept the new one because of its superior explanatory power. Rather, at a philosophical level the two are incommensurable (Pawson and Tilley, 1998: 74): they represent different epistemological and ontological assumptions. But, as Pawson and Tilley (1997) note, only part of the argument is conducted at the philosophical level, and the relevance of Kuhn's insights are that the prevailing view in the criminological research community will be as much determined by the distribution of power and influence between key stakeholders, such as those who fund research and gatekeepers to academic journals, as they are about the resolution of philosophical questions about how we understand the world, and its nature.

This raises the question, to what extent are the 'paradigm wars' in criminology (Crow, 2001: p. 52) a dispute about methodology or a battle for academic status between protagonists informed by their own values and with a lot of their own status invested in the outcome? Tilley (2000: p. 110) has already 'come clean' about how his own values include "two sources of contemporary unease: about that aspect of postmodernism which casts doubt on the possibility of objective knowledge; and about that aspect of modernism that promises universal unconditional truths". To these we have to add the value judgments of the policy-making community and practitioners. One could also apply the idea of a paradigm to a CMO configuration itself: in which case, if the criteria of falsification are unclear, they are also socially constructed.

Recognition of the importance of values in selection of research paradigms might support one version of the 'theory of change' approach to evaluation in which the views of key stakeholders on the validity of methods determine their selection:

> The theory of change is a prediction about what leads to what; plausibility to relevant people is critical. They validate in advance; face validity is always important but especially where change [produced by the intervention] is likely to be small. Credibility of

> result is related to stakeholders having agreed not only ultimate
> outcomes, but also interim ones — i.e. if they agree at the start that
> activities abc, properly done, should lead to outcomes xyz — then
> if abc and xyz all occur as expected, they will have confidence that
> the outcomes are due to the interventions. Stakeholders agree in
> advance the standard of evidence which will convince them.
> (Astbury and Knight, 2003: p. 41 quoting Connell and Kubish, 1998)

The importance of stakeholders' views on methodology might be acknowledged by Pawson and Tilley (1998: p. 75) when they state that:

> All research design is a balancing act between the commitment
> to a particular research strategy [presumably the researcher's
> commitment] and the pragmatism needed to match a sponsor's
> expectations [presumably meaning expectations of how the research
> is conducted] and funding.

If the object of evaluation is to change policy, key stakeholders are those who
have power to do this in the policy community, and their views will be
recognized by the design of the research.

Conclusion

The discussion above shows that a conclusion will reflect both one's personal
philosophical position, and one's own values. In this respect I have
considerable affinity for Pawson and Tilley's position. It accords very closely
to the approach I was taking to evaluation research before I was aware of
their own theoretical contribution, for example, in an evaluation of a sports
counselling programme (Nichols and Taylor, 1996) in which I juxtaposed
qualitative and quantitative questions to ask not only if a programme had
an impact, but how and why it did so. In doing this I started from theory
to inform the research design, and added to it. I am in sympathy with the
understanding of 'generative causality' and of the purpose of research to
inform policy. Thus, I must accept that where I agree with an understanding
of a policy *problem* as deserving of research attention, my own value
judgments on what is a *problem* must accord with those of the policy makers.
Of course, this does not preclude disagreement with policy makers over the
definition of a problem, and in this case it will be harder for me to gain funds
to research it.

I sympathise with Tilley, and I am sure with Coalter (2002), in that I want to avoid the extreme relativism of postmodernism which casts doubt on the possibility of objective knowledge. However, in the same way as scientific realism acknowledges the imperfection of a progress of knowledge towards the truth, I have to acknowledge my own imperfect knowledge of the philosophic justification of the approach to knowledge. The methodological limitations, identified above, in a scientific realist position, remain. Given this, I can only 'nail my flag' to the mast of scientific realism as the best we can do so far. However, while advocating a scientific realist approach, one still has to acknowledge that much of the theory that has informed the CMO configuration that underpinned the approach to researching Sportaction, and the development of the map of causal relationships between sport and economic and social benefits used by Coalter (2002: p. 23) has itself been derived from 'quasi-experimental' methods, which have aspired to the classical experimental paradigm.

References

Astbury, R. and Knight, B. (2003) *Fairbridge research project, final report*. London: Charities Evaluation Services.

Bhaskar, R. (1975) *A realist theory of science*. Leeds: Leeds Books.

Bryman, A. (2001) *Social research methods*. Oxford: Oxford University Press.

Bovaird, T., Nichols, G. and Taylor, P. (1997) *Approaches to estimating the wider economic and social benefits resulting from sports participation*. Birmingham: Aston Business School, Research paper 9705.

Catalano, R. and Hawkins, J. D. (1996) 'The social development model: A theory of antisocial behaviour', in Hawkins, J.D. (ed.) *Delinquency and crime*. Cambridge: Cambridge University Press, pp 149–197.

Coalter, F. (2002) *Sport and community development: A manual*. Edinburgh: Sport Scotland.

Collier, A. (1998) 'Critical realism', in *Routledge Encyclopedia of Philosophy*. London: Routledge.

Collins, M. with Kay, T. (2003) *Sport and social exclusion*. London: Routledge.

Connell, J.P. and Kubish, A.C. (1998) 'Applying a theories of change approach to the evaluation of comprehensive community initiatives: Progress, prospects and problems', in Fullbright-Anderson, K., Connell, J.P. and Kubish, A.C. (eds.) *New approaches to evaluating community initiatives: Theory, measurement and analysis*. Washington, DC: Aspen Institute.

Crow, I. (2000) 'Evaluating initiatives in the community', in Jupp, V., Davies, P. and Francis, P. (eds) *Doing criminological research*. London: Sage, pp 114–127.

Crow, I. (2001) *The treatment and rehabilitation of offenders*. London: Sage.

Department for Culture, Media and Sport / Strategy Unit (2002) *Game plan: A strategy for delivering Government's sport and physical activity objectives*. London: Cabinet Office.

Emler, N. (2001) *Self-esteem, the costs and causes of low self-worth*. York: Joseph Rowntree Foundation.

Farrington, D. (2000) 'Explaining and preventing crime: the globalization of knowledge — the American Society of Criminology 1999 Presidential Address', *Criminology* Vol. 38, No. 1: 1–24.

Farrington, D. (1998) Evaluating 'Communities that Care', *Evaluation* Vol. 4, No. 2: pp. 204–210.

Farrington, D. (1996) 'The explanation and prevention of youthful offending', in Hawkins, J.D. (ed) *Delinquency and crime*. Cambridge: Cambridge University Press, pp 68–148.

Huskins, J. (1998) *From disaffection to social inclusion*. Kingsdown: Huskins.

Kuhn, T. (1970a) *The structure of scientific revolutions*, 2nd edition. London: University of Chicago Press.

Kuhn, T. (1970b) 'Logic of discovery or psychology of research', in Lakatos, I. and Musgrave, A. (eds) *Criticism and the growth of knowledge*. London: Cambridge University Press, pp 1–24.

Lakatos, I. and Musgrave, A. (eds) (1970) *Criticism and the growth of knowledge*. London: Cambridge University Press.

Long, J., Welch, M., Bramham, P., Hylton, K., Butterfield, J. & Lloyd, E. (2002) *Count me in: the dimensions of social inclusion through culture and sport*. Report to the Department for Culture Media and Sport. http://www.lmu.ac.uk/ces/lss/research/countmein.pdf .

Nichols, G. (1999a) 'Developing a rationale for sports counselling projects', *The Howard Journal of Criminal Justice* Vol. 38, No. 2: pp. 198–208.

Nichols, G. (1999b) 'Is risk a valuable component of outdoor adventure programmes for young offenders undergoing drug rehabilitation?', *The Journal of Youth Studies* Vol. 2, No. 1: pp. 101–116.

Nichols, G. (2000) 'Risk and adventure education', *Journal of Risk Research* Vol. 3, No. 2: pp. 121–134.

Nichols, G. (2001a) 'A realist approach to evaluating the impact of sports programmes on crime reduction', in McPherson, G. and Reid, G. (eds) *Leisure and social inclusion: New challenges for policy and provision*. Eastbourne: Leisure Studies Association.

Nichols, G. (2001b) 'The use and limitations of reconviction rate analysis to evaluate an outdoor pursuits programme for probationers', *Vista* Vol. 6, No. 3: pp 280–288.

Nichols, G. (2001c) 'The difficulties of justifying local authority sports and leisure programmes for young people with reference to an objective of crime reduction', *Vista* Vol. 6, No. 2: pp. 152–163.

Nichols, G. (2004) 'A model of the process of personal development through the medium of outdoor adventure', in Barnes, P. and Sharp, B. (eds.) *The RHP Companion to Outdoor Education*. Lyme Regis: Russell House Publishing, pp 34–42.

Nichols, G. and Booth, P. (1999) 'Crime reduction programmes supported by local authority leisure departments', *Local Governance* Vol. 25, No. 4: pp. 227–236.

Nichols, G. and Taylor, P. (1996) *West Yorkshire Sports Counselling, Final Evaluation Report*. Halifax: West Yorkshire Sports Counselling Association.

O'Hear, A. (1989) *An introduction to the philosophy of science*. Oxford: Clarendon Press.

Pawson, R. (2003) 'Nothing as practical as a good theory', *Evaluation* Vol. 9, No. 4: 471–490.

Pawson, R. & Tilley, N. (1997) *Realistic evaluation*. London: Sage.

Pawson, R. & Tilley, N. (1998) 'Caring communities, paradigms polemics, design debates', *Evaluation* Vol. 4, No. 1: pp. 73–90.

Tashakkori, A. and Teddlie, C. (1998) *Mixed methodology*. London: Sage.

Tilley, N. (2000) 'Doing realistic evaluation of criminal justice' ,in Jupp, V., Davies, P. and Francis, P. (eds) *Doing criminological research*. London: Sage, pp. 97–113.

Yin, R. (1994) *Case study research*. London: Sage.

EVALUATING SPORTS-BASED INCLUSION PROJECTS: METHODOLOGICAL IMPERATIVES TO EMPOWER MARGINALISED YOUNG PEOPLE

Jacquelyn Allen Collinson, Scott Fleming, John Hockey and Andy Pitchford
University of Gloucestershire

Introduction

The primary focus of this paper is a methodological approach for the evaluation of sports-based inclusion projects, set within the interpretivist and phenomenological traditions. Importantly though, the approach has the potential to be transferred to other empirical contexts which may (or indeed may not) involve young people and/or other marginalised or disempowered individuals or groups. First we discuss briefly some of the debates informing social inclusion and social exclusion, as well as the academic literature on the role of sport as a social inclusionary force, problematising some of the underlying assumptions regarding the motives and aspirations of young people in sports contexts. A series of key principles is subsequently identified which may be deployed in order to facilitate a more sophisticated analysis of the use of sports within social inclusion policy initiatives with young people. The paper concludes with the delineation of a range of measures which can be used to facilitate the involvement of young people in such research projects, and their subsequent evaluation.

Social inclusion and social exclusion

Theories of social exclusion represent a move away from the narrowly focused concept of poverty, with its primary emphasis upon the lack of resources at the disposal of a household or individual, to a more encompassing definition of social inequality. Here the focus is upon relational issues: inadequate social participation, lack of power and lack of social integration (Room, 1995). Despite some difficulty in establishing a consensus on the definition of social exclusion (Democratic Dialogue, 1995; Bittman, 1998), many definitions relate to processes which restrict or deny people participation within society (de Haan & Maxwell, 1998; Burchardt *et al.*, 1999).

The causes of social exclusion are numerous, multi-faceted and interconnected, including for example geographical, educational, economic and cultural variables. People experience exclusion, and thus marginalisation, as a result of a diverse variety of factors, including (often in combination) poverty, homelessness, unemployment, lack of opportunities to participate in public life, lack of fluency in the English language, lack of familiarity with bureaucracies that provide services, or the lack of supportive social networks. Persons are often categorised along different dimensions, and many experience multiple disadvantages which can result in alienation and distance from aspects of the 'mainstream' society (Duffy, 1995). The concept of social exclusion highlights the primary responsibility of the wider society for the condition of its more marginal members, and of the need of all to share equally in the fruits of citizenship (Democratic Dialogue, 1995).

The UK Government has gone some way to addressing this problem since the late 1990s with the setting up of a Social Exclusion Unit (cf. Social Exclusion Unit, 1999) with the remit of achieving a better understanding of social exclusion, and with the eventual aim of formulating and implementing policies which have a focus upon the social inclusion of those defined as excluded. Social inclusion is conceptualised as emphasizing the values and principles of social communities which are tolerant, aware, interdependent, compassionate, based on mutual respect and commitment, and which value diversity (cf. McVicar, 2000). A central feature of UK Government policy is to address social exclusion amongst young people, on the grounds that prevention is better than cure, in terms of those with potential for future exclusion. Significantly, research on young people[1] who are deemed vulnerable to social exclusion points to their position being linked to multiple disadvantages, lack of advice and low self esteem, as well as to the importance of adopting a holistic approach to tackling social exclusion and joblessness, and the need for more accessible and independent advice during the transition from school to work (McVicar, 2000). This attempt at re-integrating the young who are excluded from the labour market has also been accompanied by policies which take a more cultural approach to facilitating their social inclusion. Community-building and the fostering of individual self-esteem, through, for example, the arts and sport, constitute another Government-sponsored strategy (White & Rowe, 2000).

The use of sport as a palliative to the apparent problems of youth has a long history in the UK. Agencies and institutions with a spectrum of motives have viewed sports and recreation activities as a source of distraction, discipline and morality. Ever since evangelical churches at the end of the nineteenth century promoted rational recreation (Holt, 1989), sport has provided institutions with a potential solution to moral panics (after Cohen, 2002) created by debates over the nature and propriety of the behaviour of young people.

The positive view of the virtues of sport is still widely held and provides much of the rhetoric that is often deployed to justify the role and inclusion of Physical Education in the school curriculum[2]. Sport can, it is argued, provide constructive, disciplined activity which provides a focus for the troublesome energy of youth. Competitive team sports, with their core values of teamwork, determination, dedication, respect for authority and loyalty, are construed as preparing young people for the vicissitudes of the labour market, instilling a work ethic which will help to secure and maintain employment. Inclusion in sport, it is held, can lead to inclusion in the labour market, and therefore active engagement with the core structures of society. There is insufficient space here to capture the full complexity and scope of the debates surrounding this particular conceptualisation of sport (but see, for example, Jarvie & Maguire, 1994; Morgan, 1994; Giulianotti, 2004). A brief mention, however, is necessary regarding some of the trenchant sociological critiques which were, in the first instance, descended from a Marxist interpretation of sport as a medium of social control. Young people are, in this view, distracted from meaningful political activity by the opiate of sports participation and spectating. Neo Marxists extend this analysis by considering the role sports play in perpetuating hegemonic power relations, inculcating conservative values which support authority and the status quo (Brohm, 1976). Hegemonic analyses are also used by feminist theorists *inter alia* to explain the historic and contemporary exclusion and marginalisation of women in sporting contexts (Hargreaves, 1994) and also by scholars seeking to examine the position of ethnic minorities in relation to institutionalised sports (Carrington & McDonald, 2001).

While the nuances and subtleties of these interpretations continue to cause disquiet in academic circles, their central thrust is clear. That is to say, mainstream, competitive sports are essentially exclusive activities, supported by membership institutions which regulate entry and access (Hargreaves, 1986). Subordinate classes, or 'minority' groups, are allowed access to these institutions only on the terms of the dominant groups. However, these essentially structural explanations may fail to account for the ability of individuals and communities to resist the intentions of dominant groups and institutions, and actively to construct their own meanings and values. Sub-cultural analysis of young people in sport, inspired by the ethnographic studies of working class youth in the 1970s by Willis (1977) and Corrigan (1979), offer an account of sport as a contested site, in which young people can find enjoyment and challenges which allow them to evade and subvert the intentions of the dominant institutions. From this perspective it is possible to interpret more fully and effectively the motives and experiences of young people in sports settings, while accounting for the range of sports and physical activities chosen — or rejected — by young people at different times and in different places.

Sports-based inclusion projects

In the past five years in particular, academic writing on sport as a device for social inclusion has proliferated. In the UK, sociological and policy-oriented contributions from writers such as Collins (2003), Coalter *et al.* (2000) and Long & Sanderson (2001) have focused on a range of factors including, delivery mechanisms; the apparent lack of evidence-based policy; and questioning the utility of mainstream, institutionalised sports for such programmes. The refocusing of sports resources and the rationalisation of some aspects of sports policy at central Government level has facilitated the development of a number of sports-based inclusion projects, many of which focus on marginalised young people. These inclusion projects are characterised by a range of approaches, but in the main projects are either based on referral systems, counselling and advice or neighbourhood outreach work. In the context of this kind of sports development policy, the failure of this approach is clearly mapped out by the work of Murray (1988), and Carrington (1997), who demonstrate how minority communities have contested and resisted many of the unsubstantiated assumptions which underpin much mainstream policy.

During the same period, Lentell (1994) has questioned the ability of sports development workers to engage effectively with community development agendas. This theme has since been further developed by Hylton and Totten (2002), who argue that community intervention by sports development workers can be based on a series of competing assumptions and ideological positions. Thus, community-based delivery in the sports sector can be *inter alia*:

- a social control mechanism;
- a paternalistic social welfare tool;
- an attempt to democratise culture (to include those who are currently excluded from mainstream cultural practices); or
- an attempt to promote cultural democracy (the devolution of power, resources and responsibility to marginalised groups and individuals).

Critics of sport in contemporary society (Brohm, 1976; Hargreaves, 1986, Hargreaves, 1994; Eitzen, 2001) have highlighted the social exclusion of youth from sport as being linked to gender, social class, and 'race'. However, as indicated above, such structural explanations often fail to account for the active constructions and reconstructions of meaning and values by more marginal individuals and communities. It seems clear that any assumptions made about the motives and aspirations of young people in sports contexts are susceptible to variations in local circumstance, politics, culture, geography, education and socialisation, not to mention class, gender, ethnicity, and so on. Sports inclusion schemes are, necessarily, situated in complex social environments which, for a variety of reasons, demand researchers to take account of local circumstances and to invest in research approaches which counter the prevailing assumptions about sport, and life in general, in these settings.

There are various methodological issues which need to be addressed in researching such schemes, and one research approach in particular constitutes the methodological focus of this paper.

Participatory methodology

Participatory methodology is a research approach within the qualitative tradition, which advocates the involvement of the research stakeholders in the majority, if not the entirety, of the research process. This may include the initial definition of the problem or topic to be researched, through project design, data collection and analysis, to the final written account and evaluation of the research project.

'Methodology' in this sense is not necessarily always applied in its strict social scientific sense — that is, including the underlying philosophy behind the selection of methods. Rather, it may, in some instances, focus more upon the practical, technical aspects of the research project and the utilisation of appropriate methods to ensure that participant-stakeholders do not merely participate as providers of information (for example, as interviewers and/or interviewees), but engage fully in the construction and execution of the research project (e.g., Evans *et al.*, 2000).

In common with other interpretivist approaches, researchers working within the participatory paradigm are committed to seeking an understanding of the social world from the perspective of the social actors who inhabit that world, through their own subjective meanings and experiences. So, for example, researchers focussing upon children and young people would advocate entering the world of the young people as far as practicable, in order to 'tease out' and analyse their subjective meanings and experiences.

In doing so, however, there are (at least) three sets of issues that are encountered. First, there are epistemological debates around the centrality of experience *as* understanding. This has been elaborated upon *inter alia* by Cashmore (1982) and Pryce (1986). The crux of one extreme position that we eschew (and which may be referred to as rampant empiricism), is that it is necessary to experience the social world at first hand to understand it properly and fully, Garfinkel's (2002: p.175) 'unique adequacy requirement'. For Cashmore and others who have attempted to study socio-cultural groups of which they are not a part, have never been a part or are unlikely ever to be a part (e.g., those studied by Fleming, 1995; Howe, 2001), subscribing to this epistemological position would bring into question the validity and status of their work. Even for Pryce, a black researcher from the Caribbean studying a black community in Bristol, there was still the reality of being a University researcher that made his experience different from those of the participants in his study. The point to be inferred from this, then, is that researchers are never going to experience the social world in exactly the same way as their participants unless they study the social world of researchers also studying each other. The practical absurdity of this position is even more transparent when the argument is extended; for if this were the case, it would follow that the only researchers who could experience (and therefore understand) the social worlds of children and young people would be children and young people[3]. Empirical work in the sociology of education (in particular) has evidenced that this is simply not the case (Willis, 1977; Corrigan, 1979; Scraton, 1987). The wider point of principle is also made plain from the domain of sport and leisure studies in which ethnographic accounts (e.g., Willis, 1978; McConnell, 1999; Borden, 2001), and especially those in the investigative tradition (e.g., Sugden, 2002; Sugden & Tomlinson, 1998, 2003) have demonstrated that this position is far too crude, simplistic and unsophisticated.

An alternative approach, one that does not privilege first-hand experience as a precursor to understanding, emphasises the importance of empathy in order to generate understanding. The corollary of this, of course, in contrast to some anthropological approaches, is that minimising 'social distance' as far as practicable increases the likelihood of empathy and understanding. That is to say, when more and more layers of social distance are factored into an attempt to generate understanding, the analysis becomes increasingly susceptible to *mis*understanding.

Second, there are empirical issues which are illuminated by Fetterman's (1989) notes of caution about entering the social worlds of children and young people: "A consistent disregard or lack of concern for the group's basic cultural values will severely impede research progress" (p.55), and "Acting like an adolescent does not win the confidence of adolescents, it only makes them suspicious" (p.56). This is a theme to which the discussion will return.

Third, there are also significant ethical issues about the ways in which the worlds of children and young people can be entered by adult researchers. Of primary importance amongst these is participants' right to exercise voluntary informed consent (cf. Homan, 1991)[4]. Furthermore, however, for children and young people (under the age of 16) there are additional 'conditions' that must be met before research should proceed. As potentially vulnerable populations, there are clear guidelines that should inform the design of ethically responsible research — not least securing voluntary informed consent from parents/guardians as well as organisational gate-keepers (see Sieber, 1992; British Educational Research Association, 2004).

The point here is *not* that covert or deceptive research is always unacceptable, even with children or young people; but there are two essential criteria that should be met before engaging in the practice of covert research[5]:

- the research question(s) should be worth asking;
- no alternative data collection methods exist that could answer the same question without the need to violate voluntary informed consent.

Notwithstanding these sets of issues, providing they can be resolved satisfactorily, it is the intention of researchers adopting this kind of participatory approach that ultimately children and young people are enabled and empowered (Williamson, 1995) to examine critically their own worlds, to identify and research topics of concern, problems and possible solutions, and in general to learn from the research experience.

A commitment to a participatory methodology also implies strongly a willingness to share widely the research findings in accessible formats and fora with the communities involved, so that the results of the project are available for evaluation by stakeholders and the communities they represent and serve, and also can be fed into future projects (see, for example, the recent Football Association-funded study of child protection — Brackenridge *et al.*, 2003; Pitchford *et al.*, 2004, Brackenridge *et al.*, 2004; Russell, 2004).

Key principles

Commensurate with participatory methdology, a series of key principles has been identified which may be deployed in order to facilitate a more sophisticated analysis of the use of sports within social inclusion policy initiatives with young people. These principles include the need to:

- consider the social worlds of youth from an insider-member perspective;
- chart and analyse the subjective experiences of young people themselves;
- provide young people with the social space in which to give 'voice' to their thoughts and feelings (cf. Hollands, 1995; Brackenridge *et al.*, 2003);
- counteract the 'democratic deficit' in ensuring more effective participation and citizenship of young people (Evans, 1998; Cutler & Frost, 2001).

These principles can work to enhance the research conducted on social inclusion projects, sports-based or more general, in a number of ways. As Wadsworth (1998) has pointed out, a collaborative research process can help to:

1) improve the relevance of the inquiry to those who share the problem;
2) sharpen the focusing of the research questions;
3) enhance the relevance of the inquiry to service providers (funders, sports development officers, etc).
4) increase the effectiveness of the research design;
5) improve the meaningfulness of the information gained (the researched can evaluate the accuracy of the data);
6) increase the power of any theory developed to analyse and understand the problem.

Facilitatory factors

There are a number of measures which can be used to facilitate the involvement of young people in such research projects, and their subsequent evaluation. The first involves establishing an understanding that the research project is a collaborative venture between professional researchers and the particular group/community. All parties will have mutual authority and responsibility. In this way researchers seek an equivalent voice in the research process rather than a dominant one. Thus the expertise of young people is incorporated integrally within the 'natural history' of the project in terms of evaluating its success or failure from their own insider perspective. This might, for example, involve young people making joint decisions with the research team regarding the content of the final report, its evaluation, format, and possibly also its diffusion.

Second, there is a need to ensure that stakeholder-participants understand the value of their local knowledge (Geertz, 1993) for the success of the research venture itself. This involves facilitating young people in their use of the stock of local knowledge as they begin to evaluate the sports project present in their area. Again the interaction here is collaborative.

Third, the provision of some training in fieldwork methods and research ethics is needed so as to allow and encourage their use of local knowledge as an evaluative tool. Part of this will be exposure to various data collection techniques, to allow the young people and their peers to give 'voice' in relation to the sports projects in their locale. These techniques may cover both the orthodox (e.g., systematic observation, sociometry, individual interviews, focus groups, participant observation) and the more innovative[6] (e.g., performance art, still photography, video diary, 'vox pop', texted notes). Given that young people are often particularly receptive to media and new technology, consideration should be given to the use of various audio and visual means of documentation.

Fourth, there is a need to employ a common communication vocabulary[7] so that stakeholder-participants understand both the project and its evaluation. This will involve coming to a shared purpose, namely coming to understand not just for its own sake, but in order to change things for the better via action; and may be achieved by what Pink Dandelion (1997) has described as the 'overt insider to the context' (see Figure 1).

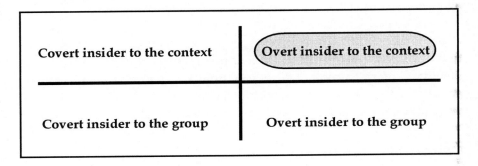

Figure 1:   A typology of 'insider research'
              Source: Pink Dandelion (1997: p. 182)

"That's all very well, but in the real world ... "

What we have sketched out in the previous sections reflects a set of principles and commitments that are intended to facilitate the empowerment of children and young people by 'giving them a voice'. That, in itself, is not enough. It is also important that those who seek an informed view from children and young people listen very carefully, and act in an appropriately empathetic manner. Importantly too, we are acutely aware of the operational and logistical difficulties and tensions associated with the participatory approach that we have described. These may be summarised as either empirical or ethical (though, of course, they intersect), and a brief note on each is therefore required.

Empirical difficulties may be identified as being concerned either with research design or with implementation. In the principles outlined above there is an explicit intention to have the participants involved throughout the process. The reality is that very often an evaluation of the effectiveness of a strategy or policy is undertaken *post hoc*. Logically, that would seem to be a truism. Yet that does not *necessarily* prevent the detail of its implementation being planned from the outset. By identifying those persons likely to be involved in the evaluation process, they can themselves become more sensitized to it, and thus more effective at it. Additionally, evaluation is often undertaken by an agency that was not responsible for the delivery of the strategy/policy. This too brings its own inherent difficulties — especially when the apparent independence that this provides takes primacy. Finally, there is a clear tension that exists in the 'real world' of commercial research between, on the one hand, the most academically rigorous and robust empirical research (which is inevitably more resource-intensive than some alternatives); and on the other hand, competitive cost-effectiveness.

The second set of issues may be thought of as concerned with research ethics. Involving children and young people in the entire process in the ways that have been described *does* present pragmatic challenges for securing voluntary informed consent effectively from all relevant stakeholders (see above). These challenges should not, though, be seen as insurmountable — for they are not. And in any case, in whose interests are the safeguards in place?

Concluding comments

In this paper we have sought to portray the potential of a participative methodological approach for researching and evaluating sports-based inclusion projects in order to address some of the criticisms levelled at some of the extant academic studies of young people in sports contexts. A series of key principles has been identified, together with some of the potential benefits of collaborative research. Finally, a range of measures to facilitate the involvement of young people in research projects, and their subsequent evaluation, has been advanced. Participatory methodology is proposed as an approach which can facilitate a more sophisticated analysis of the use of sports within social inclusion policy initiatives with young people. This approach seeks to give full voice to a group of marginalised social actors who have traditionally been 'silenced' within many fora, including much of the research and other literature. It is hoped thereby to enable and empower them to examine critically their own social worlds. This may of course provide a trenchant critique of, and challenge to dominant received discourses.

Acknowledgement

We are grateful for the contributions from delegates at the Leisure Studies Association annual conference at Leeds Metropolitan University in July 2004 where a version of this paper was presented and discussed.

Notes

1 Whether research is done 'on', 'about' or 'with' young people is more than mere semantics over prepositions. There has been a tendency to do research *on* young people, implying (at best) some kind of paternalism. In this paper we argue for a more central and significant role for research *with* young people.

2 The irony is, of course, that those positive features of Physical Education [PE] are often more accurately those that are promoted and celebrated in only one part of one aspect of a broad, balanced PE curriculum — major team games. The misunderstandings are concerned with two sets of conceptual conflations: first, PE as sport; and second, team games as PE.

3 Or, perhaps even worse still, on the basis that every adult researcher had at some point been a child and a young person, they were all sufficiently qualified and experienced to do research with children and young people.

4 In a pragmatic sense, it may be helpful to think of other substantive themes in research ethics as risk and harm, confidentiality, anonymity, privacy, data protection. All of these may be captured in the 'permission' that is provided in completely voluntary, fully informed, consenting approval.

5   It is inevitable that in some instances the requirements of voluntary informed consent are incompatible with socially beneficial research — and in such instances consequentialist arguments are often advanced. As Hollway and Jefferson (2000: p.7) explain, there are also some modified forms of consent that have been used to overcome some of the concerns without (apparently) undermining the ethical integrity and propriety of particular projects. These include ex- post facto consent (getting approval of research subjects retrospectively), proxy or presumptive consent (getting approval from mock subjects), and prior general consent (getting general approval for deceptive procedures before the experiment).

6   Many of the techniques/methods that may be deployed are not, in themselves, innovative. Indeed they may be even thought commonplace in other disciplinary conventions and subject fields (e.g., media studies — see Pink, 2002; Bolton *et al.*, 2001). The innovation, such as it is, lies in their use for this kind of strategy/policy evaluation.

7   This should not involve adult researchers merely copying the vernacular or mimicking the vocabulary of young people inauthentically. Rather, it should involve recognition of the sophisticated and nuanced manner in which young people attach particular meanings to words.

References

Bittman, M. (1998) 'Social participation and family welfare: The money and time costs of leisure'. Paper from *6th Australian Institute of Family Studies Conference — Changing families, challenging futures.* [http://www.aifs.org.au/external/institute/afrc6papers/bittman.html]

Bolton, A., Pole, C. & Mizen, P. (2001) 'Picture this: Researching child workers', *Sociology*, Vol. 35 (2): pp. 501–518.

Brackenridge, C., Pitchford, A., Russell, K., Nutt, G. & Allen Collinson, J. (2003) *Child Protection in Football Project 2003. Final report on year two — review.* Glasgow: Celia Brackenridge Ltd.

Brackenridge, C., Pitchford, A., Russell, K., Nutt, G., Bringer, J. & Pawlaczek, Z. (2004) 'The Football Association's Child Protection Research Project 2002–2006: rationale, design and first year results', *Managing Leisure,* Vol. 9: pp. 30–46.

Borden, I. (2001) *Skateboarding, space and the city.* Oxford: Berg.

British Educational Research Association (2004) *Revised ethical guidelines for educational research.* London: BERA.

Brohm, J. M. (1976) *Sport: A prison of measured time*. London: Pluto Press.

Burchardt, T., Le Grand, J., and Piachaud, D. (1999) 'Social exclusion in Britain 1991 — 1995', *Social Policy and Administration*, Vol. 33 (3): pp. 227–244.

Carrington, B. (1997) 'Community, identity and sport: an exploration of the significance of sport within Black Communities', paper presented to the *British Sociological Association Annual Conference, 'Power/Resistance'*, University of York, April 1997.

Carrington, B. & McDonald, I. (eds) (2001) *Race, sport and British society*. London: Routledge.

Cashmore, E. (1982) 'Black youth for whites', in E. Cashmore & B. Troyna (eds) *Black youth in crisis*. London: George Allen & Unwin, pp.10–14.

Coalter, F., Allison, M. & Taylor, J. (2000) *The role of sport in regenerating deprived urban areas*. Edinburgh: University of Edinburgh.

Cohen, S. (2002) *Folk devils and moral panics*. 2nd edition. London: Taylor & Francis.

Collins, M. (2003) *Sport and social exclusion*. London: Routledge.

Corrigan, P. (1979) *Schooling the Smash Street kids*. London: Macmillan.

Cutler, D. & Frost, R. (2001) *Taking the initiative: Promoting young people's involvement in public decision-making in the UK*. London: Carnegie Young People Initiative.

de Haan, A. & Maxwell, S. (1998) 'Poverty and social exclusion in North and South', *IDS Bulletin*, Vol. 29 (1): 1–9.

Democratic Dialogue (1995) *Social Inclusion, Social Exclusion*. [*http://www. democraticdialogue.org/report2/report2.htm.*]

Duffy, K. (1995) *Social exclusion and human dignity in Europe. Background report for the proposed initiative by the Council of Europe*. Brussels: CDPS.

Eitzen, D. S. (ed) (2001) *Sport in contemporary society: an anthology*. New York: Worth Publishers.

Evans, K. (1998) *Shaping futures: Learning for competence and citizenship*. Aldershot: Ashgate.

Evans, L., Hardy, L. & Fleming, S. (2000) 'Intervention strategies with injured athletes: An action research study', *The Sport Psychologist* Vol. 14 (2): pp. 188–206.

Fetterman, D. (1989) *Ethnography step by step*. London: Sage.

Fleming, S. (1995) *"Home and away": Sport and South Asian male youth*. Aldershot: Avebury.

Garfinkel, H. (edited by Warfield Rawls, A.) (2002) *Ethnomethodology's program: Working out Durkheim's aphorism*. New York: Rowman & Littlefield.

Geertz, C. (1993) *Local knowledge*. New York: Fontana Press.

Giulianotti, R. (ed) (2004) *Sport and social theorists: A plurality of perspectives*. London: Palgrave Macmillan.

Hargreaves, John (1986) *Sport, power and culture*. Cambridge: Polity Press.

Hargreaves, Jennifer (1994) *Sporting females — Critical issues in the history and sociology of women's sports*. London: Routledge.

Hollands, R. (1995) *Friday night, Saturday night*. Newcastle: Newcastle University Press.

Hollway, W. & Jefferson, T. (2000) *Doing qualitative research differently: Free association, narrative and the interview method*. London: Sage.

Holt, R. (1989) *Sport and the British — A modern history*. Oxford: Oxford University Press.

Homan, R. (1991) *The ethics of social research*. London: Longman.

Howe, P.D. (2001) 'An ethnography of pain and injury in professional rugby union: The case of Pontypridd RFC', *International Review for the Sociology of Sport*, Vol. 35 (3): 289–303.

Hylton, K. & Totten, M. (2002) 'Community sports development', in K. Hylton, P. Bramham, D. Jackson & M. Nesti (eds) *Sports development: policy, process and practice*. London: Routledge.

Jarvie, G. & Maguire, J. (1994) *Sport and leisure in social thought*. London, Routledge.

Lentell B. (1994) 'Sports development: Goodbye to community development?', in C. Brackenridge (ed) *Body matters, images and lifestyles*, LSA Publication No 47. London: LSA, pp. 141–149.

Long, J. & Sanderson, A. (2001) 'The social benefits of sport: Where's the proof?', in C. Gratton & I. Henry (eds) *Sport in the city*. London: Routledge, pp. 187–203.

McConnell, R. (1999) *Inside the All Blacks*. London: Willow Collins.

McVicar, D. (2000) *Marginalised young people and social inclusion policy in Northern Ireland*. Working Paper No 54. Northern Ireland Economic Research Centre, Belfast: NIERC.

Morgan, W.J. (1994) *Leftist theories of sport: A critique and reconstruction*. Chicago: University of Illinois Press.

Murray, K. (1988) 'The Brixton Leisure Centre: An analysis of a political institution', *International Review of the Sociology of Sport* Vol. 23 (2): pp. 125–138.

Pink, S. (2002) *Doing visual ethnography*. London: SAGE.

Pink Dandelion, B. (1997) 'Insider dealing: Researching your own private world', in A. Tomlinson & S. Fleming (eds) *Ethics, sport and leisure: Crises and critiques.* Aachen: Meyer & Meyer Verlag.

Pitchford, A., Brackenridge, C., Russell, K., Nutt, G., Bringer, J. & Pawlaczek, Z. (2004) 'Children in football: Seen but not heard', *Soccer in Society* Vol. 5 (1): pp. 43–60.S

Pryce, K. (1986) *Endless pressure.* 2nd edition. Bristol: Bristol Classical Press.

Room, G. (ed) (1995) *Beyond the threshold: the measurement and analysis of social exclusion.* Bristol: The Policy Press.

Russell, K. (2004) Opportunities for playing? Gendered structures of youth football. Paper presented at the Leisure Studies Association annual conference, Leeds Metropolitan University (July).

Scraton, S. (1987) '"Boys muscle in where angels fear to tread" — Girls' sub-cultures and physical activities', in J. Horne, D. Jary & A. Tomlinson (eds) *Sport, leisure and social relations.* London: Routledge & Kegan Paul, pp.160–186.

Sieber, J.E. (1992) *Planning ethically responsible research.* London: Sage.

Social Exclusion Unit (SEU) (1999) *Bridging the gap: new opportunities for 16–18 year olds not in education, employment or training.* Report by the Social Exclusion Unit. London: HM Stationery Office, CM 4405.

Sugden, J. (2002) *Scum Airways. Inside football's underground economy.* London: Mainstream.

Sugden, J. & Tomlinson, A. (1998) *FIFA and the contest for world football. Who rules the people's game?* London: Polity.

Sugden, J. & Tomlinson, A. (2003) *Badfellas. FIFA family at war.* London: Mainstream.

Wadsworth, Y. (1998) 'What is participatory action research?, Action Research international, 2. [Available at: http://www.scu.edu.au/schools/gcm/ar/ari/p-ywadsworth98.html]

White, A. & Rowe, D. (2000) *Sport for All — the United Kingdom experience.* Unpublished report, Sport England.

Williamson, H. (ed) (1995) *Social action for young people: accounts of SCF youth work practice.* Lyme Regis: Russell House.

Willis, P. (1977) *Learning to labour: How working class kids get working class jobs.* Farnborough: Saxon House.

Willis, P. (1978) *Profane culture.* London: Routledge & Kegan Paul.

IMPOVERISHED LEISURE EXPERIENCES: HOW CAN ACTIVE LEISURE PROGRAMMES MAKE A DIFFERENCE?

An analysis of the use of leisure life histories in programmes for young offenders

Fiona McCormack
Buckinghamshire Chilterns University College

Introduction

The rationale for active leisure interventions in juvenile delinquency is based on traditional theories where outcomes are linked to provision of physically demanding activity, self discipline and competition. This is closely linked to the theories of constructive leisure activity, that is leisure activity that conforms to society's norms and offers benefits to the participant. It has developed from rational recreation which was an early attempt to control the activities of the working class through their leisure time, by instilling the Protestant work ethic: leisure as a reward for work, to be used to improve oneself. Hargreaves (1986: p. 22) summarised the early philosophy of rational recreation as:

> ...'improving', 'educational', respectable and more refined than the boisterous and dissolute pursuits of popular culture. The alternative model offered was a more privatised family centred recreation and wholesome entertainment, catered for by respectable institutions under the supervision of dominant groups.

A century later, contemporary applications advocate the power of constructive leisure activities as a tool for teaching social skills to young people at risk of offending. This relies on the concept that recreation is an effective tool with which to instil the values and behaviour accepted by society in

61

general, and which helps young people to develop self respect and a sense of physical well being. Examples such as the Scouting movement are used to support this idea. Constructive leisure behaviour can therefore be defined in terms of activities which offer positive impacts for the individual and society; examples can be either participating, such as swimming, or creative such as arts and music. Non-constructive use of leisure time includes activities which harm society or the individual such as vandalism and drug abuse. Constructive leisure behaviour continues to be encouraged through public sector subsidised provision and contracted services from private companies.

Politicians and government policy have embraced this theory for many decades. This can be traced back to the Scarman Report (1982) which suggested that the Brixton riots were closely linked to a lack of constructive leisure opportunities for young people. Young offenders have also acknowledged the importance of leisure. In an Audit Commission survey (1996) 13% said that sports participation and 11% said that leisure activities would prevent other people offending. Although these figures are a relatively small proportion of the sample, response rates to this questions were low and ideas somewhat limited, thus making these observations worthy of note. The importance of early experiences is supported by Roberts (1999: p. 140):

> ...childhood and youth leisure socialisation are crucial. Most people base the rest of their leisure lives on interests, which may be subsequently built upon, to which they were initially introduced when young.

He suggested that although leisure learning is not restricted to childhood, the process during adulthood is incremental and relies on building from childhood experiences. Since leisure patterns appear to have such an important impact on young people's life styles this paper will consider whether there should be greater support for the idea of leisure education. It will also examine how life history profiles can help to deliver appropriate leisure counselling interventions.

Firstly the importance of leisure education will be considered within its theoretical and contemporary contexts. Given the increased level of free time experienced by young people, particularly through unemployment, should education not only prepare young people for work but also for leisure? This idea has been expressed for many years. Bacon (1982) raised a concern about the lack of preparation of young people for leisure, a concern that was reiterated by Roberts (1983: p. 58):

Are today's young people being better prepared for their futures? ...we have still not developed effective means of delivering recreational interests to all young people, especially girls, and male and female early school leavers, mainly from working- class homes.

In contemporary society this argument can be supported by the high levels of youth unemployment, which leaves thousands of young people with no direction, little money and plenty of free time. However, preparing young people to benefit from this free time has generally been ignored both by schools and the youth service. This left the responsibility for leisure education to the family. In most families this was adequately provided. However in the often chaotic family structures of many socially excluded communities this process cannot be relied upon. For these young people the assimilation of positive and constructive use of leisure time from a supportive family is unlikely. Many socially excluded families will have little experience of the choices and processes by which leisure opportunity is accessed.

The process of leisure education became unfashionable in the 1980s since it was viewed as importing or teaching what is a worthy or wise use of time. This has been conceived from the concept of rational recreation developed in the 1800s to support the provision of leisure services, particularly for young people. However the approach to leisure education currently reflects "a total movement to enable individuals to enhance the quality of their lives in leisure" (Mundy & Odum, 1979: p. 2). This should result in "increasing the individuals' options for satisfying quality experiences in leisure" (Mundy & Odum, 1979: p. 13). What leisure education no longer seeks is to "communicate predetermined standards concerning what is good or bad, worthy or unworthy uses of leisure". Nor does it seek to advocate "a leisure-style for everyone" (Mundy, 1998: p. 7).

Mundy (1998: p. 9) identifies two philosophical premises which are fundamental to the implementation of effective leisure education programmes:

1 The essence of leisure is freedom, therefore leisure education must above all else facilitate individual self determination.
2 The leisure experience is a uniquely individual experience; therefore the individual should be the primary focus: recipient of values, evaluation of outcomes; and agents of the leisure education process.

By providing an individual development model, Mundy suggests that greater understanding of the impacts of leisure choices not only on their own lives but also on the community will be achieved. She proposed a three tier process for leisure education to involve leisure awareness, self awareness and leisure skills.

Constructive leisure participation offers benefits in terms of interest, opportunity for self expression, and social interaction. Unlike sport and physical recreation, constructive leisure need not test physical ability, nor offer an enforced sense of competition. Examples of leisure education and community based constructive leisure can be found in the USA as identified by Witt and Crompton (1996). Their study included the example of Madison School Community Recreation department, who through providing multiple strategies for reaching at risk youth, demonstrated improvements in a number of protective factors for at risk young people including greater participation in activities, attention to school study and an increased amount of time spent with adults and peers in positive activity.

This research therefore sought to explore the impact of leisure education informed by life history profiling on a group of socially excluded young people. This was completed by using the Hampshire Probation Service's Sports Counselling programme, a well established programme which had emerged from a Sports Council National Demonstration Project. The project was the brain child of a committed local businessman and magistrate in the Solent area. He was convinced that many of the young people referred to him through the courts needed support for constructive leisure and an opportunity to burn up energy through physical activity. With the support of a Methodist minister in Portsmouth, he set up the Solent Sports Counselling Project in 1983. This project could be seen as political protest against the growing lobby for harsher penalties for young offenders, and reflected the political ideology of the founders. It gained the support of the Manpower Services Commission, which funded one staff post. From this the project expanded and became one of the longest surviving examples of this style of intervention.

Although some previous studies have contained individual participants' profiles and a general analysis of their offending background (Tungatt, 1990; Taylor & Nichols, 1996), there has been little attempt to analyse the existing leisure patterns of young people joining sports and active leisure schemes, or to examine the processes by which these patterns emerged. Life histories were recorded using semi-structured interviews and a pro forma adapted from the City Sport Challenge project (Brodie, Roberts and Lamb, 1991). The interview format covered broader leisure behaviour, leisure biographies and motivations or constraints. These were supplemented by additional interview questions.

As with the City Sport analysis, participants were asked to report the patterns of their leisure behaviour from 10 years old. Activities earlier than this may be distorted by memory and are mainly influenced by external forces. Each pro forma was entered into a database and processed using the spreadsheet package, Excel. Individual pro formas were then analysed, and factors related to changes in leisure behaviour were mapped. Life history charts derived from Hedges (1986) were used to record the interview and provide a visual map.

An important element of the Hampshire project was to achieve sustainable constructive leisure patterns among participants. Seventy percent of the sample had joined the Scheme as a conscious decision to improve their health and fitness. However, the process of leisure education was a lengthy one, in many cases requiring more than the standard four sessions. Half of the sample reported that the Scheme provided sufficient contact for them. The average number of sessions was eight for completed participants. Most of the clients who successfully altered their leisure patterns required long-term contact, often for as many as ten sessions. Rather than creating client dependence on the counsellor, this seemed to ensure that changes in behaviour were established before contact ceased.

By using life history profiles it was possible to identify individual leisure experiences and common themes among the sample. There was little evidence in the life history profiles of existing constructive leisure before starting the Sports Counselling Scheme. This was demonstrated by the fact that 46% of the sample had never visited a leisure centre. Furthermore, recreation club membership among participants was very low, only 8% of the sample had joined clubs prior to referral, and many of these were snooker or gambling clubs. This aspect of leisure behaviour remained virtually unchanged; only one of the follow up sample successfully joined a club as a result of the sports counselling, as shown below.

This participant had a complicated offending history and was the oldest participant in the sample. He had committed an array of petty offences but also had had more serious schedule 1 offences in the past which had resulted in long terms in custody. He was suffering depression and needed help to adopt positive leisure patterns. He had enjoyed sport before custody including football and golf. He had also tried badminton and fitness training in custody, but had failed to pursue them on release. He had no previous use of leisure centres. He saw a lack of company and knowledge of facilities as his greatest constraints to participation. He completed ten sessions with the Scheme and reported sustained changes to his leisure during the follow-up period. He tried bowls and pitch and putt during the Scheme and was introduced to a bridge club. He continued to attend the bridge club and to play bowls throughout the follow up period. In this example the scheme had encouraged him to mix outside the pub network, which made a significant impact on many life style choices. By developing interests outside the pub network the participant was able to control his alcohol consumption with positive impacts on his depression. He was able to build a new peer group with positive role models and support. He also experienced improved physical health.

A total of 88% of those who completed the Scheme reported an intention to continue to participate in the exit interview. Seventy nine percent of participants intended to continue to use leisure centres after the project ended. They reported that the Scheme had significantly improved their confidence and perception of leisure centres from a common initial perception that "they are too expensive, really only there for people with jobs and money who play well" (Stuart, interview Portsmouth, 1997).

However the follow up also revealed cases where although leisure patterns had been changed, this ingrained perception of leisure centres remained unchanged. This was demonstrated by a young man in his mid twenties who had already completed a custodial sentence and had a record of aggravated bodily harm, possession of a weapon, and other alcohol-related offences. His Probation Officer felt that he needed help to develop more constructive leisure interests, which could help him to channel his aggression by improving his self esteem and fitness. He was concerned to counter boredom and wanted to get fitter. He chose weights and running as activities, both of which he had tried before, but dropped due to lack of company and encouragement. He had enjoyed football at school and tried weight training on several occasions.

He spent ten sessions with the Scheme, somewhat longer than anticipated, but during this time he trained for the Great South Run. He and other participants on the Scheme completed the Run successfully. He enjoyed the preparation and found the Run was a goal to aim for. He felt that his self esteem was greatly enhanced having managed to stick at something and achieve the objectives: "I think that the sessions were good because they gave me a goal to aim for" (Paul, Portsmouth, 1997). Since completion he had managed to keep the running going through a winter but decided not to use leisure centres, which he still felt were inaccessible, elitist and expensive.

The success of the scheme in changing leisure behaviour was assessed by reviewing patterns over a 12 month period after completing the scheme

Table 1: Patterns of continued participation

Past leisure patterns	Intended to continue at exit stage	After 6 months	After 12 months
Previous leisure centre use	100%	67%	58%
Non participant	75%	67%	33%
Total	88%	67%	46%

is shown in Table 1. After 6 months, two thirds were still participating in activities introduced by the project. The Scheme was more successful at re-establishing constructive leisure than working with non participants. It is important to note that the intention to continue after completion was short-lived for previous non-participants; after 12 months only 33% were participating. After optimistic commitment from all with prior leisure use, there was sustained activity for 58% of the sample after a year. The reason for drop out at 12 months was often related to new work commitments. The options set up by the scheme were targeted at the unemployed, therefore once in employment their ability to continue was reduced.

The case studies revealed many predictable factors that enable continued participation in leisure activities introduced during the project, such as reducing cost and improving physical accessibility. However, in depth interviews showed that, although these were important, the most significant constraints to participation were lack of confidence and company. Therefore the participants reported greater success in activities where either company was unnecessary such as weight training and swimming, or where follow-up, drop in sessions were arranged, for example, football in Southampton, and badminton in Portsmouth and the Isle of Wight.

Approximately 90% of participants who completed four or more sessions reported trying at least two different activities while on the Scheme. The greatest number of activities was five, and in this case the participant had failed to continue with any of them on completion. When the contact time is short, the results showed that one or two activities repeated more frequently were more likely to result in continued participation. If no time constraints existed, then trying a wide range of activities might be an excellent start, but when the number of sessions was limited, repeating the activity selected helped to achieve continued participation.

Regular sessions with one to one contact and encouragement most effectively addressed the issue of self-confidence. However the target of completing the Great South Run was reported as a major incentive and confidence booster for those involved. In many cases self confidence to access local leisure facilities was simply boosted by accompanying the participants until they were familiar with the systems in place such as payment, lockers, gym induction and use of apparatus. These observations further emphasise the need for informal leisure education since many at risk young people lack both the confidence and knowledge to access facilities in their local area.

The analysis of leisure patterns of young people at risk of offending showed that leisure experiences and levels of participation were very limited. Costs and lack of money were significant constraints on their participation. The research showed that after offending young people became isolated, and a lack of information about opportunities became a more significant factor influencing leisure behaviour. The incidence of mental health problems, noticeably depression, was also a significant feature. Many convicted young offenders in the research reported currently being treated for depression. This significantly altered their dependence on the sports counsellor or mentor and often resulted in a need to use a one to one volunteer to offer longer term contact.

These reported constraints to participation, combined with the life history profiles of past leisure behaviour, demonstrated that such young people need adult support to create effective sports and leisure opportunities. Young people at risk of offending were shown to have little knowledge of discount schemes such as the Leisure Pass in Southampton. This was traced to the limited role of parents or carers in childhood, showing that parents had little input into leisure patterns. Siblings and peers were the most common mentors.

Young people also reported that many activities on offer were team or course based — aiming at performance level sport — and so they felt excluded. Young people at risk of offending often demonstrated ties to social settings and levels of deprivation which precluded such levels of commitment and support. Current styles of leisure provision created frustration for these young people, who wanted to play sport simply for recreation, and on demand.

The formal recording of life history profiles for participants has been shown to clarify the complex array of life events that have contributed to the situation faced by participants when they enter a scheme. This provides three important sets of information to assist providers:

- The relationship between life events and participation in leisure activity. This helps in designing sustainable individual programmes and identifying constraints to participation. It identifies previous interests which may be re- established.
- The sample of life history profiles provides clear visual evidence of the impacts of life events on the development of leisure patterns.
- The life history chart provides a focus for leisure counselling, as part of the leisure education process.

By recording life experiences and leisure participation graphically, it is easier to explore the relationship between life events and participation in leisure activity. For example, the chart may reveal the sudden absence of a previously popular activity. In the follow up interview by cross referencing the life events, counsellors can examine with participants the reason for stopping leisure pursuits. Participants may then make connections to other life events such as truanting, moving home or school exclusion. This helps participants to reflect on past experiences and possibly see them in a more positive way. For example, if an activity stopped the young person may have thought it was because they were no good at it or that they did not like it; but by making connections to life events they may realise that the activity had stopped for other reasons beyond their control. This discussion may help to rekindle past interests and tailor sustainable individual programmes while identifying constraints to participation. Results from the research suggest that sustained participation is more likely to occur from activities where the participants had some prior experience. Re-establishing activities is easier than introducing new activities.

The life history chart provides a focus for leisure counselling as part of the leisure education process. The chart can be used to demonstrate to young people the reasons for and strengths or weaknesses of their previous leisure choices. This can help them to take control of leisure choices and reduce the drift into anti social leisure. This is shown in the following example, which demonstrates the importance of the counselling and continuing support through casual drop in sessions. These were instrumental, not only in providing ongoing support, but also as a way for the participant to have a sense of responsibility and purpose.

One participant was a young man in his early twenties with a history of drug and alcohol abuse. These habits had contributed to his offending behaviour. He identified boredom as a major problem and another contributory factor in his offending. Both he and his Probation Officer identified that he had problems controlling aggression, which was attributed to general frustration. His youth had been spent in comprised a unstable family with frequent changes in his domestic situation. As a result he had lacked direction and guidance with his lifestyle choices, including use of leisure time.

On joining the project he was keen to reduce boredom and return to badminton which he had enjoyed in the past. He identified lack of support as a key factor limiting his choice of leisure activities. His involvement with the Scheme was sustained as on completion he remained to help at a regular badminton session, which he felt gave him the sense of responsibility that he needed to rebuild his self esteem. After 12 months he reported regular participation in football, badminton and fencing. He reported: "I found the benefits to be immense ... they include increased health and fitness also an increase in self esteem and self confidence...".

This paper has identified the need to provide leisure education for some socially excluded groups within society. Without this intervention many of these young people will lack the confidence, skills and knowledge to access leisure opportunities. For older adolescents and adults the use of leisure life history profiles in the counselling process can increase the effectiveness of the intervention by identifying individual needs and constraints. This is supported by Mundy's (1998) emphasis on the need for self determination and individualism in the leisure education process. However for socially excluded groups some styles of leisure provision remain inaccessible. In particular they want more opportunities for casual participation, open access or drop sessions. Young people from these groups found clubs and sports courses to be too formal with too great an emphasis on competition and performance.

The research therefore indicates the benefits to be derived from taking time in the initial stages of a sports or leisure counselling process. By collecting life history data in an initial interview, analysing and presenting this in a simple visual format and then discussing the results in a second interview, the counsellor can facilitate a negotiated programme which more accurately meets the needs of an individual. These conclusions are supported by Collins (2003) who advocates the longer term benefits of tailoring provision to individual needs. Although this is a more costly option he suggests that without mentoring, services may be "devoured by active, informed, mobile and more affluent residents" (Collins, 2003: p. 96).

The cost of this style of intervention is likely to remain a problem for providers. The sports counselling scheme no longer exists — it was merged into the standard referral process, a compulsory Community Links Assessment. This consisted of three sessions with the Community Links officers. In session one there was a health assessment and the City Council's leisure pass scheme was explained and issued. If further support was required then the volunteer system was used to provide a leisure mentor. These developments may illustrate the problems facing an individual leisure counselling approach to interventions. The scheme was outside the statutory requirements of the probation service, costly in staff time and, despite large scale research programmes, direct links to recidivism were difficult to establish. However the qualitative evidence suggests that individual leisure counselling can make a significant difference to the lifestyles of socially excluded, at risk young people.

References

Audit Commission (1996) *Misspent youth — young people and crime*. Audit Commission, Abingdon, Oxon.

Bacon, W. (1982) *Leisure and learning in the 1980s* (LSA Publication No. 14). Eastbourne: Leisure Studies Association.

Brodie, D., Roberts, K. & Lamb, K. (1991) *City sport challenge*. Cambridge: Health Promotion Research Trust.

Collins, M. (2003) *Sport and social exclusion*. London: Routledge.

Hargreaves, J. (1986) *Sport, power and culture*. Cambridge: Polity Press.

Hedges, B. (1986) *Personal leisure histories*. London: Sports Council and ESRC.

Mundy, J. & Odum, L. (1979) *Leisure education: Theory and practice*. New York: Wiley & Sons.

Mundy, J. (1998) *Leisure education: Theory and practice*. Second Edition. Champaign (Ill): Sagamore Publishing.

Roberts, K. (1983) *Youth and leisure*. London: Allen and Unwin.

Roberts K. (1999) *Leisure in contemporary society*. Wallingford (Oxon): CABI Publishing.

Scarman, Lord (1982) *The Scarman Report*. London: Penguin.

Taylor, P. & Nichols, G. (1996) *West Yorkshire Probation Service Sports Counselling Project Final Evaluation Report*. Sheffield: Sheffield University.

Tungatt, M. (1990) *Solent Sports Counselling Project, Hampshire Probation Service, final evaluation*. Manchester: North West Sports Council.

Witt, P. & Crompton, J. (1996) *Recreation programs that work for at risk youth: The challenge of shaping the future*. State College (Pennsylvania): Venture Publishing.

II

EVALUATING POLICY
AND PRACTICE

EVALUATING PROGRAMME IMPACTS: CHAMPION COACHING ON MERSEYSIDE -- PATHWAYS TO OPPORTUNITIES?

Barbara Bell

Edge Hill College of Higher Education, Ormskirk

Introduction

Over the last 20 years in the UK there have been numerous projects, programmes and initiatives that have attempted to tackle the 'problems' of youth sport, first highlighted by the report of the Wolfenden Committee (CCPR, 1960). Internationally, there has been growing literature in youth sport, covering a range of social and psychological perspectives of this issue (de Knop *et al.*, 1996; Smoll and Smith, 1996). Four areas of concern were highlighted by Wolfenden in 1960 and throughout the intervening years these have been core to the 'problem' of youth sport in the UK:

- the lack of opportunities available to young people at the right price and the right time;
- the weakness of the links between schools and clubs for young people
- the lack of a "performance ladder" for coaching, training and personal development;
- the lack of a co-ordinated approach between governing bodies of sport and other bodies.

One of the key problems identified has been the tendency for involvement in organised sport to reduce as young people, particularly girls, move through adolescence. Whether this is perceived as a problem is clearly dependent on the perceived desirability of such activity. Recent government policy has

75

indicated such engagement in organised sport is not just desirable, but central to achieving targets for participation and activity, particularly for school aged children (DCMS/Strategy Unit, 2002; DfES, 2003). However, as pointed out by Coalter (2001), many claims were made for the benefits of sport participation, for which there is only limited evidence. Despite this lack, numerous projects, programmes and initiatives have sought to address the issue of sport participation by young people. One such programme was the Champion Coaching Scheme, managed by the National Coaching Foundation (NCF), which operated from 1991–1999.

Davies *et al.* (2000) described a growth of evidence-based policy (EBP) which resulted from the expansion of social science knowledge, the decline in deference to government and the demand for greater public accountability, and a corresponding growth in demand for well-focused evidence to explain and reflect the increasing complex society in which public policy operates. Such demands have led to increasing interest in techniques and approaches which can bring "more finely grained understanding" of policy impacts and processes, according to Annan (in Davies *et al.*, 2000, p: vi). This paper outlines a realist approach to the evaluation of Champion Coaching, focusing on case studies completed on Merseyside and attempts to draw out some implications for sport programmes and their evaluation, based on the results of the evaluation of participation (Bell, 2004).

The background of Champion Coaching

Champion Coaching's underlying assumption was that in order to improve the standards of sport for young people, we first had to address the issue of the quality of their initial experience of coaching — and indeed, give more young people such opportunities. Coaching and the importance of coaches to performance pathways had been identified in *Coaching Matters* (Sports Council, 1991) which led to the increased interest in developing qualifications, education and training for coaches, particularly those working with young people.

The concept of a performance ladder, or pathway, represents an ideal progression from basic movement literacy to the pinnacle of sporting achievement (Campbell, 1993). It is central therefore to the model of sports participation represented by the Sports Development Continuum (SDC), originally developed by the Sports Council (Sports Council, 1993). A simplistic and idealistic assumption underpinning performance pathways is that the complex web of agencies and individuals involved in them is planned and managed in a co-ordinated way, and that key roles are agreed and well resourced. Furthermore that such 'pathways' are clearly signposted to young people, seeking opportunities in dynamic and diverse sporting networks.

However, as pointed out by Kirk and Gorelly (2000) simple metaphors describing models of pathways and ladders, hide increasingly diverse and complex experiences of young people. A development of the basic pyramid model, showing diverse routes into elite performance and the different needs of performers at different levels was proposed by Cooke (1996), in a "House of Sport" model. Coaching was central to the concept of performance pathways and any important step up to the next level of performance implied an increase in both the level and quality of coaching received by young performers. There appears to be consensus that coaches can, and do, exert significant socialising influences on the progress of young performers along a performance pathway, as they occupy a "central and influential position in the athletic setting" (Smith and Smoll, 1996: p.125).

One of the significant reasons for the emphasis on improving the levels and quality of coaching, particularly for young people, was the recognition of the possible impact on drop out or attrition rates, i.e. how far coaches could influence children to stay involved in sport. Such failure to progress was not likely to improve standards of excellence and performance and could be evidence of deficiencies in coaching opportunities. The conversion of 'players' to committed 'performers' was perceived therefore to be an indicator of the outcomes of 'quality' coaching. The tracking of sport from adolescence to adulthood had also been found by Roberts and Brodie (1992) as well as Yang *et al.* (1996) and Vanreusel *et al.* (1997). But the work of Roberts and Brodie implied that the range of sport experiences rather than their nature, whether recreational or competitive, was important. However, the quality of the sporting experience began to be the focus of sports policy in the 1990s, hence the development of Champion Coaching.

The original mission of Champion Coaching was: "to promote quality coaching for performance motivated children within a co-ordinated community structure" (NCF, 1996: p.3). The Scheme operated from 1991–99 and at its peak in 1998; over 145 Local Authorities were involved in delivering sport programmes in 16 sports. It was reported to have involved over 8,500 coaches, though the actual numbers of coaches was likely to have been less as many coaches were engaged over several years or programmes. Local Authorities had registered 80,000 or more children, but again, due to repeat enrolments, the true figure is almost impossible to estimate (NCF, 1997). Despite these difficulties, this was undoubtedly a very extensive extensive scheme, into which considerable sums of money were invested, but for which reported outputs gave only limited information about impacts. Collins and Buller (2000) reported on one of the largest countywide schemes, in Nottinghamshire, which highlighted both successes and concerns. It appeared that though good proportions of children went on to join clubs, those accessing the scheme had not been representative of the population of young people in Nottinghamshire, especially as those from the more deprived parts of the county were less likely to take part.

This research (Bell, 2004) was particularly interested in the legacy of Champion Coaching at different levels, that of the individual and of the organizations concerned, and in particular understanding *how* it worked and *for whom*, to achieve its outcomes. In the realist tradition, it is important to understand the 'causality of mechanisms' in seeking to use lessons for subsequent schemes and improve practice (Danermark *et al.*, 2002; Archer *et al.*, 1998).

A central concept, identified above, was the 'performance pathway', which was difficult to define and operationalise, as it appeared part of the received wisdom or jargon of sports development practitioners. However, the disposition or interest to get involved with organised club sport has been considered by sociologists to be related to their conceptions of personal and economic capital, derived from the work of Bourdieu (1978, 1988). He considered that perceptions of the social capital accruing to individuals due to their engagement in sport, was part of what he termed their 'habitus'. This is a set of acquired patterns of thought, behaviours, dispositions and tastes. Participation in sport, as with many behaviours, is a consequence of the internalisation of specific manners, deportment, and demeanours in childhood (Bourdieu, 1978). This is also the approach taken by Bandura (1977) in his theory of social learning. This implies that a disposition towards sport participation is not fixed but subject to change and many influences, both internal and external, over time. According to Bourdieu, tastes and dispositions for particular sports are highly influenced by home circumstances and the interpretations of the suitability or appropriateness of some sports to any given class or group in society:

> Class habitus defines the meaning conferred on sporting activity,
> the profits expected from it; and not the least of these profits is the
> social value accruing from the pursuit of certain sports by virtue of

the distinctive rarity they derive from their class distribution. (Bourdieu, 1978: p.835)

Bourdieu was concerned with how people acquire the 'taste' for sport and why they prefer one to another. It was also important to consider sporting practices in their context:

Sporting consumptions ... cannot be studied independently of food consumptions, or leisure consumptions in general. The sporting practices apt to be recorded by a statistical survey can be described as the outcome of the relation between a supply and a demand, or more precisely, between the space of products offered at a given moment and the space of dispositions. (Bourdieu, 1988: p.155)

Without this understanding of *habitus*, it is unlikely such opportunities will be seen as appropriate or desirable by those for whom they are designed. Bourdieu (1978, 1988) posits that different meanings and functions were given to the supply of sport and sporting practices by different classes and class fractions. This implies that the early socialisation of young people towards participation in certain sports is an influential factor in determining future participation, and inclination for 'performance' or 'club based' activity may be seen a feature of this *habitus*. However, as with many sport programmes, such engagement and outcomes of sustained participation take time to emerge and coaching and the experiences on sport programmes could influence the perceptions of young people of their competence and capability. Central to sports development interventions therefore, is the development of self-efficacy beliefs, as proposed by Bandura (1997). These beliefs would be influenced by experience, when young people perceive they would have the necessary 'personal capital' to engage in club-based sport, through their involvement in appropriately motivating sport programmes.

Collins *et al.* (1999) reported on the lack of outcome oriented evaluations and confirmed that such research was important, but difficult to establish, as Coalter (2001) later concurred. Outcome measures were therefore derived by looking at the Programme Impact Theory (Rossi *et al.*, 1999) of Champion Coaching. This idea was based on the analysis of documentation from Champion Coaching and implied or inferred claims supporting the scheme. The outcome measure identified as central to the Merseyside programme impact theory was the membership of a sport club and regular, sustained sport participation after Champion Coaching. Club membership could also be seen as evidence of the success of 'pathways' to lead young people to opportunities in performance oriented sport.

Methods and approaches in the evaluation

The evaluation started with questionnaire-based surveys of participants and their parents, which were mailed to all those with details on the lists supplied by the two local authorities who agreed to co-operate. For St Helens, this was to children taking part from 1996–1999 in five sports; in Knowsley this was to children taking part in 1999 in seven sports. These surveys took place between 2–3 years after involvement in the last course to allow sufficient time to have elapsed to demonstrate sustained participation outcomes. A second phase of the research involved group and individual discussions with pupils and teachers, and face to face and telephone interviews with coaches and sports development officers. This final phase explored whether these outcomes had been achieved and if any legacy from the scheme could be evidenced.

This multi-method realist approach had both a theoretical and practical basis, as it contributed to a Context-Mechanism-Outcome (CMO) con-figuration for each case and an overall CMO for the Scheme. These config-urations are the basis of the 'scientific realist' approach to evaluation proposed by Pawson and Tilley (1997) and have been used by others looking at sport programme impacts (Nichols, this volume; Obare and Nichols, 2001). Essentially, scientific realist approaches try to focus on how and why a programme has certain impacts or outcomes in different contexts. Realists are essentially pluralist in their approach to methods, as depending on the nature of the investigation and the data involved, different methods may be required. This methodological pluralism has both a philosophical and pragmatic rationale. Social processes are not easily understood through positivist methods, which focus on that which can be measured, and have limited ability to infer causal relationships. As social reality can be perceived differently by the different actors involved, so realists accept the 'multiple realities' often found in social programmes, and attempt to uncover the 'mechanics of causality' (Danermark *et al.*, 2002).

By 2003 most of the children who had taken part in Champion Coaching would have been in year 10/11 (or had left school), so this was the age group selected for interviews in the schools. Both authorities had high percentages of girls involved in Champion Coaching because they had been specifically targeted; therefore, though small, the samples achieved in surveys were representative, based on gender and sport, of their populations. Only limited statistical analysis was possible, due to the small samples when broken down by sport and the categorical data collected. A geographical analysis was based on all registrations in the sample in an attempt to minimise the bias that may be associated with survey respondents. This used the postcodes of participants to locate their ward and converted participation to a ratio of the target population, based on 2001 Census figures. The Index of Multiple Deprivation (IOMD) was derived from various indicators by the Department of the Environment, Transport, Local Government and the Regions (DETLR, 2000), and it is expressed as a score, which is highest in the most deprived wards. The IOMD score across wards was then compared to see if areas of high deprivation attracted proportional numbers of participants onto the scheme, as Collins and Buller (2000) had suggested this was unlikely. The limitations of this approach to inferring individual deprivation need to be recognised, as it is based on a 'proxy' measure, rather than a direct measure of deprivation. Methods of geo-demographic classification based on home address, such as ACORN or MOSAIC are widely used to infer lifestyle or material resources, and though they remain a rather 'gross' measure, they have been used in analyses of access to Higher Education (Tonks and Farr, 2003) and in other social policy. However, not all of those living in deprived wards are deprived, or perceive themselves to be, as shown by Townsend *et al.* (1992). The impact this may have on sport participation is a complex one and relatively poorly understood (Collins, 2003). For example, though the issue of social inclusion is central to the ethos of 'Sport for all' which underpinned much sports development work, many programmes like Champion Coaching did not address the issue of material deprivation or poverty specifically, and often assumed that opportunities offered were accessible to *all*, rather than making any particular efforts to address this issue.

Following performance pathways

The exit routes from Champion Coaching showed that children continued on recreational routes (playing for fun) and significantly, also joined competitive pathways (Youth Games or Development squads) and joined clubs. Almost half of the St Helens group joined a club after Champion Coaching, compared to about a third in Knowsley (see Table 1). Therefore, this was a profile of performance orientation, very similar outcomes in both groups, but with some key differences due to different local circumstances and potential opportunities. Very few young people gave up playing

Table 1   Exit routes from Championship Coaching

Exit Route	St Helens %	Knowsley %
Playing for fun	68	80
Join local club	46	32
Join new junior club	7	6
County squad	15	11
Development squad	12	4
Playing for school — out of lessons	70	65
Youth Games squad	42	22
Give up playing	8	2
Other involvement in sport	9	2

(Respondents could choose more than one alternative)

Table 2   Club membership by gender and scheme

Scheme	Girls club member %	Boys club member %	Club overall member-ship %	N=
St Helens	66	81	70	74
Knowsley**	47	76	59	53
Sport England National Survey*	36	56	46	

*   National average for all (boys and girls) under 16
      (Mori/ Sport England, 2002)

**   Pearson Chi-Sq .291signif at 0.05

completely and clearly, this initiative had been a stepping stone (to use another metaphor commonly associated with sport) to county and development squads, competitive and representative sport.

When current club membership was compared with the national picture provided by Sport England national surveys (Mori/ Sport England, 2002), these groups had higher rates of club membership, considering their age, time since the course and the proportion of girls in the groups, than their peers.

The results did show however that despite the positive outcomes for club membership, girls in Knowsley were still less likely to join a club (see Table 2). This indicated that their pathways into organised sport were not as secure or as well signposted, despite their interest and new skills. Children find out about their clubs from a relatively narrow range of sources and clearly Champion Coaching was not all that important to many. For children without a socialising influence from their parents, or in schools where they had less encouragement, this might have been more important. This was an issue explored with school visits.

Table 3 shows that the more important sources of information about clubs were peers and teachers – and Champion Coaching was not the most important in either case. It appeared to be more important to participants in Knowsley, as clubs were not as accessible there as they had been in St Helens. Parents were less important in both groups due to the age of children (average age between 15 and 16) for whom peers are often assumed to be more influential (Hendry *et al.*, 1993). This also implied that these were not children who would otherwise have gone to a club, as parents had not already introduced them. Consequently, whether or not parents rated Champion Coaching positively had no significant impact on club membership.

Champion Coaching helped young people to achieve positive outcomes of club membership and regular sport participation well into teenage years, which, according to the findings of Roberts and Brodie (1992) and others (Malina, 1996; Yang *et al.*, 1996), should result in good levels of sport participation later. Participants followed a range of routes to maintain an engagement in sport outside of school, which was particularly important for girls.

Table 3   How children found out about their club

Source	St Helens (n=55) %	Knowsley (n=34) %
Friend	41	32
Teacher	24	44
CC Course	13	21
Parent	5	3
Already member	3	0
Advertisement	3	0
Other	3	0

What clearly emerged from the surveys was the important role teachers played, compared to parents, in encouraging children to join clubs. But club membership was only one pathway, and the youth games emerged as another, which helped sustain engagement where clubs may not have been available or accessible. This engagement extended the involvement in organised sport and helped to lock them in to sport organisations. Therefore, the integration of the Merseyside Youth Game (MYG) and Champion Coaching together helped to sustain better outcomes than might have been anticipated at the outset.

Did Champion Coaching reach 'all' young people?

Geographical analysis showed that the ratio of participation compared to local populations was different in the two areas (see Table 4). There were clear differences achieved by the local authorities, as children in Knowsley lived in some of the most deprived wards in the country let alone the district, yet they still accessed the scheme in similar proportions to other ward populations of under 16s. There was some relationship to ward level deprivation in St Helens, as more participants came from the least deprived areas.

Table 4   Participants and populations compared

Participants by Scheme	St Helens %	Knowsley %
U16 living in most deprived wards	26.49	20.78
CC participants in most deprived wards	13.25	21.13

To understand how this was achieved, the different approaches to promotion and recruitment were analysed, in the specific local contexts of sport and the diverse opportunities available. Each area had a unique combination of 'sporting capital' or resources (physical and organisational as well as human in the form of coaches) through which pathways had to be identified and negotiated by young people.

Children's perceptions of pathways and opportunities

In order to gain some insight into how young people perceived such opportunities, a series of visits to schools were undertaken in both districts.

These school visits involved small group interviews with 74 young people in Knowsley and 57 in St Helens. Other key informants included LEA advisor on PE in St Helens and the P.E. Curriculum Leaders group in Knowsley.

These interviews helped to explain how Champion Coaching had worked for the children who had attended, and how they had been attracted onto it. They also helped to explain how and why different schools achieved different referral rates. Clearly different schools promoted and encouraged out of school activity in different ways and with varying degrees of success. High referral schools were successful, as they had been more engaged with the process and found that the Champion Coaching courses were complementary to their own provision. The schools recognised that the significance of parental support in terms of material resources and interest in sport varied greatly across the district, so that not all of those offered the chance took up the opportunity to do Champion Coaching. Low referral schools had a low priority for after-school sport, or were more distant from many of the venues used for courses. Even in these schools, there were children who were motivated and interested in sport, but Champion Coaching was not something they would take part in, as it did not involve their sport, or they preferred to do their own thing, with their 'mates'. There was little evidence of a legacy from Champion Coaching in club links from low referral schools, with a similar cohort of young people that had accessed Champion Coaching.

Teachers suggested that this was related to perceptions of sport by 'middle class' parents, who would be more able and willing to support children attending sport programmes after school, in the evenings or at weekends. Even if 'working class' parents were supportive in principle, in practice they would struggle to get their children to programmes taking part outside of school times, across districts, as they may not have access to suitable transport. Levels of car ownership were low and approximately 35% of children in Knowsley lived in families receiving benefits of some kind.

In both case studies children suggested that there were plenty of opportunities in their area – though girls were more likely to mention their opportunities were more limited than the boys. Both girls and boys attributed any lack of participation to lack of interest and motivation rather than any lack of opportunity. Teachers were generally regarded as being very important and supportive in encouraging those with an interest or talent in sport to take it further outside school. Also, many young people were interested in getting involved in sports not included in Champion Coaching or similar programmes – for example, girls were interested in diverse activities like swimming, dance, or martial arts, not all of these in clubs or competitive environments. Similarly boys could be interested in 'going to the gym', boxing or rock climbing – some were linked to their school experiences but others were clearly not. The pattern of affiliations and interests expressed by young people in these areas were therefore a result of a complex mix of influences, based on home and family, peers and school experiences, mediated by the diverse range of facilities, clubs and services available to them in their neighbourhoods.

Both sets of children also indicated that the influence of teachers and schools was particularly important, where parental resources were more limited or where they had limited family links to clubs. Many children talked about the expense of sport opportunities as putting them off, or the fact that by age 16, they were often classed as adult, though without the resources to pay adult prices (even in local authority facilities). On the other hand, even if the services were on their doorstep, many children said they would not be interested in organised sport, as they had 'better things to do'. Schools and teachers were important to generate the motivation and interest in young people, but it depended on the interest and motivation of individual teachers, to go beyond merely providing information, with advice and guidance for development to individual children. This was particularly important for 'performance motivated children' but had implications for any children with an interest in after-school sport, particularly if they were in families with little or no sporting background.

Schemes varied in how they promoted their sports, the choice of sport, pricing and location of venues. St Helens offered a more limited range of courses but achieved good outcomes in club membership. With more limited clubs available in the sports selected by Knowsley, they nevertheless achieved club membership outcomes with little relationship to the ward level deprivation, by locating their courses in different parts of the borough, and with a 'pay as you go' approach to pricing, so that those on low incomes would not be deterred from enrolling. Though this facility was available on request in St Helens as the scheme developed, it was not advertised or promoted as 'pay as you go', so some children or parents could have been discouraged from applying.

Using a context-mechanism-outcome approach helped to match what mechanisms worked when applied in different ways in their different contexts. Clearly even if the courses were successful in developing self-efficacy beliefs, (coaching mechanism) if no clubs were available, children from the more deprived areas were going to struggle to demonstrate that particular outcome. However, they could demonstrate that even several years after the programme, they were still playing sport on a regular basis. It was clear that many variables, not all of which could be accounted for in this study, influenced the outcomes that were achieved, particularly as the scheme overlapped with many others operating in these areas and in after-school sport.

Conclusions and implications for practice

The most recent agenda for sport is to drive up participation, meeting both health-related and performance targets in a 'twin track' approach (Game Plan, 2002). This research, as it related to both areas, may contribute to the evidence base for sport, as club membership is being used as a key indicator for the success of current policy in after-school sport (DfES, 2003; 2004). Schools are increasingly becoming a site of importance in starting children on pathways to sporting engagement, particularly in organised and competitive sport. But overcoming the lack of clubs or outlets was something Champion Coaching could do little to address. The mechanism it represented, of bridging school to club-based participation, was shown to have some success, in demonstrating a performance orientation of children after the Scheme. However, the choice of sports and clubs needed to 'fit' with the *habitus* of local youth for such outcomes to be successful in the long term. It would have been possible to achieve better results in outcomes by focusing on sports with existing 'sporting capital' and a base in clubs, but this was not what Champion Coaching set out to address in these areas. It was clearly used to make up perceived deficiencies in provision, particularly for girls, and attempted to develop the sporting capital in these areas. In this it was only partly successful, as gains made at the time were not always sustained once Champion Coaching funding was withdrawn.

These local sports development units sought to develop more opportunities for new groups or those underrepresented in club sport, in other words, more challenging targets. They did not specifically address equity based on ward deprivation or targeting areas of need. But by targeting girls and sports that could widen pathways to sport, such as girls' football, these cases achieved good results of sustained sport participation into late adolescence, which could indicate greater likelihood of continuing into adulthood. Nevertheless, to widen and strengthen pathways to opportunity, we need more 'bottom–up' policy, driven and shaped by local needs and better research into local circumstances, as centrally devised models of pathways may not actually fit well into local implementation. The use of sports specific local planning is evidence of such 'bottom up' implementation. Baseline research was lacking in both cases, in that even now, it is not known what level of club membership is the 'norm' in these areas, or in selected sports, without the intervention of Champion Coaching or its successor scheme, Active Sport. Given that netball was played by virtually all girls in school, in both cases, exit routes to clubs have been difficult to sustain, as clubs often lacked the resources, and sometimes the will to extend opportunities to greater numbers of young people, when Champion Coaching funding was withdrawn.

A 'bottom-up' approach should also include more autonomy for schools, to help deliver increased after-school activity, which is both planned and delivered for and by local young people. The school as a site for multi-sport clubs, offering quality coaching will certainly attract those young people who seek organised and structured activity. But there may continue to be resistance to such organised activity if this is perceived as an extension of school, rather than a link to clubs in the community, as young people seek sites to express their autonomy and personal choices. Based on these interviews, teachers certainly feel that their ability to develop such opportunities is limited while they have to deliver the National Curriculum, examination based PE and open extra-curricular clubs, and for this reason, additional resources, are essential. However, while a lack of clubs limits the potential achievement of programmes like Champion Coaching, efforts to help clubs become more 'youth friendly' must continue outside of schools, to provide more integrated pathways for young people.

Currently, after-school sport is being co-ordinated through two sets of partnerships; school partnerships, centred on sport colleges and school sport co-ordinators, and Active Sport partnerships, based on counties and selected sports (in this case Merseyside). Arguably, this should increase co-ordination, but this may also hinder achievement of outcomes due to fragmentation and dilution of resources, across sports, districts and two sets of partnerships. Better monitoring and more thorough evaluation of the sports partnerships will therefore need to build on the conclusions presented here about Champion Coaching and test out whether the partnerships are working effectively to increase opportunities and access.

This research has also highlighted the need for better data and more of a culture of evaluation in sports development, as in other aspects of sport. It is no longer sufficient to simply count participants, or programmes. Sports practitioners must demonstrate who uses these services and track their subsequent development. Unfortunately such longitudinal data, though more effective than the snap-shots provided by surveys, is more difficult and costly to collect and sustain. The use of more qualitative approaches is also necessary to better to understand *how* programmes work, particularly with different groups of young people. Again however, the resource implications for this may preclude such approaches being more widely applied. Despite the limitations of postcode based analysis of participation, this can be a useful starting point to demonstrate at least the representativeness of those taking part in programmes. With added features of the Census services, including the designation of Super Output Areas (which are based on the aggregation of data from Enumeration Districts), such measures are likely to be more widely used to allow more finely grained detail of populations and their use of services from a range of policy areas. Sport risks losing the ground more recently gained, if it is unable to capitalise on this trend of evidence-based policy and increased reflexive policy-making.

References

Anann, R. (2000) 'Forward', in Davies, H. T. O., *et al.* (eds) *What Works?* Bristol: The Policy Press. pp.v-vii.

Archer, M., Bhaskar, R., Collier, A., Lawson, A. (eds) (1998) *Critical realism: Essential readings.* London: Routledge.

Balyi, I. (2001) 'Sports system building and long term athlete development', *Best Practices Quarterly* Vol. 18, Issue 1: pp. 1–1.

Bandura, A. (1977) *Social learning theory.* Englewood Cliffs, NJ: Prentice Hall.

—— (1997) *Self efficacy: The mastery of control.* New York: WH Freeman.

Bell, B. (2004) 'An evaluation of the impacts of the Champion Coaching Scheme on youth sport and coaching' . PhD thesis, University of Loughborough.

Bourdieu, P. (1978) 'Sport and social class', *Social Science Information* Vol. 17: pp. 819–840.

—— (1988) 'Program for a sociology of sport', *Sociology of Sport Journal* Vol. 2: pp. 153–161.

Campbell, S. (1993) 'Coaching education around the world', *Sports Science Review* Volume 2, Issue 2: pp. 62–74.

CCPR/Wolfenden Committee (1996) *Sports and the community.* London: Spottiswood.

Coalter, F. (2001) *Raising the potential of cultural services.* London: Local Government Association

Collins, M. F. (2003) *Sport and social exclusion.* London: Routledge.

Collins, M. F., Buller, J. (2000) 'Bridging the post school institutional gap: Evaluating champion coaching in Nottinghamshire', *Managing Leisure* Volume 5, Issue 4: pp. 200–221.

Collins, M. F., Henry, I., Houlihan, B., Buller, J. (1999) *Research Report: Sport and social exclusion, A report to the Policy Action Team 10, March 1999.* London: Department for Culture, Media and Sport

Cooke, G. (1996) 'Pathways to success: A new model for talent development', *Supercoach* Vol. 8, Issue 2: pp. 10–11.

Danermark, B.,Ekstrom, M., Jakobsen, L., Karlson, J. C. (2002) *Explaining society: Critical realism in the social sciences.* London: Routledge.

Davies, H. T. O., Nutley, S., Smith, P. C. (eds) (2000) *What works?* Bristol: The Policy Press.

De Knop, P., Engstrom, L.-M., Skirtad, B., Weiss, M. (eds) (1996) *World wide trends in youth sport.* Champaign Ill: Human Kinetics.

Department for Education and Skills (2003) *Learning through PE and sport: A guide to the PE, school sport and club links strategy.* London: DfES/DCMS.

Department for Education and Skills (2004) *High quality PE and sport for young people: A guide for recognising and achieving high quality PE and Sport in schools and clubs.* London: DfES/DCMS.

Department for Environment, Transport, Local Government and the Regions (2002) *Regeneration research summary. Indices of deprivation 2000.* Number 31 online at: Department of Transport, Local Government and the Regions, www.regeneration.dtlr.gov.uk/rs/03100/index.htm, accessed on 06.02.02

Hendry, L., Shucksmith, J., Love, J. G., Glendinning, A. (1993) *Young people's leisure and lifestyles.* London: Routledge.

Kirk, D., Gorely, T. (2000) 'Challenging thinking about the relationship between school physical education and sport performance', *European Physical Education Review* Vol. 6, Issue 2: pp. 119–134.

Malina, R. M. (1996) 'Tracking of physical activity and physical fitness across the lifespan', *Research Quarterly for Exercise and Sport* Vol. 67, (Supplement 3) pp. 48–57.

Mori/Sport England (2002) *Young people and sport in England.* London: Sport England.

National Coaching Foundation (1996) *Champion Coaching: The guide.* Leeds: National Coaching Foundation.

———— (1997) *Champion Coaching summary report 1996/97.* Leeds: National Coaching Foundation.

Obare, R., and Nichols, G. (2001) 'The Full Sporty — The impact of a sports training programme for unemployed steelworkers', *World Leisure Journal* Vol. 43, Issue 2: pp. 49–57.

Pawson, R., Tilley, N. (1997) *Realist evaluation*. London: Sage.

Roberts, K., Brodie, D. (1992) *Inner city sport: Who plays and what are the benefits?* Culemborg: Giordano Bruno.

Rossi, P. H., Freeman, H. E., Lipsey, M. W. (1999) *Evaluation: A systematic approach.* Thousand Oaks: Sage Publications.

Sanderson, I. (2002) 'Evaluation, policy learning and evidence-based policy making', *Public Administration* Vol. 80, Issue 1: pp. 1–22.

Smith, R. E., Smoll, F. L. (1996) 'The coach a focus of research and intervention in youth sports', in Smoll, F. L. & Smith., R. E. (eds) *Children and youth in sport: a biopsychosocial perspective*. London: Brown and Benchmark. pp.125–141.

Smoll, F. L., Smith., R. E. (eds) (1996) *Children and youth in sport: A biosychosocial perspective.*: Brown and Benchmark.

Sports Council (1991) *Coaching matters: A review of coaching and coach education in the U.K.* London: Sports Council.

———— (1993) *Sport in the nineties: New horizons.* London: Sports Council.

Strategy Unit (2002) *Game Plan: A strategy for delivering Government's sport and physical activity objectives*. London: Cabinet Office.

Tonks, D., Farr, M. (2003) 'Widening access and participation in UK Higher Education', *International Journal of Education Management* Vol. 17, Issue 1 26–36.

Townsend, P., Whitehead, M., Davidson, N. (1992) *The Black Report and the health divide*. London: Penguin Books.

Vanreusel, B., Renson, R., Beunen, G., Claesens, A.L., Lefevre, J., Leysens, R., Eynde, B. (1997) 'A longitudinal study of youth sport participation and adherence to sport in adulthood', *International Review for the Sociology of Sport* Vol. 32, No. 4: pp. 373–387.

Yang, X., Telema, R., Laasko, L. (1996) 'Parental influence on the competitive sports and physical activity of young fins: A 9 year follow up study in physical education and sport', in Doll-Tepper, G., Brettschneider, W.D (eds) *Changes and challenges. World Congress,PE and Sport 1994, AIESEP.* Aachen: Meyer & Meyer Verlag.

THE IMPACT OF SCHOOL SPORT CO-ORDINATORS IN DUNDEE: A CASE STUDY

Grant Small and Christine Nash
Division of Sport and Leisure, University of Abertay Dundee

Introduction

Participation in regular physical exercise has long been established as being an effective method of reducing the risks of various degenerative diseases. The Scottish Executive have identified that many of Scotland's health problems are directly linked to a lack of regular physical exercise (Scottish Executive, 2000).

The education sector has been viewed as a key provider of sport and physical activity through a range of ages and abilities. There have been a number of initiatives aimed at raising activity levels (Scottish Executive, 1999a); in particular the Active Schools Co-ordinators have been introduced to primary schools. This introduction has only been a part of the School Sport Co-ordinators (SSC) scheme, which links physical activity, community involvement and sport in an attempt to make Scottish children more active (sportscotland, 2000). The aim of this study is to evaluate the impact of the active school co-ordinators within the City of Dundee, in respect to current policy initiatives within two sports, football and swimming.

Background to initiatives

At present Scotland's population have been highlighted as having one of the poorest health records in the world. The Scottish Executive has made a commitment to reduce the levels of disease in Scotland with the publication of the public health White Paper 'Towards a Healthier Scotland' (1999b). One of the key aims of this initiative is to reduce the number of deaths under the age of 75 years old by 50% from the year 1995 to 2010 with the expected result of a healthier Scottish population.

Within this strategic plan for health improvement, the white paper identifies the need for increased levels of physical activity and states that:

> The Government will set up a Task Force to develop a National Physical Activity Strategy for Scotland. It will bring together key agencies in sport and leisure, education, health, fitness, exercise and play, in joint action to help people of all ages and walks of life to enjoy the benefits of physical activity. (Scottish Executive, 1999b: p.32)

Support for this positive strategy came from the Department for Education and Skills (DfES) and the Department for Culture, Media and Sport (DCMS) following the publication of Learning through PE and Sport (2003). The rationale for this document was to outline a national strategy for physical education (PE), school sport and club links (DCMS, 2004: p.1). The aim of this strategy is to deliver a key government target to:

> Enhance the take up of sporting opportunities by five to 16 year olds by increasing the percentage of school children who spend a minimum of two hours each week on high quality PE and school sport within and beyond the curriculum from 25% in 2002 to 75% by 2006.

This positive campaign to increase physical activity levels has resulted in sport now being viewed as a tool for improving the health of the nation, maintaining a more active outlook on life and encouraging more children to participate in sport (Scottish Executive, 2000, Department of National Heritage, 1995, The Scottish Office, 1995). Within both primary and secondary schools one of the key factors in raising the profile of extra-curricular sport has been the appointment of school sport co-ordinators and active primary school co-ordinators. Education is highlighted within many strategy and policy documents as being a key partner in promoting and facilitating access to both structured and unstructured sporting opportunities (Department of Culture, Media and Sport (DCMS), 2001, Scottish Sports Council, 1998, sportscotland, 2003a).

The introduction of active primary school pilot programme resulted from the publication of *Youth Sport Strategy for Scotland* and the sportscotland Youth Sport Group discussions of Sport 21 (sportscotland 1998). This initiative has resulted in close links with the aims stated within the Scottish Executives

Physical Activity Task Force (2002) The intention of the Active Primary School Pilot Programme is to "increase the range and quality of opportunities for children to become more physically active" (sportscotland 2004 p1). This programme works in conjunction with school sport co-ordinators (secondary schools) to develop and enhance extra-curricular sport in schools. There has been significant funding input with this programme receiving £2.8m over a three-year period, to be distributed amongst 250 Scottish schools (sportscotland 2003b). This funding is further supported by TOP play and TOP sport, initiatives introduced to assist primary schools and community organisations. Since 2001, sportscotland have distributed over £2m of lottery funding to the TOP programme.

Remit of Active School Co-ordinator

The School Sport Co-ordinator Programme (SSCP) was a collaborative launch between the Scottish Executive and sportscotland in 1999, with the majority of funding coming from sportscotland's lottery fund. The initiative was launched with the aim of improving the access and provision of sport within Scotland, concentrating on the development of sport outside school hours.

As a result of the success of this programme, sportscotland launched the Active Primary School Pilot Programme (APSPP) in 2000, which was later extended in 2001 with additional resources allocated by the Scottish Executive. This programme was specifically aimed at primary school children with the need for such a programme, highlighted the publication '*Let's make Scotland more active*'. This stated that:

> The health of two thirds of the Scottish adult population is now at risk from physical inactivity. (Scottish Executive, 2000: p.10)

This increased risk clearly highlighted the need for positive action to increase physical participation amongst Scotland's school children. As a result the four main areas of the Active Primary School Pilot Programmes are to provide:
- Active Playgrounds
- Classroom Movement Activities
- TOPS — After School Clubs
- Active Routes to School

Whilst the aim of the APSPP is clear, the roles and responsibilities of the active primary school co-ordinators are dependant upon local needs, however sportscotland describe a broad remit of Active Primary School Co-ordinators as being:

- Co-ordination of extended curricular activities
- Working with appropriate local authority departments, school sport associations and national governing body staff and volunteers
- Recruiting, supporting and developing teachers, coaches and leaders
- Creating links between schools and clubs
- Working closely with community clubs
- Working closely with associated primary schools
- Monitoring participation levels.

Although the remit from sportscotland is broad, it differs considerably from that posited by the Department for Education and Skills (DfES) Strategic Planning:

- To develop and implement a PE and school sport strategy as part of school development plans, through working in partnership with key strategic organisations and providers in the area.
- Primary Liaison: To improve PE and school sport programmes by establishing and developing links within and between the clusters of schools.
- Out of School Hours: To provide new and enhanced out of school hour opportunities (out of hours) for all young people in the partnership, including out of hours learning, non-competitive participation and competition.
- School to Community: To increase all young peoples participation in community sport through creating and strengthening links with sports clubs, leisure facilities and community providers.
- Coaching and Leadership: To provide training, support and deployment opportunities in leadership, coaching and officiating for senior pupils, adults other than teachers and teachers.
- Raising Standards: To raise standards of pupils achievement in all aspects of their school life through increased participation and improved performance, motivation and attitudes.

This programme is now in place in 250 schools across 21 local authorities throughout Scotland. Within Dundee there are currently 2 full time Active primary co-ordinators, both qualified and registered teachers, working with a number of support staff.

Sport Commitment Model

If school sport schemes, designed to attract children into sport and physical activity, are to be successful then they must consider not only the reasons why children participate but perhaps more importantly the reasons why they leave or dropout. The Sport Commitment Model, illustrated in Figure 1, investigates the psychological processes which govern involvement in sport and physical activity. It categorises the motives for involvement but also highlights the attractiveness of other activities. These categories include sport enjoyment, involvement opportunities, involvement alternatives, personal investments and social constraints.

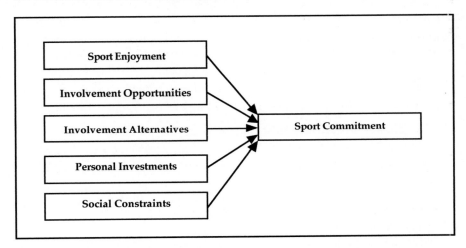

Figure 1   Sport Commitment Model (Scanlan, Carpenter, Schmidt, Simons & Keeler, 1993)

Enjoyment has been cited in many studies as the main reason why children participate and continue to participate in sport (Starkes, 2000, Carpenter & Scanlan, 1998, Lee, 1993). Involvement opportunities can be defined as the benefits related to participation for example, being with friends and health benefits. The involvement alternatives, however, refer to other activities, not necessarily sporting, and their appeal to the individuals in question. Time and effort are the most common examples of personal investments, although it could also refer to monetary investment. Social constraints characterise pressure to remain in the activity, in this case peer pressure is a common reason for children to continue to belong to a group or activity even if they are no longer interested (Kramer, Trew & Ogle, 1997).

Background of Dundee

Dundee is situated on the North East coast of Scotland and is one of Scotland's largest cities. The most recent population survey found that Dundee's population is estimated to be 144,180 with a split of 52.6% female and 48.4% male (General Register Office 2002). It has been involved with, and indeed, implemented government led initiatives to reduce instances of social exclusion. In 1997 Dundee City Council in conjunction with the Scottish Executive launched the Social Inclusion Partnership (SIPS) programme, which encourages joint working to tackle social exclusion in some of the most deprived communities within Dundee. Each SIPS area has a Partnership Board with representatives from the community, public, private and voluntary sectors. This programme identified a total of fifteen communities/ areas as being socially excluded, with key indicators being low employment, high crime rates, high mortality rates and low educational achievement:

> The cluster of communities that provide the focus for Dundee's Priority Partnership Area (PPA), represent the areas where the largest proportion of the most disadvantaged people in Dundee are resident. (Dundee City Council, 1999: p. 26)

The aim of the SIPS programme is to regenerate these communities using all resources at their disposal.

Economic Factors

Within the city of Dundee several key areas have been identified as contributing to this level of deprivation:
- Income — within Dundee average gross weekly income is lower than any of the other main cities within Scotland, and Britain as a whole. (Office for National Statistics, 2003)
- Employment — the employment sector within Dundee has a higher proportion (per head of population) of 'manufacturing' and 'public administration' than any other Scottish city (Dundee City Council 2003),
- Unemployment — the rate of unemployment is currently 1.9% higher than the national Scottish average of 3.3% (Dundee City Council 2003), of those unemployed within Dundee 26.2% are under the age of 25 years old.

Long-term unemployment is also significantly higher than the national Scottish average with 20.9% unemployed for over 12 months, this compared to the national average of 14.1% (Dundee City Council 2003)

- Education — the number of children attending school within Dundee during 2002 was recorded as being 19,654 with 10,990 attending the 41 primary schools whilst the remaining 8,664 pupils attended the 10 secondary schools (Dundee City Council 2003). Within Dundee whilst a lower than national average percentage of the population enter higher education, there is a significant difference in students entering into further education. Of those leaving school to find employment only 17% were successful, compared to the Scottish average of 24%.

- Health — An annual report from the Scottish Executive entitled 'Health and Well Being in Tayside' published in 1999 found that Dundee had a higher percentage of deaths due to cancer and coronary heart disease than the national Scottish average. The study also found however that instances of stroke were lower in Dundee than any other major city (per head of population). These figures show a direct correlation with Dundee's higher than average mortality rate. During 2002 Dundee had a mortality rate of 12.7%, whilst other Scottish cities had an average of 11.5%.

Methodology

Participants

The participants in this study were selected from the following groups:
- Active Primary School Sport Co-ordinators
- Participants in APSPP programme
- Parents of participants

Data collection and analysis

The data collection procedures for this study were divided into two parts.
Part 1: A questionnaire was developed and distributed to the participants (n=107). This questionnaire was designed to obtain basic information from 10–11 year olds, specifically utilising the constructs from the Sport Commitment Model to categorise responses.
Part 2: Primary school coordinators were selected for an interview (n=2). Each interview lasted approximately 1.5 hours. The interview approach adopted was that of open-ended, semi-structured questions. The aim of the interviews was to elicit more detailed information on issues than could be

provided in questionnaires. Questions asked included the effectiveness of the SSC activities, the constraints they feel impact upon their position and the links established between schools and clubs offering further provision.

The parents of participants were randomly selected for an interview (n=4). Each interview lasted approximately 1.5 hours. The interview approach adopted was that of open-ended, semi-structured questions. The aim of the interviews was to elicit more detailed information on issues than could be provided in questionnaires. Questions asked included the reasons why their children participate, the support they offer to their children and the burdens that this places on the family.

The completed questionnaires were analysed using the Statistical Package for Social Sciences (SPSS, version 8.0).

Results

The results shown in Table 1 were analysed from data gathered from the returned questionnaires (Table 2). Further information gathered from the interviews is presented in the discussion section.

Discussion

The results obtained from research into the Active Primary School Pilot Programme (APSPP) highlighted many factors associated with the Sport Commitment Model highlighting reasons for sports participation/non participation (Scanlan *et al*, 1993). As can be seen from this study, the sporting activities children take part in out of school time show significant differences to the Scottish national figures. Although the most popular sports were similar to national statistics (sportscotland 2002), less popular sports varied considerably. This research showed that whilst football was the second most popular sport for girls within Dundee it is actually the fourth most popular sport throughout Scotland (sportscotland 2002) and also highlighted that female participation in gymnastics is significantly higher within Dundee than nationally. Recently there has been significant investment in gymnastics in Dundee, both financially and in human investment terms.

There are also differences in participation levels amongst males, namely the second most popular sport for males nationally is swimming (sportscotland 2002). Within Dundee, swimming is ranked fourth behind rugby and hockey, although on a national scale, rugby is ranked eleventh

Table 1   Ranked table of activities

Favourite Activities at School			Favourite Activities outside School Time		
Overall	Male	Female	Overall	Male	Female
Football	Football	Football	Football	Football	Swimming
Swimming	Swimming	Swimming	Swimming	Rugby	Football
Non-Stop Cricket	Non-Stop Cricket	Hockey	Hockey	Hockey	Gymnastics
Hockey	Rugby	Non-Stop Cricket	Rugby	Swimming	Hockey
Rugby	Hockey	Playground Games	Basketball	Basketball	Badminton
Playground Games	Rounders	Rugby	Athletics	Table Tennis	Athletics
Rounders	Playground Games	Rounders	Badminton	Athletics	Basketball
Basketball	Basketball	Running			
Athletics	Gymnastics	Badminton	*		
Running	Athletics	Running			
Athletics	Netball	Table Tennis	Sailing	*	
Volleyball	Volleyball	Basketball	Sailing	Skate Boarding	**

*   denotes no choice — only a limited number of choices were selected by both males and females

**   other activities noted by females but not included in table were music lessons such as piano and violin, brownies and drama

Table 2   Reasons for participation

Construct	Overall %	Male %	Female %
Enjoyment	32	36	28
Involvement Opportunities	19	24	14
Social Constraints	17	12	22
Personal Investments	19	16	22
Involvement Alternatives	11	14	8

whilst hockey is thirteenth. Dundee has a tradition within hockey and rugby, developing national level performers on a regular basis. This could explain the participation within these sports as a result of enhanced local media coverage. There were significant differences within levels of participation in cycling as nationally cycling is recognised as being the third most popular sport. This research found that within Dundee cycling was not found to be within the top ten sporting activities but this could be attributed to the age of the participants and the environment.

The figures shown within this research can be directly compared to the reasons for participation in sport (Table 2) and the Sport Commitment Model (Figure 1). The Sport Commitment Model highlights the enjoyment of sport as being one of the main reasons for participation, supported by Starks (2000) and Carpenter & Scanlon, (1998). This current investigation further supports this research by finding that 32% of the children questioned took part in sport due to the levels of enjoyment. When asked what they enjoyed the answers reflected other constructs e.g. because friends were there, parental expectations, they had been going to the club for a long time and it was what they did on Saturday mornings. A few female participants did state that they participate in football because "the coach was cute".

The impact of social constraints upon sports participation is another key finding as only 12% of males felt that they were unable to take part in sport because of peer pressure. With the exception of athletics and sailing the top ten male sports do not require any expensive or inaccessible facilities, which could relate to the economic background of the Dundee population. There were however, differences in the response from females as non-participation in sporting activities due to social constraints made up 22% of the responses. This may be related to the perception that there are fewer activities available to females as a result of peer pressure but could also be due to the increased cost of gymnastic facilities and equipment, in contrast to the relatively low cost of male participation sports.

With regard to the specified sport of swimming, it was found that the numbers attending swimming lessons have greatly increased over the last five years. Since the establishment of the active primary school programme, a scheme has been initiated whereby children can join a learn-to-swim scheme for £1 per session. This has proved to be a great success as all of the spaces have been filled to capacity, which has resulted in a greater number of children from swimming lessons progressing into competitive swimming. The reasons for this are twofold:

- bigger base leads to more progression
- perceived success of swimmers in club therefore more people wanting to participate resulting in a trickle down effect.

It was also stated that the swimming club has expanded in size as two clubs had folded meaning that this amalgamation of two swimming clubs has also resulted in an expansion of the clubs lessons programme. This increase in children progressing into competitive swimming can again be related back to the sport commitment model as personal investments, in terms of time and money, have been identified as being a major factor in participation levels within sport.

It has also been shown that there has been a difference in the attitude of swimmers, which can again be related to the Sport Commitment Model as involvement opportunities increase via competitions. This results in the child becoming more focussed, whilst setting themselves competitive targets within the sport. One of the swimming coaches interviewed further supported the concept of involvement opportunities by stating that:

> "Instead of 18 time wasters and 2 serious swimmers it's now the opposite — 18 serious swimmers and 2 time wasters — which makes it a lot easier to deal with."

Within football it was found that the number of development programmes had increased significantly since the establishment of the school sport co-ordinator. This research found that the barrier created by constraints was avoided by providing football coaching at little or no cost specifically within areas identified as SIPS. The football coaches interviewed during this research felt that the increase in provision has had a definite impact on the clubs ability to retain children within their programme.

During this investigation, parents of children who participated in sports outside of school time were interviewed, but it should be made clear that it is only parents of participants who were interviewed as it was not possible to gain access to parents of non-participants. These parents were questioned as to their perception of sporting provision for their children since the establishment of primary school co-ordinators. Parents' perceptions that "...as my children progressed through primary school there were more opportunities available for them to participate" further supported the Sport Commitment Model. The parents stated that they were happy that there was an increase in the number of school clubs/after school clubs such e.g. the MAGIC club (MAGIC stands for Most Active Guys in Craigie, one of the secondary schools in a SIPS area).

Interestingly of the parents interviewed, excluding those parents with children involved within football, many wanted their children to enjoy sport rather than specialise, providing them with good opportunities for future personal investment. Football is an interesting example, as it seems to provide an excellent progressive pathway within the sport but appears to insist on early specialisation within the sport.

An example of financial constraints was highlighted whilst interviewing parents. The factor of involvement alternatives, contained within the Sport Commitment Model was identified when one of the parents stated that:

> "Sometimes I cannot afford to let my daughter go to all the activities she want to — she also has piano lessons that are more expensive than sports – but I feel she needs a balance."

The impact of the APSS programme within Dundee has undoubtedly increased participation levels across the city, however this research has found that concerns have been raised directly from the co-ordinators regarding the framework designated by sportscotland. This research also discovered that recent changes to the role of an active primary school co-ordinator have been met with a great deal of scepticism from the current co-ordinators.

As previously stated, the socio-economic factors and constraints affecting sporting participation within Dundee have a major influence on sporting participation within the city. Dundee's population has a household income of approximately £22,700, which is lower than the national Scottish average of £26,500. The lower average income indicates a clear constraint to children participating in sport, one that is identified by an Active School Co-ordinator as not being supported by Dundee City Council. The provision and therefore subsequent payment for facilities was an area highlighted by the sports co-ordinators. The internal framework of Dundee City Council was criticised as being a major constraint to children taking part in sport, with a sports co-ordinator stating that:

> "The leisure and arts department gets to use an educational facility for free, but will charge the education department for using a leisure and arts facility, despite being all one part of Dundee City Council."

When questioned further on this subject the co-ordinators felt that this was beyond their control and required structural change within Dundee City Council or at least some acknowledgement of a cohesive programme.

The framework produced another concern from the co-ordinators who they felt that the flexibility within the programme required review. The co-ordinators stated that whilst they were aware of what was expected from sportscotland, the socio-economic factors within Dundee had a major bearing on the actual job function as many of the social constraints within Dundee are locally devised rather than related to national averages. The co-ordinators felt that this lack of flexibility was something that restricted their progress.

A further point raised by the sport co-ordinators was the recent change in sportscotland policy, stating that co-ordinators no longer have to be registered with the General Teaching Council for Scotland (GTC). As a result of this six new co-ordinators have been employed by Dundee City Council, none of whom are qualified teachers. The current co-ordinator within Dundee commented that this change could have a detrimental effect on the programme, stating that:

> "In my experience, unless you are a teacher you are going to find this job very, very difficult, I don't know how successful sport-scotland's new posts will be because they are not teachers."

This change to the programme has been greeted with uncertainty, particularly as sportscotland has identified Dundee as being one of the more successful programmes set up within Scotland. As the current primary sport co-ordinators are all qualified teachers this change is a risk, which has led to the resignation of both the current co-ordinators with one commenting that:

> "I think that they [sportscotland] are making the wrong decision [by allowing Co-ordinators who are not teachers], I think the way to impact on every child's activity levels is to do it through changing the curriculum and changing the way we teach."

Although the six new co-ordinators are not qualified as teachers they are educated to degree level and may prove to be successful, however this change in policy has left sportscotland open to criticism should the altered programme prove to be unsuccessful.

Conclusion

The impact of primary school co-ordinators within Dundee has clearly improved the provision of sport within the city as well as improving participation levels amongst children. This has been highlighted by the responses from both the school age participants and the parents. Both emphasise the difference that they have perceived as a result of the Active Schools Programme.

Dundee would appear to have set an example for implementation of their SSC programmes. This research has found however, that there are a number of fundamental concerns within the framework of the programme that may be inhibiting the success of the primary school co-ordinators, although many of these concerns are outside the remit of the SSC. There does appear to be serious misgivings concerning the sportscotland role in defining the role and function of the SSC.

Findings of this study have generally reflected the findings of the Sport Commitment research. There do, however, appear to be anomalies between male and female reasons for participation, which could benefit from further investigation. There would also appear to be significant variation between the patterns of participation within Dundee and the national average.

References

Carpenter, P.J. & Scanlan, T.K. (1998) 'Changes over time in the determinants of sport commitment', *Paediatric Exercise Science* 10: pp. 356–365.

Department for Culture, Media and Sport (2001) *Game plan: A strategy for delivering Government's sport and physical activity objectives*. London: UK Crown copyright.

Department for Culture Media and Sport. (2002) *The coaching task force — Final report*. London: DfES publications.

Department for Culture Media and Sport. (2004) *High quality PE and sport for young people*. London: DfES publications.

Department for Education and Skills (2002) *Guidelines on teaching gifted and talented pupils – Physical Education*. London: DfES Publications.

Department for Education and Skills (2003). *Learning through PE and Sport: A guide to the Physical Education, School Sport and Club Links Strategy*. London: DfES Publications.

Department of National Heritage (1995) *Sport — raising the game*. London. HMSO.

Dundee City Council (1999) *Priority Partnership Area and Regeneration Project: 1999–2006 strategy document*. Dundee City Council

———— (2003) *About Dundee: Demographics, statistics and reference material*. Dundee City Council.

General Register Office (2002) *2002 Mid-year population estimates*.

Kramer, J., Trew, K. & Ogle, S. (1997) *Young people's involvement in sport*. London: Routledge.

Lee, M. (1993) *Coaching children in sport: Principles and practice*. London: E&FN Spon, English Sports Council.

Scanlan, T.K., Carpenter, P.J., Schmidt, G.W., Simons J.P. & Keeler, B. (1993) 'An introduction to the sport commitment model', *Journal of Sport & Exercise Psychology* 15: pp. 1–15.

Scottish Executive (1999a) *Health and well being in Tayside. Annual report for the director of public health*. Edinburgh.

Scottish Executive (1999b) *Towards a healthier Scotland — A White Paper on health*. Edinburgh: The Stationery Office.

Scottish Executive (2000) *"Lets make Scotland more active" – A strategy for physical activity*. Edinburgh: Physical Activity Task Force.

Scottish Sports Council (1998) *Sport 21: Nothing left to chance*. Edinburgh: Scottish Sports Council.

sportscotland (2002) *Sports participation in Scotland*. Edinburgh: sportscotland.

sportscotland (2003a) *Sport 21 2003–2007 The national strategy for sport: Time to speak up: Consultation Document*. Edinburgh: Scottish Executive, UK.

sportscotland (2003b) *An evaluation of the school sports co-ordinator programme in Scotland*. Edinburgh: sportscotland.

sportscotland (2004) *Evaluation of the active primary school pilot programme*. Edinburgh: sportscotland.

Starkes, J. (2000) 'The road to expertise: Is practice the only determinant?', *International Journal of Sports Psychology, 31, 431–451*.

The Office for National Statistics (2003). *Regional trends No. 38* (2003 Edition). London: The Office of National Statistics.

The Scottish Office (1995) *Scotland's sporting future: A new start*. Edinburgh: Scottish Office Publication.

- lead to improved socialisation with peers and adults
- can help participants "enjoy improved scholastic attendance and performance" (Collins, 2003: p. 169).

Personal development and self esteem

Wurrdinger (1994) suggests that outdoor education is different from traditional education; the delivery of outdoor education through practical experience offers children an alternative mode of learning, particularly for those who are not successful in traditional classroom subjects. This approach supports the development of the whole person, through the development of different styles of curriculum (Eisner, 1996) or multiple intelligences (Gardner, 1983).

There is a growing body of empirical evidence that indicates the importance of self-esteem for positive personal development. Huskins (2003; 2001; 2000) argues that self-esteem development is one of four "priority social skills" along with the ability to recognise and manage feelings, empathise with others, and explore values. He states that these skills are important for an effective personal development curriculum that aims to promote the inclusion of young people in their schooling and reduce alienation and disaffection. Emler (2003; 2001) has recently challenged the notion that low self-esteem can act as a causal factor in delinquency, substance abuse, educational under-achievement, and by implication social exclusion. He claims that self-esteem raising programmes are not the 'magic bullet' (Katz, 2000), or a "social vaccine" for social ills (CTF, 1990), that they are often thought to be. His statement that programmes are " ... unlikely to be what we need most, and very unlikely to deliver the benefits promised", is somewhat disconcerting given the sheer volume of personal development interventions that refer to objectives related to self-esteem.

However, Emler's (2001, 2003) provocative conclusions can be rebuffed by highlighting his rather uni-dimensional and dismissive analysis, his failure to evaluate properly alternative approaches to research, and his exclusive and extremely narrow definition of self-esteem. One may also point out, as Peel (2003), has that his approach is 'too simplistic to have anything of value to contribute to the practical issue of how we should work with young people'. Yet, Emler's (ibid.) critique is a useful reminder of the dangers of exclusivist definitions of concepts of self, however alluring they may appear. Furthermore, his work reminds us that self-esteem is not the only contributory factor to delinquency or social exclusion.

Social exclusion and delinquency

McCormack (2003) has offered a series of external (structural) and internal (agency) factors that can contribute to the production of social exclusion and delinquency. These include:

- Poverty
- Residential Setting
- Parental control
- The influence of peer groups
- Boredom
- Status and hence self-perception
- Excitement
- Labeling

The influence of some of these factors on social exclusion and youth behaviour has, according to Collins (2003: p. 159), been examined thoroughly. For example, Scarman's (1982) report suggested that the inner city riots of the late 1970s were partly caused by a lack of constructive leisure opportunities for young people. According to Collins (2003), this comprises another version of 'The devil finds work for idle hands' thesis. Yet Glyptis (1989) demonstrated that recreational activity programmes could not replace the role of work in alleviating boredom by filling time, providing a structure to life, and providing a sense of achievement. If boredom is not the only causal factor of delinquency, as McCormack (2003) suggests, then preventive programmes aimed merely at alleviating boredom are unlikely to be successful. However one could go even further and examine the notion of boredom as a separate causal factor for deviancy by comparing the assumption that 'boredom' is simply about having too much free time, with Sartre's (1938) existentialist perspective of the problems of human freedom and existence. Perhaps the most productive approach is to accept that delinquency has multiple influences, rather than deterministic causes, which are interlinked.

Outdoor activities have a recent but intensive history of being used to address delinquent or anti-social behaviour, and particularly at secondary (Diversion and Socialisation) or tertiary (Rehabilitation, Retribution and Atonement) levels of intervention (Hardy and Martin, 2004a; Hardy and Martin, 2004b). Outdoor activities or Sports-based interventions have been used much less frequently at a Primary level, or for Diversion and Welfare objectives (Collins, 2003; McCormack, 2003). Examples of primary level initiatives include holiday schemes, youth clubs and community centre projects but determining the outcomes of such projects has been problematic (Collins, 2003). After all one cannot use recidivism rates for preventive schemes as the young people have not, by their nature, been involved with the criminal justice system. Few primary level schemes have been evaluated, and where they have they often involve sport as opposed to outdoor activities. However the potential for outdoor activities for engaging disaffected youth may be greater, and more inclusive, than sport due to its non-competitive nature (McCormack, 2003) particularly if used as vehicles for socialisation, diversion or welfare objectives. This is supported by McKay's (1993) review of research conducted in the US, which concluded that those at risk preferred adventure activities to conventional team sports. The programmes which are the subject of this article were designed mainly as Primary and Secondary level interventions and hence operated mainly as vehicles for Welfare, Diversion and Socialisation.

The Outdoors Against Drugs (TOAD) and Children's Fund (CF) in context

Social exclusion is a difficult term to define particularly as there appears to be much disagreement about processes of exclusion and the nature of excluded groups or underclasses (Macnicol, 1994). Furthermore, various political ideologies have generated overlapping and competing discourses of social exclusion (MacDonald, 1997). These discourses comprise those based upon economic deprivation and redistribution, moral turpitude, and the relationship between the individual and labour (Collins, 2003: pp. 7–10). Thus, individuals are excluded because they have no money, no morals or no jobs! Consequently the solutions to social exclusion have been various. For example, approaches to juvenile crime management have swung between a focus on punishment and retribution, and reformation (Collins, 2003: 163).

The Scarman Report (1982) included one of the earliest references to the link between delinquent behaviour and a lack of constructive leisure opportunities. Several years later specific support for outdoor activities in formal education was indicated by the presence of Outdoor and Adventure Activities in the national curriculum (DfEE, 1989) and Inspectorate reports (HMI, 1990). 'Adventure 2000' (UK) is perhaps one of the most prominent of more recent initiatives which aimed to develop forward planning and 'life skills' for sixteen-year-old pupils. 'Positive Futures' (www.drugs.gov.uk) initiated in March 2000 aimed to use sport to involve and engage young people in active sports participation with the intention of "preventing today's young people becoming tomorrow's problematic drug users" (Ramello, 2004). The reference to physical activities in policy documents, both in the form of sport and outdoor recreation, demonstrates the commitment of government to this form of youth development during recent times.

Birmingham Children's Fund (BCF) was established in 2001 with the potential to reach 30,000 in the target area using preventive services aimed at reducing the risk of social exclusion amongst young people. With a total budget of £6.6M in 2002–2003 it was able to fund 75 new services including 42 short-term projects addressing at least one of the following themes:

- isolation and access
- aspiration and experience
- economic disadvantage
- children's voices, (allowing young people the opportunity to express their own opinion) (BCF, 2003)

Combined with this, Birmingham Drugs Action Team (DAT) was established in 2002 in order to bring together local agencies that could co-operate in dealing with drug abuse in their areas. Amongst the projects they were responsible for monitoring and reviewing were 'Positive Futures' and Health Education with a focus on neighbourhood and locality needs. Birmingham Outdoor Education Centre (BOEC) was ideally located to develop bespoke programmes that would fulfill some or all of the objectives of the Birmingham DAT and the BCF. This was because they were situated on or very close to priority areas, indicated by poverty and deprivation indices, or other information provided by consultation with funding agencies, and others. The BOEC developed two programmes to address the desired outcomes of the BCF and DAT, namely The Children's Fund and The Outdoors Against Drugs. The key elements of the two programmes are compared in Table 1.

Only two of the centre's programmes were evaluated in this research. The work of the BOEC is much wider than these two programmes although the income provided by them was significant for the centre and accounted for the employment of several full and part time teaching staff. The programmes appear very similar in many ways and they contained many elements that were transferable between the two contexts. After all they were working with similar young people from similar backgrounds. The differences were evident in the way the activities were conducted and this can be seen partially at least from a discussion of the explicit aims of the programmes, contained in Table 2.

Table 1   Description of BOEC Programmes

Children's Fund	TOAD
Funded by Birmingham Children's Fund/ DfES	Funded by Birmingham Drugs Action Team/Inter-departmental Home Office 'Led' Funding
Children in years 5–8 at risk of social exclusion.	Children in years 5–8, at risk of becoming involved in drug taking.
A ten-week programme of outdoor activities in an urban and rural setting. Half / full day release, including a residential experience	
Designed in consultation with the young people in the Hodge Hill and Erdington wards.	Designed in consultation with the participants and stakeholders.
Post programme follow-up achieved through links with partner agencies, but mainly through BOEC.	Supports continuation of the activities at a range of levels Integrated into the lives of the participants through links with partner agencies.

Table 2   Aims of BOEC Programmes

Children's Fund	TOAD
To provide the opportunity for children to experience a variety of outdoor activities.	To develop new skills by introducing young people to new activities.
To improve self-confidence and motivation.	To develop self-confidence
To develop a greater respect for themselves, others and the environment in the city and beyond. Increased interest in schooling with improved behaviour, attendance and achievement.	Improving communication skills. Improving problem solving skills. mproving teamwork
A reduction in anti-social behaviour (vandalism, criminal activities and drug misuse).	Improving the ability of young people to resist the powerful influence of the drug culture.

The BOEC programmes were unusual, if not unique, in that they:

- used the local environment as well as rural non-local areas outside of the city;
- incorporated residential trips which involved staying overnight at accommodation ranging from campsites in the Peak District and North

Wales, to self catering cottages in the Wyre Forest and the Lake District;
- were delivered over a relatively long period (ten weeks);
- supported continuation of the activities at a range of levels, after the programmes were completed;
- were integrated into the lives of the participants through links with partner agencies such as schools, after school clubs and holiday schemes;
- were designed in consultation with young people.

The programmes were based on a range of activities including orienteering, rock-climbing, canoeing, skiing, sailing and problem solving. These were all particular specialisms of the BOEC and they had many years experience of delivering these activities in a variety of environments and contexts. The programmes were arranged in cooperation with schools in the prioritised areas, with the task of identifying participants being the responsibility of the school staff, normally teaching staff.

Methodology

Much of the literature described above investigated relatively short courses operating in wilderness or rural areas, in environments non-local to the participants, although the value of long term programmes is evident in Ofsted reports (Clay 1999). Furthermore, much of this research was carried out in North America or Australia. Recent studies carried out in the UK have followed this trend by researching short-term, non-local programmes. Paradoxically perhaps, recent research (Tucker, 2003; Humberstone, 2003) has identified the importance of maintaining links with the young person's home environment and familiar supporting service such as the youth service or school, upon programme completion. Therefore it would not be unreasonable to question whether delivering one-off, short-term activities in non-local environments is the best way of achieving transferable personal development objectives. However, not only can the mode of provision be questioned, it is also important to examine the methods used to generate empirical data that underpin evaluations of informal outdoor education provision. In fact, there is little empirical support for programmes that operate within local environments and comprise medium to long-term interventions.

Unsurprisingly perhaps, evaluations of outdoor education experiences have tended to be positivistic in style, conforming to a technocratic rationality that reflects the rationality of the wider society (Giroux, 1992). Thus, evaluations have been generally concerned with providing 'measurable' evidence and results that are universally 'valid' and 'reliable'. The work of Neill (1997; 2002; 2003) and Hattie *et al..* (1997) are good examples of this emphasis. Naturally, such a rationality permeates every aspect of the phenomenon and many 'therapeutic' programmes are concerned with 'treating' deviancy (McCormack, 2003) without ever questioning the notion of 'deviance' itself. Discussions of the nature of 'deviance' and how this impinges upon outdoor activity programs have been virtually invisible until very recently (see Humberstone *et al..*, 2003) and socially conservative and normative behaviour modification programmes have become accepted practice. Consequently there is much potential for outdoor activity programmes that adopt methodologies of delivery that are more considerate of young people's perspectives and contexts, and naturally adopt commensurate methodologies of evaluation.

Research Aim

The BOEC research aimed to
- deepen understanding of the ways in which the behaviour of pupils has been influenced by the programmes in the short-term;
- outline the effectiveness of different aspects of the programme for changing the behaviour of pupils;
- examine the place of the BOEC outdoor programme in the national regional and local framework for supporting the development of young people;
- suggest ways in which the programme could be developed to maximize benefits to young people.

The principle style of enquiry employed was 'grounded theory', based on the analysis of a range of qualitative and, perhaps unusually, quantitative data gathered from interviews, observations and questionnaire surveys with outdoor education field workers, school liaison staff, the pupils involved in the project, and staff from partner agencies. This takes into account the relationship between the micro and macro within any research project as identified in the 'conditional/consequential matrix' (Strauss and Corbin 1998), each level of the matrix was investigated, with field observation simultaneously investigating both individual and sub-organisational levels (see Table 3). This approach was guided by the conviction that programmes of the sort being investigated cannot lead to a clear deterministic and measureable end but are part of an interactive and ongoing process.

Table 3   Research Methods adapted from the Conditional Matrix
(Strauss and Corbin, 1998)

Conditional Matrix level	Aspect of investigation	Primary methods employed	Supplementary sources
Individual	'Significant moments' for participants during, and as a result of, the programme Development of children's social and learning skills. Children's attitudes regarding self-perception, the environment, schooling and anti-social and criminal behaviour.	Pupil group interviews Attitude Survey	Letters of thanks, written accounts and review materials written by pupils following the programme
Family	Development of children's social and learning skills (self-confidence, self esteem, teamwork, communication, problem solving)	Parent interviews Parental questionnaires	Letters from parents commenting on the influence of the programme on children
Sub-organi-sational	Development of children's social and learning skills (self-confidence, self esteem, teamwork, communication, problem solving)	BOEC staff, Teacher interviews. Field observation	Planning and proposal documentation from BOEC. BOEC programme plans
Institutional	Policy implementation. Views on effectiveness of the outdoor programmes in Birmingham.	Birmingham Dugs Action Team, Birmingham Childrens' Fund, West Midlands Police	Funding and policy documents from regional and national government agencies Ofsted reports.

Factors enhancing data

- The research was commissioned by the organization which operated the programme and was perceived as being part of the process of review and programmed development, thus the researchers were not seen as separate to, but as a specialist part of, the programme.
- The recognition of the researchers as practitioners in the field of outdoor education and qualified teachers as well as researchers allowed the development of empathy and shared professional understanding.
- The researchers were therefore 'indwellers' (Patton 1980) capable of putting themselves in the place of the interviewees, aiding both the posing of questions and later identifying the significance of the answers given.
- The interviews were held in the natural setting of participants (Lincoln and Guba 1985) This had a number of practical benefits that aided the research: the rapport developed with the schools staff facilitated the arranging of pupil interviews which took place in a quiet room within the school; staff seemed to view the pupil interviews as an opportunity for pupils to broaden their education by interaction with the researcher; in one case the interviews were carried out by a researcher through informal discussions with pupils during their activities.

Interviews

Interviews were held either in the workplace of the professionals involved, at the school of pupils and varied from 35 to 45 minutes, they were recorded and transcribed. Interview questions were open ended thus encouraging participants to share their experiences, thoughts and feelings about the programme. Data was analysed using QSR's Nvivo software package.

Questionnaire Surveys — Pupils

Neill's "Life Effectiveness Questionnaire" (Neill 2004 after Rosenberg 1965) was chosen to identify changes in nine personal development objectives. It was adapted to gauge the programme participants' personal development retrospectively by self-reported responses to 18 questions, two for each objective. A list of the nine personal development objectives assessed by the questionnaire is given in Table 4. 120 pupil questionnaires were administered by schools and 47 of these were returned, representing a good response.

Questionnaire Surveys — Parents

Once again, the LEQ was used to gather data, but the LEQ-Observer version (LEQ-O) was adapted and used with parents. This version was used to gauge changes in seven personal development objectives. A list of these seven objectives is given in Table 5. 120 parent questionnaires were distributed via schools with stamped addressed envelopes. 15 were returned after two months. This is not surprising as a return rate of 15–50% is not uncommon (Burns, 2000). Preliminary statistical analysis was performed upon the

Table 4   Scale Items and Descriptions for the LEQ P (Pupils)

Scale	Description
Communication Skills	Communicates effectively with others in interpersonal and group settings.
Cooperative Teamwork	Cooperates well working with other team members.
Self-esteem	The belief that one's actions are successful and effective.
Self-confidence	The degree of confidence in abilities.
Risk Taking	Takes healthy risks, neither too cautious nor too risky, for the sake of personal growth and well-being.
Problem Solving	Effective at solving problems
Effective Leadership	Leads effectively when a task needs to be done.
Conflict Resolution	Effectively heads off and resolves interpersonal and group conflicts
Locus of Control	The belief that one has self-determination and choice about one's behaviour

Table 5   Scale Items and Descriptions for the LEQ-O (Parents)

Scale	Description
Social Competence	The degree of personal confidence and self-perceived ability in social interactions.
Achievement Motivation	The motivation to achieve excellence and put the required effort in to attain it.
Intellectual Flexibility	The ability to be adaptable and flexible, or pragmatic
Emotional Control	The ability to maintain emotional control in potentially stressful situations.
Active Initiative	The desire to initiate action in new situations
Self-confidence	The degree of confidence in abilities and the success of actions.
Locus of Control	The belief that one has self-determination and choice about one's behaviour

questionnaire data; the correlation between factors is too weak to form any statistically significant conclusions as the poor response rate is likely to be a major contributory factor. Consequently, the data has been presented in visual form and only general conclusions have been drawn.

The use of a parent questionnaire on its own is probably not an efficient method of collecting information and future evaluations would need to use a wider range of interviews.

Results — Quantitative

Life Effectiveness Questionnaire: Observer (LEQ-O) – Parents

In general, parents thought that children's personal and social development, as rated by the seven scale items, had improved. This data is included in Table 6.

Table 6 LEQ-O Scores for the seven scale items

	Activity Initiative	Achievement Motivation	Emotional Resilience	Intellectual Flexibility	Locus of Control	Social Competence	Self-Confidence
	AI	AM	ER	IF	LC	SC	SE
i= LEQ-O item score	Frequency						
3	0	0	1	0	0	0	0
4	1	0	0	0	0	0	0
5	0	0	0	0	0	0	0
6	0	1	2	0	1	1	0
7	1	1	3	1	0	3	0
8	0	2	2	2	4	0	3
9	6	4	4	6	6	5	7
10	5	3	2	6	3	4	2
11	1	3	0	0	1	2	3
12	1	1	1	0	0	0	0
positive	87%	87%	60%	93%	93%	73%	100%
negative	13%	13%	40%	7%	7%	27%	0%

Table 6 shows the number of children (frequency) that received a particular score for that particular scale item of the questionnaire. Essentially, these indicate the extent to which the observer (parent) thought that their child's attitudes or behaviour had 'improved' since completing the BOEC programme. Each question was scored from one to four. Four represented 'strongly agree' and one 'strongly disagree'. There was no option for a neutral response. Scores from all three questions were aggregated to give a maximum score of 12 and a minimum score of three. Hence a score of nine shows a positive result, or an average response of '3–agree' for each question. A score of seven or eight was inconclusive as to whether or not change had occurred. A score of 6 indicated an average response of '2–disagree' for each question.

All observers thought that Self-Confidence had improved. Intellectual Flexibility, Locus of Control, Activity Initiative, and Achievement Motivation were thought to have improved by a large proportion of responses (87% or more). Most observers (73%) noticed an improvement in Social Competence. The least conclusive development was in Emotional Resilience which showed that 60% of parents thought that they had observed a positive change.

Aggregated Totals

Each of the seven scale items was placed into three broader categories that would reflect changes in characteristics of personality development that were more closely related to the programme objectives. These categories were:
- Self-confidence and Motivation
- Autonomy
- Relationship Building

A final category was used to summarise the total score from the LEQ-O. The aggregated totals, combined with the way in which scores for these categories have been calculated, is given in Table 7.

Table 7 Aggregated totals for the LEQ-O Scores

	Self-confidence and Motivation	Autonomy	Relationship Building	Total
	SE+AM+AI	AI+LC+SE	AI+ER+IF +SC+SE	AI+AM+ER +IF+LC+SC +SE
i= LEQ-O item score.	FREQUENCY			
3	0	0	1	1
4	1	1	1	1
5	0	0	0	0
6	1	1	3	5
7	2	1	8	9
8	5	7	7	13
9	17	19	28	38
10	10	10	19	25
11	7	5	6	10
12	2	1	2	3
Mean Score	9.29	9.13	8.92	8.97
Positive(3 to 7)	91%	93%	83%	85%
Negative(8 to 12)	9%	7%	17%	15%

The results of this aggregation are illustrated by Figure 1 to Figure 4. These show that each of the three characteristics was judged to have at least improved, by the majority of observers. There were few aggregated negative responses, the highest being for Relationship Building, but this was heavily influenced by one item, Emotional Resilience. Furthermore, the distributions are skewed, being clustered around a mean that is over the borderline in all cases, marked on the graphs with a dashed line.

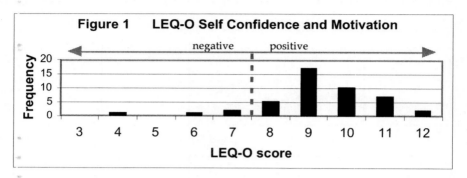

Figure 1   LEQ-O Self Confidence and Motivation

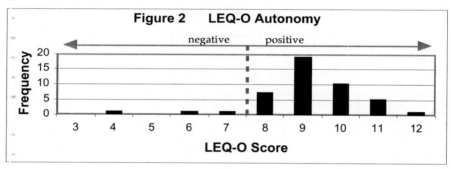

Figure 2   LEQ-O Autonomy

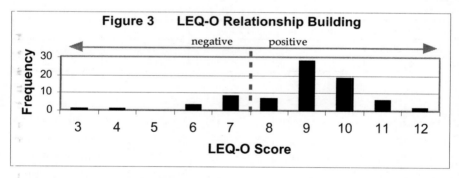

Figure 3   LEQ-O Relationship Building

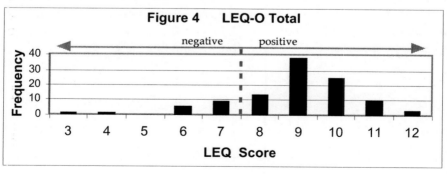

Figure 4   LEQ-O Total

Life Effectiveness Questionnaire — Pupil

The correlations between LEQ scores and the factors of age, gender and school were examined and the results are summarised in Table 8.

Table 8   A Summary of Total LEQ Scores

LEQ Scale Item	Mean	St Dev
Communication Skills	14.09	2.44
Cooperative Teamwork	13.60	3.18
Self-esteem	13.40	3.27
Self-confidence	13.35	2.48
Risk Taking	13.21	3.33
Problem Solving	12.07	3.34
Effective Leadership	11.91	3.29
Conflict Resolution	11.82	3.94
Locus of Control	10.90	3.12

- *Age, Self-esteem and Self-confidence.*   The effect of TOAD on the self-esteem of the students varied. Older students appeared to benefit slightly more in terms of self-esteem following the activities than younger pupils. Overall the activities appeared to improve the self-confidence of students although this was more noticeable in younger students. Older students' scores tended to be more variable. Clearly the effects of positive learning experiences on pupils' self-esteem are complex and cannot be reduced to a single causal factor.
- *Locus of control.*   For younger students (9,10,11) it was noted that the activities had allowed students to feel as if they were more in control of their lives and what they do, possibly due to a feeling of success in an activity which they were anxious about doing. Older students' scores were more variable.
- *Communication.*   Communication appeared to have improved during the activities. This could be the outcome of students communicating with each other in different environments on a different level. Age did not appear to be a factor in the improvements in LEQ score for communication.

- *Teamwork.* Teamwork was seen to have improved after the activities, notably in younger students. Older students also seemed to have benefited from the activities but not to the same degree.
- *Conflict Resolution.* Age did not appear to be a significant factor in the responses to this item.
- *Leadership.* Younger students' leadership scores improved during the activities possibly because this may have been the first time they have had the opportunity to work in this context, leading to greater perception of the development of skills of effective leadership. Older students' answers were more variable and no relationship was discernible.
- Problem solving. Post activity scores showed an improvement in the problem solving ability of younger students (9,10,11), although older students' answers were more variable and inconsistent.
- *Risk Taking.* Younger students' perceptions of risk taking appeared to have consistently improved, showing that they were generally more aware of themselves and the risks which they take, since they took part in the activities. Again, older students' answers were less consistent.
- *Gender.* In general the gender of students did not appear to have any effect on changes which occurred during the activities. There were very slight differences but these were not statistically significant. Although there was not a great difference, male students did seem to think that their communication skills had improved more than females since taking part in the activities. This is possibly as a result of seeing one another in different ways and talking about things which they would not usually talk about. Males were generally more positive about their improvement in problem solving. Following the activities both males and females felt as if they had more self-confidence, however females were slightly more positive in their responses. This could be attributed to success in new activities that they would not have otherwise thought that they could do. Where team-work is concerned male students were more likely than females to feel that their teamwork improved during the activities. This could be related to communication where male students felt that their communication had also improved during the activities.
- *School.* There were differences in the answers given by pupils from different schools that responded to the questionnaire however these also included a number of contradictory responses which suggests that there were issues with the completion of the LEQ. This is an important point

to note for future evaluations and methods should take account of issues such as question phrasing and readability in order to make the instrument more inclusive.

This illustrates that, in general the mean scores were positive or very positive, with the most improvement noted for Communication Skills, Cooperative Teamwork, Self-esteem, Self-confidence, Risk Taking and Problem Solving. Even the lowest mean score represented a significant change.
As the programme seems to be successful in the short term, a key priority is to gauge its effectiveness in the longer term.

Results — Qualitative

An interpretive paradigm based on what Weber termed *erklarendes verstehen* (Weber 1949) or what Patton (1980) and others have referred to as 'indwelling' was used in order to find significance within the data. Interviews were transcribed and organized using the NVivo software programme where they were coded in order to identify key concepts, ideas or intellectual reactions which emerged from the data. The emerging concepts were then modeled using the NVivo analysis facility to build inter-related concepts which were complimentary or significant to the effectiveness of the programme (see Table 9).

Table 9   Common themes emerging from the data

Structural Factors supporting Positive Learning Experiences
• Biographies of staff involved   • Selection of groups
Positive Learning Experiences

• Fun/enjoyment and anomie
      • Cooperative atmosphere
      • Support and responsibility continuum
      • Teamwork
      • Continuity/access and the use of local facilities

Structural Elements supporting Positive Learning Experiences

Staff biography

The development of confidence in young people relies as much on style and personal conviction as in technical competence of staff. BOEC staff show a strong personal conviction based on their personal and professional experience in the value of using outdoor education as a developmental tool. Comments made by BOEC staff during interviews clearly demonstrate that their personal and professional experiences have equipped them to empathise with the problems experienced by young people both growing up in a city and in the school setting.

The conviction and empathy that result in a very supportive atmosphere for pupils are illustrated by both observations made during the Peak District visit and by interview comments. The following typical comments from interviews illustrate the personal conviction and empathy that are vital to the success of the programme.

> "My first realisation of this was when I first started teaching and we were talking to a child who said he'd spent his summer holidays on the balcony ... ."

> "I've been involved since I started teaching basically, about thirty years ... taking groups walking or sailing or working with groups doing orienteering, since I've been a Head at this school, which is thirteen years."

> "I was at five secondary schools. I also went to two primary schools ...That is where ... I can relate to some of the children."

The in-depth knowledge of the situation in which the pupils live is a vital element in the success of this process. Thus to know where the children are 'coming from' and be able to empathise with that is a vital element in effective management capable of developing self-esteem amongst pupils.

Selection of group

Interviews with school staff and the following case study illustrate the importance attached to group composition. This selection process in itself could work against the developing of self-esteem and self-confidence and subtle approaches were sometimes employed to avoid stigmatising a group. In one instance pupils were invited to volunteer and those identified as in need were selected. The interview comments from pupils in this school indicate that the strategy was successful as pupils when asked why they were on the programme said:

" ... because we volunteered to go on it ... we paid ... "

There were some examples where a school "selected the ten worst children from the year because they feel they need it most." However, interviews with other staff during field observation in the Peak District revealed a very clear position that challenged this strategy on group selection.

Development of selection strategy – case description

Groups were initially selected on the basis of those children who were perceived by staff as being most 'at risk' that is children with behavioural problems, who in most/many instances were brought up with little parental influence or where one or both parents had a problem e.g. drugs. This selection strategy was changed to one where groups were drawn from a wider range of backgrounds. This was felt to be more effective by school staff as it provided pupils 'at risk' with peer support and role models; problems were more manageable and school staff motivated to get involved with the programme. It was also seen as fair by all pupils and reduced the risk of stigmatising groups.

Positive Learning Experience

An important element in the success of the BOEC programme was that it provided, perhaps for the first time for some of these young people, positive learning experiences linked to the locality and the pupil's school.
Positive attitudes towards the programme experience from both teachers and pupils are clearly illustrated by the comments of one teacher describing pupils' attendance on the BOEC course:

"Our attendance was below the government guidelines, (as defined by Ofsted) but on this course the attendance was 100% ... children had to give up a weekend of their own time and a day of ... holiday ... We said be here at ten, they were here at quarter to, if we said be here at nine, they were here at quarter to."

Fun, enjoyment and anomie

The importance of fun and enjoyment of the activities was highlighted during interviews with pupils and staff. This was most often concerned with low skill level activities rather than those activities requiring high skill levels. Low skill level activities were typified by activities with minimal structure such as jetty jumping and night walks, both activities incorporated into the outdoor programmes. High skill level activities were activities such as rock climbing or kayaking that are defined by a structure of rules required for safe and effective pedagogy. In this context the young people were socialised in the following ways. The explicit need to manage their behaviour by employing a framework of safety rules. Secondly, by accepting the management of their behaviour, they implicitly acknowledged the right of the instructors to do this. Within the BOEC programmes both of these processes were important. In rock climbing, for example, young people defer to the authority of another, the instructor, and learn how to behave in ways appropriate to the rules, in this case for safety reasons.

The significance of young people's vivid recall of low skill activities, such as the jetty jump, is thus related to the relaxation and apparent subversion of "normal" rules. Whilst this may appear to approach a state of anarchy it is, however, sanctioned and encouraged by authority, in this case the authority of the instructor. The apparent paradox is not unimportant; young people, arguably, learn to conform by not conforming.

The inclusion in pupils' accounts of activities that lead to fun and exhilaration featured frequently, with activities ranging from abseiling to jetty jumping and night walks. Thus the most fun and most memorable activities, in terms of generating intense feelings of enjoyment or perhaps even ecstasy, were often not those that involved skill development or particular physical commitment. They were often the ones that allowed the pupils to behave in ways contrary to the 'rules' that had been laid down during the activity sessions. Thus socialisation rules were deliberately reversed, and behaviour that had been proscribed earlier, such as jumping off the jetty jump or walking around late at night, was now prescribed.

"I liked it because we went on a night walk, it was proper dark and J. told us a scary story".

Activities such as this are often the simplest to set up but may have the most effect in generating positive feelings as they are inclusive, require little physical skill or commitment, but may require emotional support from peers and adults. They are considered to be 'fun' because both the young people and the adults are complicit in exposing the contradictions of the adult world to the young people. Furthermore, children learn how to control risks, but also this control may be safely relaxed by proper management. It is likely that the exploration of the boundaries of different ways of controlling the same risk will contribute to a better developed approach towards healthy risk-taking.

Cooperative atmosphere

The creation of a relaxed 'easy going' atmosphere was observed, depending in part on the factors described above, and seemed to be an important element in the success of the programme; this is referred to in other reports as an important issue in supporting the success of the activities (Counterpoint, 2000). Staff biography (see above) was a common factor which appears to have a positive impact on this atmosphere. Centre staff reported empathy with the problems of young people who had educational problems based on their own educational background, school staff had an understanding of the outdoor experience based on their own biography. This was supported by the development of positive relationships with an adult in a joint goal. In this case the adult was recognised both as leader and participant as staff regularly involved themselves directly alongside the pupils.

Support and responsibility continuum

The empowering of young people by developing their responsibility through simple practical tasks was a characteristic evident throughout the programme. It is most clearly evidenced in Table 10.

Table 10   Progressive Development of Pupil Autonomy

Stage in pupil autonomy	Example
Discussion of need for mutual support	Preview of activities and discussion of affective purpose
Taking responsibility for selves	Kayak and orienteering practical activities and equipment
Taking responsibility or other individuals	Belaying each other in rock climbing
Taking short term group responsibility	Making a raft in order to solve the task set
Taking long term group responsibility	Planning food including barbeque etc. for two day residential and camping trip

This is exemplified when one instructor gave the following description of the start of a programme: "I have got a new group of ten people, I then take them, you know, to a local park and (we) talk about what they are going to be doing on the programme"; whilst another described the organisation at a later stage in the programme: "we give them a budget ... , we might say to the children that your budget is £50.00. We are going away for two days, ... so get all your foods. If you get to the check out and it's £58.00 — £60.00 there is no worry about that. ... That is a success in itself ... working with a budget."

This developed a feeling of ownership of the programme amongst the group. Such empowerment of pupils is a consistent characteristic of the programme and closely matches Huskins (2003) curriculum development model which he argues supports positive development of young people.

Teamwork

LEQ scores for problem solving, effective leadership, cooperative teamwork, communication skills and conflict resolution were obtained separately. The maximum possible score for each item was 16, a neutral score was in the range of 8–10, and a minimum score would have been 2. All elements showed a score greater than 10 indicating a positive change, with means between 11.8 and 14.0 with 16 being the mode in each case.

This is supports an Ofsted report which stated that " ... the TOAD project helps children in year 5 develop their teamwork skills and self-esteem in order to deal with the pressures of the outside world" (Martin, 2004: p. 17). This was reinforced as pupils interviewed spoke very clearly of the importance of teamwork and communication and the development of new levels of communication. In some interviews it was the most prominent issue raised by pupils in discussion.

Continuity and the use of local facilities

Sessions were organised at a number of local venues including Edgebaston Reservoir, Ackers Trust ski slope, the 'Rockface' in Birmingham city and canals within the city limits. This has two main advantages. Firstly it maximises the amount of time spent on the activities, and secondly, it demonstrates how pupils as individuals may gain access to these venues themselves. As well as advice BOEC offers practical support for pupils whilst they develop their independence. One teacher said:

"Particularly, for example, the rock climbing, because some of them have carried that on at a club, it's run on a Friday by A___ from the Outdoor Ed. They don't get taken there, they have to make their own way there, there's at least three of them who have been on the course that have gone back to the climbing."

A health education advisor carrying out a review with the group explained:

"I'm trying to get them to realise a) that there are things out there for them to do, so it's like diversionary activities away from drug use, so look these things are available in Birmingham, you can get the number 66 bus ... " and use the Birmingham "signposts" website that provides information about activities for young people.

Continuity and parental involvement was evident from interview comments, one head-teacher explained:

"Oh yes, they say the kids haven't stopped talking about it since they got home, and some have come back and said, 'Where is the climbing wall?' I know a couple of families who do take their children onto the climbing wall now, in their free time."

Activity levels

The involvement of pupils in the planning of the programme has already been identified as an important element in the achievement of affective objectives within the programme. Independence and empowerment, already discussed, taken together with the use of the local environment allows pupils to continue the activity after the completion of the programme. There was evidence from school staff of pupils taking part in rock climbing at a local climbing wall. This involved support from parents, an additional benefit in involving parents in the activities of their children which in turn supports self esteem (Morris, 2002). BOEC provides a bridge to independent use of local facilities by running an out of school club programme.

Conclusion

The literature reviewed shows outdoor education programmes to be based on the original 'outward bound' model which approach self-confidence objectives and the use of experiential learning methodologies through a framework of adventure (Miles and Priest, 1990). Consequently outdoor programmes tended to be very short term comprising isolated one-off experiences and using areas non-local to participants, sited in rural or wilderness areas. Evaluations of outdoor programmes tended to be either polarized into anecdotal or positivistic perspectives leading to what Huskins(2003) reports as a researcher versus practitioner divide. Of the anecdotal evidence work of Huskins (2003), Walker and Minnitt (2003) and Butcher (2003) comprise particularly good examples. The positivistic evaluations were concerned with providing 'measurable' evidence and results that are universally 'valid' and 'reliable' and the work of Christie (2003), Neill (1997; 2002; 2003) and Hattie *et al..* (1997) are instructive here.

The BOEC programme, which comprises the main focus of this paper, departs from the model describe above in that it is a medium to long term programme (ten weeks), uses facilities and environments local to the young people involved and attempt to provide continuity. The evaluation was guided by empirical research principles (grounded theory) and was enhanced by being carried out by practitioners in the outdoor field. The evaluation employed qualitative and quantitative approaches, the quantitative data providing valuable triangulation with the qualitative data that gave depth and understanding on which parts of the programme contributes most to its effectiveness.

The quantitative data illustrated that in general the mean scores were positive or very positive, with the most improvement noted for Communication Skills, Cooperative Teamwork, Self-esteem, Self-confidence, Risk Taking and Problem Solving. Even the lowest mean score represented a significant change. The qualitative data provided some useful indicators for future policy development identifying; staff and pupil relationships, group selection, pupil autonomy and responsibility and programme continuity as factors important to the success of the programme.

The development of good staff:pupil relationships has been identified as a vital ingredient in the success of outdoor programmes (Counterpoint 2000) and one that in youth work is claimed to be the most crucial if least quantifiable. (Richardson 1997).

This quality of relationship was evident at BOEC appearing to be linked to strong personal conviction based on their personal and professional experience in the value of using outdoor education as a developmental tool.

The composition of groups was an important factor in the success of the BOEC programmes. Groups were initially selected on the basis of selecting children who were perceived by staff as being most 'at risk'. This selection strategy was changed to one where groups were drawn from a wider range of backgrounds. This was felt to be more effective by school staff as it provided pupils 'at risk' with peer support and role models; problems were more manageable and school staff motivated to get involved with the programme. It was also seen as fair by all pupils and reduced the risk of stigmatising groups.

The empowerment of pupils through a graduated devolution of responsibility within a structured framework is a consistent characteristic of the programme and closely matches Huskins (2003) curriculum development model which he argues supports positive development of young people. This it could be argued, cannot be achieved through short courses as the progression cannot be achieved safely without the longer preparatory period needed to develop pupil knowledge and confidence. Further, staff relationships with young people, which Richardson (1997) argues is vital to success, cannot be developed in a short period.

Support for longer courses essential for this devolution of responsibility is only likely to be viable if such courses are organised close to pupil's home locality. This has the advantage of allowing continuity of the activities as in the case of BOEC and allows continued contact between the young people and local support services identified as an important factor by Humberstone (2003) and Tucker (2003). In the case of the BOEC programmes this has the added advantage of associating school with a positive experience, often intangible but supported by individual reports on improved attendance.

This supports the argument for the development of outdoor education programmes which are locally based, long term and focused on a sensitive delivery of programmes that empowers and encourages independence of the young people involved. This refutes the argument that, 'learning objectives are achieved alongside enjoyable and challenging activities which cannot be performed in conventional settings' (Fox and Avramidis (2003: p. 268).

The reports on which this paper are based were published in March 2004 (Hardy and Martin, 2004; and Hardy *et al.*, 2004) and are currently being used to inform the development of strategy within Birmingham.

Notes

1   'Therapeutic purposes' refers, generally, to any objectives focused on changing behaviour or attitudes.

2   The R^2 value indicates the statistical reliability of the relationship between two variables (Pearson product moment correlation coefficient). An R^2 value of 1 indicates a perfect relationship; and a value of 0 indicates no relationship.

References

Barrett, J. and Greenaway, R. (1995) *Why adventure? The role and value of outdoor adventure in young people and personal and social development. A review of research.* Coventry: Foundation for Outdoor Adventure.

Birmingham Childrens' Fund (2003) *Progress Report 2001–2003.* Birmingham: Birmingham Children's Fund.

Birmingham Outdoor Education Centre. (2002) Application to Children's Fund. Unpublished Document, Birmingham Outdoor Education Centre.

Burns, R.B. (2000) *Introduction to research methods.* London: Sage.

Butcher, A. (2003) 'Insights from practice: Youth development and self esteem', in Richards, K. (ed) *Self-esteem and youth development.* Ambleside: Brathay Hall Trust, pp. 53–60.

California Task Force to Promote Self-Esteem and Social Responsibility (CTF) (1990) *Toward a state of self-esteem.* Sacramento, CA: California State Department of Education.

Clay, G. (1999) 'Outdoor and Adventurous Activities, an Ofsted survey', *Horizons* 4: pp. 83–89.

Collins, M.F. and Kay, T. (2003) *Sport and social exclusion.* London: Routledge.

Counterpoint UK Ltd (2000) *Drugs education for school excludees.* North Cheshire: Drugscope.

DfEE/QCA(1999) Physical Education, *The National Curriculum for England.* Norwich: The Stationery Office.

Eisner, E.W. (1996) *Cognition and curriculum reconsidered.* 2nd Ed. London; Paul Chapman.

Emler, N. (2001) *Self-esteem. The costs and causes of self-worth.* York: York Publishing Services.

—— (2003) 'Does it really matter if some young people have low self-esteem?', in Richards, K. (ed) *Self esteem and youth development*. P1–26, Ambleside: Brathay Hall Trust.

Fox, P.and Avramidis, E. (2003) 'An evaluation of a programme for students with emotional and behavioural difficulties', *Emotional and Behavioural Difficulties* Vol.8, No. 4: pp. 267–82.

Gardner, H. (1983) *Frames of mind*. New York: Wiley.

Gass, M.A. & McPhee, P.J. (1990) 'Emerging for recovery: A descriptive analysis of adventure therapy for substance abusers', *Journal of Experiential Education* Vol. 13, No. 2: pp. 29–35.

Gillis, L. and Priest, S. 2003 'Adventure therapy: Past, present and future' in Richards, K., and Smith, B. (Eds.) Therapy Within Adventure: Proceedings of the Second International Adventure Therapy Conference, University of Augsburg, Germany. Augsburg: Zentrum fur interdisziplinares erfahrungsorientiertes Lernen GmbH, pp. 21–37.

Giroux, H.A. (1992) *Ideology, culture and the process of schooling*. Falmer.

Glyptis, S. (1989) *Leisure and unemployment*. Milton Keynes: Open University Press.

Handley, R. (1992) 'The wilderness within: Wilderness enhanced programmes for behaviour disordered adolescents — A cybernetic systemic model', in Willis, W. & Izard, J. (eds) *Fourth national conference on children with emotional or behavioural problems*. Australian Council of Educational Research, pp. 121–131.

Hardy, D. and Martin, D. (2004) *The outdoors against drugs: An evaluation of an outdoor education intervention in Birmingham*. A report for Birmingham Outdoor Education Centre, Birmingham UK.

Hardy, D., Martin, D and Sampson, O. (2004) *The Children's Fund: An evaluation of an outdoor education intervention in Birmingham*. A report for Birmingham Outdoor Education Centre, Birmingham UK.

Hattie, J., Marsh, H., Neill, J. and Richards, G. (1997) 'Adventure education and Outward Bound; out of class experiences that make a lasting difference', *Review of Educational Research* Vol. 67, No. 1: pp. 43–87.

HMI (1990) *Adventure experiences for young people from urban areas*. London: DES.

Humberstone, B., Brown, H. and Richards, K. (2003) *Whose journey? The outdoors and adventure as social and cultural phenomena: Critical explorations of relations between individuals, 'others' and the environment*. Cumbria, The Institute for Outdoor Learning.

Huskins, L.(2003) 'Self-esteem and Youth Development: a Youth work, in Richards, K. (ed) Self-esteem and Youth Development. (pp. 53–60) Ambleside: Brathay Hall Trust.

Katz, A. (2000) *Leading lads*. London: Topman.

Lincoln,Y. S. and Guba, E. G. (1985) *Naturalistic enquiry*. London: Sage.

Luckner, J.L. Nadler, R.S. (1997) *Processing the experience: Strategies to enhance and generalize learning* 2nd Edition. USA: Kendall/Hunt Publishing.

McCormack, F. (2003) 'Adventure as an intervention for young people at risk of offending: The construction of a framework to enhance the theoretical underpinning for claimed outcomes', in Humberstone, B., Brown, H. and Richards, K. (eds) *Whose journey? The outdoors and adventure as social and cultural phenomena: Critical explorations of relations between individuals, 'others' and the environment*. Penrith: The Institute for Outdoor Learning.

MacDonald, R. (ed) (1997) *Youth, the underclass and social exclusion*. London: Routledge.

McKay, S. (1993) 'Research findings related to the potential of recreation n delinquency intervention', *Trends* Vol. 30, No. 4: pp. 27–30.

Macnicol, J. (1994) 'Is there an underclass? The lessons from America', in M. White (ed) *Unemployment and public policy in a changing labour market*. London: Policy Studies Institute.

Martin, P. (2004) Inspection under section 10 of the Education (Schools) Act 1996: Hillstone Primary School, Hillstone Road, Shard End, Birmingham, B34 7PY. Available at: http://www.ofsted.gov.uk/reports/103/103361.pdf [Accessed 22nd November 2004] In: The Ofsted Reports Database (2004). London: Office for Standards in Education. Available at: http://www.open.gov.uk/ofsted/ [Accessed 22nd November 2004]

Miles, J. and Priest, S. (1990) *Adventure education*. Pennsylvania: Venture Publishing.

Miles, J.C. Priest, S. (eds) (1999) *Adventure programming*. Pennsylvania: Venture Publishing.

Morris, E. (2002) *Insight secondary: Assessing and developing self esteem*. Gosport: Ashford Colour Press.

Neill, J. (1997) Outdoor Education in Schools: What can it achieve? Paper presented to the 10th National Outdoor Education Conference, Sydney, Australia. January 1997.

―――― (2002) Meta-analytic Research on the Outcomes of Outdoor Education. Paper presented to the 6th Biennial Coalition for Education in the Outdoors Research Symposium, January 11–13, Bradford Woods,

―――― (2003) A Meta-Analysis of Outdoor Education Research. Paper presented to the Conference on Outdoor and Adventure Education Bradford Woods, IN.

Patton,M.Q. (1980) *Qualitative evaluation and research methods*. London: Sage.

Peel, J. (2003) 'Self-esteem and youth development: The case for a person-centred approach', in Richards, K. (ed) *Self-esteem and youth development*. Ambleside: Brathay Hall Trust, pp. 53–60.

Ramello, M. (2004) *Positive Futures impact report: Engaging with young people*. London: Home Office Drugs Strategy Directorate.

Richardson, J. (1997) 'The path to adulthood' in I. Ledgerwood, and N. Kendra (eds) *The challenge of the future*. Lyme Regis: Russell House.

Rosenberg, M. (1965) *Society and the adolescent self-image*. Princeton, New Jersey: Princeton University Press.

Sartre, J-P, (1938) *Nausea*. London: Penguin.

―――― (1965) *Nausea*. Trans. Robert Baldick, London: Penguin.

Scarman,G. (1982) *The Brixton Disorders 10–12 April 1981; Inquiry Report*. London, HMSO.

Strauss, A. Corbin, J. (1998) *Basics of qualitative research: Techniques and procedures for developing grounded theory*. 2nd Edition. London: Sage Publications.

Tucker, N. (2003) Participants and practitioners experience of outdoor experiential personal and social development, in: Humberstone,B., Brown, H. and Richards, K. (eds) *Whose journey; The outdoors as social and cultural phenomena*. Cumbria, the Institute for Outdoor Learning.

Walker, F. and Minitt, M. (2003) 'Barrow community learning partnership: Strategies that support the development of self esteem in young people', in: Richards, K. (ed) *Self-esteem and youth development*. Ambleside: Brathay Hall Trust, pp. 53–60.

Weber, M. (1949) *The methodology of social sciences*. Glencoe, IL: Free Press.

Wurdinger, S.D. (1994). *Philosophical issues in adventure education*. 2ndEdition. USA: Kendall/ Hunt.

ACTIVE LIFESTYLE, PHYSICAL RECREATION AND HEALTH OUTCOMES OF YOUTH IN TWO CONTRASTING NOVA SCOTIAN COMMUNITIES

Glyn Bissix, Darren Kruisselbrink and Liesel Carlsson
Acadia University, Canada

Peter MacIntyre and Tracey Hatcher
Cape Breton University, Canada

There is growing concern over the epidemic rise of inactivity-related diseases such as obesity, Type 2 Diabetes, and cardiovascular disease among young people, and their impacts on longer term population health. Recently, some attention has been paid to the contribution of place on inactivity and its repercussions to population health (see for example Aaron and LaPort, 1997). The present study provides a preliminary examination of the relationship of lifestyle and health among youth aged 15–24, particularly physical activity and active recreation in the contrasting communities of Glace Bay and Kings County in Nova Scotia, Canada. Glace Bay is located in industrial Cape Breton, Nova Scotia; it is predominantly small town urban with a population of 21,187 (Historica, 2004). It is economically unstable with population emigration. Once sustained by commercial fishing, coal mines and a nearby steel industry, these losses were not adequately offset by economic development such as a call centre initiative. In contrast, Kings County is predominantly rural and relatively stable with vibrant agriculture, forestry, fishing, manufacturing and service industries. The County has a total population of 58,866 (StatsCan, 2001). This includes the populations of the small towns of Berwick (2,282), Kentville (5,610) and Wolfville (3,658) as well as a number of small First Nations communities (157). The differing population, economic, and social circumstances in these two communities provide interesting insights into the impact of the "character of place" on physical activity, recreation behaviour, and various health and quality of life outcomes among youth (see for comparison Perdue, Gostlin and Stone, 2003 and Jackson, 2003).

141

Specifically the present study examines:
- the extent to which youth are engaged in active lifestyles including physical recreation; and
- the impact such lifestyles has on self reported health and wellness.

Literature review

Physical activity in youth

Contradictory definitions and guidelines for optimal levels of physical activity for health promotion create confusion for people to know just how much physical activity is enough to obtain health benefits. Guidelines on the frequency and intensity of exercise necessary differ. While the American College of Sports Medicine Guidelines for Healthy Aerobic Activity calls for 40–65 minutes, three to five times per week (n.d.), *Healthy People 2010* maintain that "adults should strive to ... engage in moderate-intensity physical activities for at least 30 minutes on 5 or more days of the week *or* ... engage in vigorous-intensity physical activity 3 or more days per week for 20 or more minutes per occasion." (Centers for Disease Control and Prevention, n.d.). Canada's Physical Activity Guide to Healthy Active Living calls for 60 minutes per day of light physical activity, 30–60 minutes of moderate, or 20–30 minutes of vigorous activity per day (Health Canada, 1998). Despite their rather modest requirements, these activity prescriptions are not well adhered to by Canadians in general or by youth in particular. Recent statistics from the province of Ontario for example, show that as many as 14% of adolescents did not take part in vigorous enough exercise to elicit any health benefits in the previous seven days (Irving, Adlaf, Allison, Paglia, Dwyer and Goodman, 2003). This trend study showed that only two thirds of the student respondents met the physical activity recommendations of twenty minutes per day, three times a week and that grade 11 student cohorts had become less active between the 1997 and 2000 surveys.

Further inquiry into the predisposing, enabling and reinforcing factors that shape our youths' activities conducted by Wharf Higgins, Gaul, Gibbons and Van Gyn (2003) affirm that physical activity decreases with increasing age among Canadian youth. Interestingly, these authors showed a strong correlation between increased levels of physical activity and higher household incomes, better school attendance and greater social involvement. Eaton, Nafziger, Strogatz and Pearson (1994) found a high prevalence (46.2%) of sedentarism amongst youth less than 18 years old in a rural New York population despite the increased amount of what they call "sweat activity" among farmers. Although Eaton *et al.* (1994) describe the rural lifestyle as being generally more active, 48.8% remained sedentary in their leisure time. Using one of the two community Genuine Progress Index databases used in this study, Carlsson, Kruisselbrink, Bissix and Murphy (2004) made a preliminary analysis of Kings County data that is comparable to Savage and Scott's study (1998). It assessed the physical activity levels of youth in Kings County, Nova Scotia. Among youth 15 to 17 more males than females (79% vs. 73%) were sufficiently active three or more times per week. The gap widens among youth aged 20 to 24 where 85% of males and only 65% of females were sufficiently active three or more times per week. Not surprisingly, this report showed a substantially lower percentage among insufficiently active individuals that perceive their health to be very good or excellent as compared to active individuals. This finding is consistent with the work of Piko (2000) who showed that adherence to physical activity is a strong predictor of self rated health.

Physical activity, leisure resources, and quality of life

The *Dictionary of Geography* (Mayhew, 1997) defines "quality of life" as "the degree of well-being felt by an individual about his or her life-style" that includes access to amenities and their derived social benefits (Mayhew, 1997). This definition suggests then an important contributory role for amenity in a person's quality of life such that it contributes to, among other factors, self perceived health, well-being, health awareness and life satisfaction (Piko, 2000; Valois, Zullig, Huebner and Drane, 2004). Access to amenity is therefore important in stimulating active leisure, however, Lloyd and Auld (2001, p. 62) argue that the "mere proliferation of leisure resources … does not [necessarily] increase the quality of life". They contend that "once a certain level of provision has been reached leisure resources may no longer be central to one's assessment of quality of life". Instead, once that threshold has been reached, personal attributes such as attitudes, satisfaction, and participation dominate over place attributes such as community facilities, trails and parks.

It has been increasingly recognized that physical activity and its intrinsic health benefits do not only occur during leisure time. A citizen's ability to access work, school, and daily necessities by foot or bicycle also provides physical activity in daily life thereby, it is argued, promoting physical health. Interestingly, neighbourhood "walkability", a concept described below, positively influences social capital as well as provides physical health benefits. Social capital refers here to "the social networks and interactions that inspire trust and reciprocity among citizens (Putnam, 2000)". As measured by such factors as knowing one's neighbours, ones political and social participation, and trust in other people, social capital also contributes to a citizen's quality of life (Leyden, 2003). Leyden suggests further that more traditional neighbourhoods with local stores and sidewalks are better at empowering people to walk and are better for generating social capital than modern suburbs which foster car dependency.

Community and environmental influences on physical activity

Increasing urbanization in the nineteenth century led to the deliberate integration of public health promotion with town and country planning. Interestingly, despite accelerating urbanization during the last half of the twentieth century, this connection was largely forgotten by health officers and planners. Recently, however, given the epidemic proportions of certain diseases such as Type 2 Diabetes, there has been a resurgence of professional and academic interest in integrating health promotion and planning. Perdue, Gostin and Stone (2003) described the historical relationship between the built environment and public health. They described the public health shift of concern from infectious diseases during the industrial revolution to chronic diseases in the late 20th century which in turn has transformed the urban planning focus from zoning and decreasing urban concentration to mixed land use, nature contact and proximity. In the same issue, Frumkin, a medical officer of public health in Atlanta, Georgia reviewed the evidence surrounding the "sense of place" as a public health construct. He focused on four interacting aspects: nature contact, buildings, public spaces and urban form.

Frumkin's interest in the design of our buildings, public spaces and urban form is tied to the level of a neighborhood's "walkability" (Saelens, Sallis, and Chen, 2003). This begs the question of comparability between urban vs. rural physical activity and its relationship to health and wellbeing (see Potvin, Gauvin and Nguyen, 1997). In rural environments generally access to amenities and services are unlikely to be close enough for walking whereas some urban environments may lack sufficient security to encourage walkers. Saelens *et al.* used neighbourhood walkability as a measure of the environmental conduciveness to physical activity based on residential density, mixed land use and street connectivity. Comparing the physical activity and weight status of adults living in neighbourhoods with low and high walkability, residents of high density housing, mixed land use, high street connectivity, aesthetically pleasing and safe neighbourhoods were active for over 70 more minutes per week and had lower obesity prevalence than adults in low walkability neighbourhoods. Interestingly, more residents in walkable environments met basic guidelines of at least 30 minutes of physical activity per day, two or more days per week. Significantly, it is suggested by Leyden (2003) that walkable neighbourhood residents may contribute substantially to their personal and community health by also generating social capital.

Given the varying influences of neighborhood character and their impact on healthy behaviours, it is useful to consider how individuals become more involved in health promoting strategies. The transtheoretical model for behavioural change originally used by Prochaska and DiClemente (1983) makes the fundamental assumption that throughout any behaviour change people progress through predictable stages. These include pre-contemplation, contemplation, preparation, action and maintenance. Applying this theoretical framework, Potvin, Gauvin and Nguyen (1997) compared people's readiness for physical activity in rural, suburban and urban communities in Quebec. Their study showed that rural participants had the highest rates of readiness to begin physical activity as well as the highest rates of physical activity (action) compared to suburban and urban dwellers. Whether this contrast to reports of highly inactive rural New York State residents mentioned earlier (Eaton *et al.*, 1994) is an American/Canadian contrast, or whether this indicates the dire state of current readiness for activity in urban areas, is not clear. The results showed nevertheless, that those living in an urban setting were dominant in the pre-contemplation and contemplation stages (not yet or just beginning to consider becoming active) while those in suburban areas were most likely in the preparation stages (preparing to bring activity into their lifestyles e.g. buying running shoes).

Eaton *et al.* provided several possible explanations for the apparent decrease in readiness for physical activity as one moves from rural to urban areas. The first of these is that rural occupations such as farming are often labour intensive which might infer a greater readiness for activity. This link is by no means clear, however, as this particular study specifically examined leisure time rather than the broader phenomenon of physical activity. A second possible explanation is that suburbia decreases the leisure time available due to increased commuting time and the suburban environment's restraint over walkability. Whether close to the downtown core or in suburbia, access to dedicated activity facilities is nevertheless generally greater than in rural areas. Issues such as parking and traffic are, however, possible deterrents strong enough to diminish activity levels. Access to facilities in rural settings is not generally impeded by such factors although the overall distance to them is likely a greater deterrent. While more structured activity is likely more difficult for rural populations, unstructured activities, for those that have the time and inclination to pursue them, such as cross country skiing, cycling and walking, may be more readily accessible in rural areas.

It is important to note that Frumkin's "sense of place" as a public health construct was largely one of physical context. In a more balanced discussion of "sense of place", it is also important to consider the social dimensions of place such as socioeconomic welfare, and peace and security. In addressing some of these concerns Goodman (1999) explored the role that socioeconomic status (SES) played in explaining the differences in adolescent health in the US. Using the adolescent and parental surveys from the National Longitudinal Study of Adolescent Health (cited in Goodman, 1999), the parameters of parental education and occupation, and household income were used as SES indicators to compare with self-rated health, depression, obesity, asthma, suicide and sexually transmitted diseases. Interestingly, SES gradients were found for obesity, self-rated health and depression among adolescents whereas parental education and income were independent correlates of depression and obesity. Furthermore and of some significance to our study, it is important to note that while obesity is known to be a multifactoral disease, the prominent role of physical inactivity in obesity prevalence is also well established. Goodman's individual level approach to the economic determinants of health takes the individual differences in SES, for instance income and compares it to health. Alternately, income could be taken as a characteristic of the community and could be compared to the aggregate health of that community. Community health as a community attribute is much more difficult to conceptualize and measure. Using the community approach, poor health might be attributed to a number of factors including poor investment in health, education or social services.

West, Reeder, Milne and Poulton (2002) compared the physical activities among youth in Glasgow, Scotland and Dunedin, New Zealand, two distant communities but with similar socioeconomic attributes that combines the contributions of the physical environment, as reviewed by Frumkin (2003), with the socioeconomic environment, as discussed by Goodman (1999) and Veenstra (2002). Comparable to Veenstra's conclusions regarding community health relative to the global community, the authors found that differences in physical activity levels were not explained by the different environmental features of two British Columbian communities, but rather opportunity structures and cultural factors in the community (social factors). These cultural factors also influenced a similar gender gap identified earlier that exists in both Canadian and American youth.

As can be seen from this review, the dismal state of physical activity participation among Canadian youth as well as elsewhere, and its effects on individual and community health, and overall quality of life is beginning to have emphasis in the scientific literature. This research has further increased interest in the role that community characteristics play in our public health, and how this plays out in community design as evidence suggests that our built environment does indeed dictate much of our healthy lifestyle opportunities.

Research is necessary, therefore, to further examine the connection between physical activity and place as one piece of a much more complex puzzle that might advance this issue higher on the public health agenda. This requirement for more research into the relationship of place, lifestyle and health outcomes leads to this particular study. This study is part of a broader initiative to link our understanding of community wellbeing with policy change. In this context, it is important to understand that the physical and socioeconomic space in Kings County and Glace Bay differ substantially, especially with the recent loss of Glace Bay's primary industries. Such contrasts offer an avenue for exploring the spatial and socioeconomic determinants of physical activity and health of youth in these two contrasting communities.

Theoretical framework and methodology

This study draws upon two similar databases developed for a Community Genuine Progress Index (GPI) study in Nova Scotia, Canada. Between 2001 and 2003, Glace Bay and Kings County, Nova Scotia were involved in the design and implementation of a comprehensive community survey in partnership with GPI Atlantic, the Population Health Research Unit at Dalhousie University, and other community and university partners. The purpose of the survey, entitled "Measuring Well-being" was to collect baseline data for the monitoring of community wellbeing and progress (GPI-Atlantic, 2001). The survey instrument was comprehensive including detailed questions on a variety of topics such as household demographics, labour force activity, health, core values, caregiving, voluntary activity and community service, personal security and crime, ecological footprint, food diaries, and time use. A total of 3,606 respondents completed the 70–page survey with 1,708 respondents from Glace Bay and 1,898 respondents from Kings County giving an 82% and 70% response rate respectively. Both databases were adjusted by the Population Health Research Unit at Dalhousie University, Halifax, Nova Scotia to reflect 2001 Canadian census data. This study utilized a portion of the results of this survey to conduct a preliminary examination of issues related to youth between the ages of 15 and 24, their physical activity related behaviour, and self reported health outcomes. Specifically, we analysed the responses to questions related to leisure time physical activity, physically active commuting behaviour, physically active occupational behaviour, the presence of chronic pain, and self reported health (a full description of questions and response categories are included in the Appenix). The data were analyzed using Version 12 of the Statistical Package for the Social Sciences (SPSS).

The guiding theoretical framework for the analyses that were undertaken was developed by Evans and Stoddart (1990). This framework conceptualizes the relationship between environment and endowment in determining individual health and wellbeing (see Figure 1).

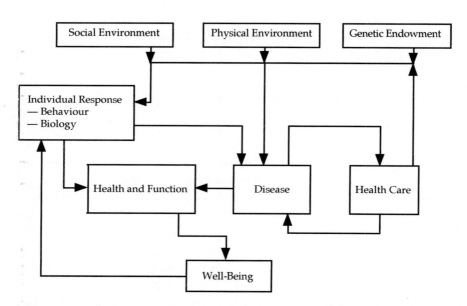

Figure 1   The determinants of health: Evans and Stoddart framework

This framework is used in this study to tie together the various contributions and attributes of health and wellbeing as measured in the two community GPI surveys. This model first recognizes biological endowment as a key health determinant; this includes age, sex and genetics. As no analysis of genetic make-up was possible in this study, an underlying assumption of this study is that random sampling avoids any skewing resulting from genetic endowment. A second key determinant of health, according to this model, is the physical/economic environment. As this study is concerned primarily with health and the attributes of place, the physical environment is a central interest of this study. According to Evans and Stoddart, a third key health determinant is the social dimension.

Data from youth 15–24 years old in Kings County and Glace Bay were compared using the Chi-square test for independent samples.

Results

Self-reported ratings of health are shown in Table 1.

Table 1   Frequencies of youth 15–24 in Kings County and Glace Bay, Nova Scotia indicating their self rated health status

Health Rating	Kings County	Glace Bay
Excellent	74	79
Very Good	130	103
Good	71	57
Fair	18	11
Poor	0	3
Total	293	253

The Chi-square test failed to reveal a difference between the Kings County and Glace Bay frequency distributions indicating that youth in Kings County and Glace Bay rated their health similarly. Analysis of participation in leisure time physical activity in the past three months showed a difference between the Glace Bay and Kings County frequency distributions, $\chi^2 (6) = 20.60$, *p*

<. .002. The largest differences were observed in the *none* and *once a week* response categories; a greater proportion of Glace Bay (22.7%) than Kings County (12.2%) youth reported not participating in leisure time physical activity, while a greater proportion of Kings County (17.0%) than Glace Bay (9.4%) youth reported participating in leisure time physical activity once a week.

A comparison between Kings County and Glace Bay communities regarding physical activity obtained while commuting to work, school, or while doing errands indicated a significant difference in the frequency distributions of the two communities, χ^2 (5) = 21.64, p < .001. More Glace Bay (36.1%) than Kings County (20.5%) youth reported not walking or bicycling to work or school or while doing errands. In rating their occupational physical activity, a non-significant chi-square indicated that Glace Bay and Kings County youth described their usual daily activities or work habits as similar.

Three questions addressed the presence and impact of pain and discomfort. Analysis revealed that similar proportions of Glace Bay and Kings County youth reported usually being free of pain or discomfort (81.9% in each community). For those not free of pain/discomfort, although more Glace Bay than Kings County youth described the intensity of their pain as moderate, and fewer Glace Bay youth described their pain as mild, the differences approached but did not reach conventional levels of statistical significance (p = .10). Additionally, more Kings County than Glace Bay youth indicated that their pain/discomfort did not prevent them from participating in activities, whereas more Glace Bay than Kings County youth reported that their pain/discomfort prevented them from participating in a few activities, χ^2 (3) = 14.70, p < .002.

Discussion and conclusions

The Evans and Stoddart's framework highlighted above allows us to conceptualize the relationship of the various determinants of health and subsequently health's impact on general well-being. Having data from two distinct communities can theoretically provide insights into the role of place on health and well-being, if we are able to control for, or isolate other influencing factors. This study's analyses represent the initial phase of an extensive plan of analyses that we hope will elucidate the relationship between physical activity and health in these two communities, and then place these in a much broader community context. This preliminary analysis provides some interesting and some puzzling perspectives on these communities. Some of our results are reflected in the literature while others contrast. This study's analyses indicate that although the physical activity patterns of Glace Bay youth appear diminished when compared to those of Kings County youth, these differences do not contribute to a systematically lower self rating of health.

More baffling was the relationship between physical activity and self reported health. The literature suggests a high correlation between inactive lifestyles and the increased incidence of inactivity related diseases such as obesity, Type 2 Diabetes, and cardiovascular disease. As a consequence, it seems reasonable to expect that those reporting greater inactivity would also report a lower health status. Given that Eaton *et al.* argue that there is also a rural/urban divide with regard to youth activity, we might expect that Kings County, which is largely rural, would have lower activity levels than Glace Bay which is largely urban. While we found no difference in the communities in youths' physical activity at work or school, we found that Kings County youth in general were more active in sport and active recreation, and walking or riding a bicycle to work or school, or in order to do errands, than their Glace Bay peers. There is clearly something else at work in determining the relationship between self-reported health and physical activity in these two communities. This we hope to uncover in future analyses. One thing that is apparent nevertheless from this study, is that Kings County youth are not receiving the expected health dividend from their greater levels of exercise. With no obvious answer to explain this, we might speculate that this is due to the greater resiliency of youth in general to disease and that any expected health disadvantages resulting from greater inactivity have yet to be manifested.

In searching further for a possible explanation for this apparent anomaly, we considered, as suggested above, a simple proxy for disease as being the absence of pain. We found our two populations to be similar in their incidence of freedom from pain while we did see a hint that Glace Bay youth had greater intensity of pain. While this latter factor might help to explain why youth in Glace Bay are less apt to be physically active — pain in this instance likely acting as a barrier to physical activity — it does nothing to explain why Glace Bay youth report similar health status to Kings County youth, despite reporting somewhat greater pain intensity.

Future analyses

Clearly this initial analysis raises more questions than it answers regarding the relationship between the self-reported health of youth and their physical activity. The breadth of the two community "Measuring Well-being" surveys will nevertheless, allow analysts to build on these early results to create an increasingly richer picture of what community attributes seems to stimulate health promotion behaviour and what provides barriers. The ultimate goal of these analyses from the community's point of view is to inform public policy at all levels of government as well as shape private, commercial and community institutions that also play a role in health promotion and health care. At this juncture, we have nothing to add in this regard.

References

Aaron, D. and LaPort, R.E. (1997) 'Physical activity, adolescence, and health: An epidemiological perspective'. *Exercise and Sport Science Review* 25: pp. 391–405.

American College of Sports Medicine (n.d.) *Guidelines for Healthy Aerobic Activity.* Retrieved December 3, 2004, from http://www.acsm.org/pdf/ Guidelines.pdf.

Carlsson, L., Kruisselbrink, D., Bissix, G. and Murphy, R. (2004) *Physical activity patterns and health outcomes in Kings County — A preliminary report.* Kentville, NS: GPI Kings County Society.

Centers for Disease Control and Prevention. (n.d.) *General recommendations for physical activity.* Retrieved Dec 3, 2004 from www.cdc.gov/nccdphp/ dnpa/physical/recommendations/index.htm.

Eaton, C. B., Nafziger, A. N., Strogatz, D. S. & Pearson, T. A. (1994) 'Self-reported physical activity in a rural county: A New York county health Census', *American Journal of Public Health* 84: pp. 29–32.

Evans, R. G. and G. L. Stoddart (1990) 'Producing health, consuming health care', in R. G. Evans, M. L. Barer and T. R. Marmor (eds) *Why are some people healthy and others not?* New York: Aldine de Gruyter, pp. 27–64.

Frumkin, H. (2003) 'Healthy place: Exploring the evidence', *American Journal of Public Health* 93: pp. 1451–1456.

Goodman, E. (1999) 'The role of socioeconomic status gradients in explaining differences in US adolescents' health', *American Journal of Public Health* 89: pp. 1522–1528.

GPI-Atlantic (2001) *Measuring well-being [in Kings County and Glace Bay].* Halifax, NS: Citizens for Community Development Society. Available at: http://gpiatlantic.org/pdf/communitygpi/kingssurvey.pdf http://gpiatlantic.org/pdf/communitygpi/glacebaysurvey.pdf

Health Canada, (n.d.) *Canada's physical activity guide to healthy active living.* Cat. No. H39–429/1998–1E; ISBN 0–662–86627–7.

Historica. The Canadian Encyclopaedia. Glace Bay, Kings County. Available at: http://www.canadianencyclopedia.ca/index.cfm?PgNm=TCE&Params=A1ARTA0003270.

Irving, H. M., Adlaf, E. M., Allison, K. R., Paglia, A., Dwyer, J. J. & Goodman, J. (2003) 'Trends in vigorous physical activity participation among ontario adolescents, 1997–2001', *Canadian Journal of Public Health* 94: pp. 272–274.

Jackson, R. J. (2003) 'The impact of the built environment on health: An emerging field', *American Journal of Public Health* 93: pp. 1382–1384.

Leyden, K. M. (2003) 'Social capital and the built environment: The importance of walkable neighbourhoods', *American Journal of Public Health* 93, 1546–1551.

Lloyd, K. M. & Auld, C. J. (2001) 'The role of leisure in determining quality of life: Issues of content and measurement', *Social Indicators Research* 57: pp. 43–71.

Mayhew, Susan. *A dictionary of geography.* Oxford University Press, 1997. *Oxford Reference Online.* Oxford University Press. Acadia University. 16 May 2004 http://www.oxfordreference.com/views/ENTRY.html?subview=Main&entry=t15.e2419.

Perdue, W., Stone, L. A., & Gostin, L.O. (2003) 'The built environment and its relationship to the public's health: The legal framework', *American Journal of Public Health* 93: pp. 1390–1394.

Piko, B. (2000) 'Health related predictors of self-perceived health in a student population: The importance of physical activity', *Journal of Community Health,* 25, 125–127.

Potvin, L., Gauvin, L. & Nguyen, N. M. (1997) 'Prevalence of stages of change for physical activity in rural, suburban and inner-city communities', *Journal of Community Health* 22(1): pp. 1–13.

Prochaska, J.O. & DiClemente, C.C. (1983) 'Stages and processes of self-change of smoking: Toward an integrative model of change', *Journal of Consulting Clinical Psychology* 51: pp. 390–395.

Putnam, R. D. (2000) *Bowling alone: The collapse and revival of american community.* New York, NY: Simon & Schuster.

Saelens, B. E., Sallis, J. F. & Chen, D. (2003) 'Neighbourhood-based differences in physical activity: An environment scale evaluation', *American Journal of Public Health* 93: pp. 1552–1558.

Savage, M. P. & Scott, L. B. (1998) 'Physical activity and rural middle school adolescents', *Journal of Youth and Adolescence* 27: pp. 245–253.

StatsCan, 2001. Kings County, Nova Scotia. Available at: http://www12.statcan.ca/english/profil01/Detailsdetails1.cfm?SEARCH=BEGINS&ID=20&PSGC=12&SGC=1207&DataType=1&LANG=E&Province=12&PlaceName=Kings%20County&CMA=&CSDNAME=Kings%20County&A=&TypeNameE=Census%20Division&Prov=

Valois, R. F., Zullig, K. J., Huebner, E. S. & Drane, J. W. (2004) 'Physical activity behaviours and perceived life satisfaction among public high school adolescents', *Journal of School Health* 74(2): pp. 59–65.

Veenstra, G. (2002) 'Income inequality and health: Coastal communities in British Columbia, Canada', *Canadian Journal of Public Health* 93: pp. 374–379.

West, P., Reeder, A. I., Milne, B. J. & Poulton, R. (2002) 'Worlds apart: A commission between physical activities among youth in Glasgow, Scotland and Dunedin, New Zealand', *Social Science & Medicine* 54: pp. 607–619.

Wharf Higgins, J., Gaul, C., Gibbons, S. & Van Gyn, G. (2003) 'Factors influencing physical activity levels among Canadian youth', *Canadian Journal of Public Health* 94: pp. 45–51.

Appendix

Items and response category options obtained from the Health and Community Questionnaire portion of Genuine Progress Index Atlantic Survey used in the present study:

1. Would you say your health is (check one):
   a.   Excellent
   b.   Very Good
   c.   Good
   d.   Fair Poor

2. Have you done any sports or physical exercise in your leisure time (not related to work) in the past three months? (For example, swimming, bicycling, jogging, exercising, walking for exercise, active yard work or gardening, dancing, basketball, hockey, other active sports, etc.)
   a.   Yes
   b.   No (skip the next question)

3. Approximately how often did you participate in this leisure time physical activity in the past three months?
   a.   At least once a day
   b.   About five times a week
   c.   About three times a week
   d.   About once a week
   e.   About once a month
   f.   Once or twice in the last three months

4. In a typical *week*, how much time do you spend walking or bicycling to work or school or while doing errands (*NOT* counting leisure time activity)?
   a.   None
   b.   Less than one hour
   c.   One to five hours
   d.   Six to ten hours
   e.   Eleven to twenty hours
   f.   More than twenty hours

5. Thinking back over the past three months, which of the following best describes your *USUAL* daily activities or work habits?
   a.   Usually sit during the day and do not walk about very much
   b.   Stand or walk quite a lot during the day but do not have to carry or lift things very often
   c.   Usually lift or carry light loads or have to climb stairs or hills often
   d.   Do heavy work or carry very heavy loads

6. Are you *USUALLY* free of pain or discomfort?
   a.   Yes
   b.   No

YOUNG PEOPLE, PHYSICAL ACTIVITY AND PHYSICAL FITNESS: A CASE STUDY OF CHINESE AND PORTUGUESE CHILDREN

Guoyong Wang, Beatriz Pereira and Jorge Mota
University of Minho, University of Porto, Portugal

Introduction

Non-communicable diseases (NCDs) such as cardiovascular disease, hypertension, obesity, diabetes, chronic respiratory diseases, and some types of cancer—are increasingly significant causes of disability and premature death across many countries. In 1999 these diseases contributed to about 60% of deaths in the world and 43% of the global burden of disease. On the basis of current estimates, these deaths are expected to account for 73% of deaths and 60% of the disease burden by the year 2020 (WHO, 2002a).

Regular physical activity is associated with a healthier, longer life and with a lower risk of NCDs (USDHHS,1996). The World Health Organization's report, *Diet, Physical Activity and Health*, indicated that unhealthy diet and insufficient physical activity are among the major causal risk factors in NCDs (WHO, 2002b).

Never before has the public been more aware of the enormous health and fitness benefits of physical activity, which have been highlighted in both the Surgeon General's report (USDHHS, 1996) and in the Healthy People 2010 study (USDHHS, 2000). The most prominent finding of the Surgeon General's report is that people of all ages can improve their quality of life through a lifelong practice of moderate physical activity. Yet, despite knowledge of these benefits, most people are still more sedentary. Worldwide, it is estimated that over 60% of adults are simply not active enough to benefit their health (WHO, 2003). In the United States, only 25% of adults reported engaging in recommended physical activity levels, 29% reported no regular leisure-time physical activity (CDC, 2000). The prevalence of physical activity during leisure time in the European adult population was similar to the U.S. estimates. Nevertheless, the amount of physical activity is low, and a wide disparity between countries exists. The highest prevalence of physical activity was found in Finland (91.9%) and the lowest in Portugal (40.7%) (Martinez-Gonzalez *et al.*, 2001).

Regular physical activity levels have also been declining dramatically both in the United States (USDHHS, 1996) and in European Countries (Freedson and Rowland, 1992). In the United States, 27% of children in grades 9–12 engaged in moderate physical activity for at least 30 minutes on 5 or more of the previous 7 days in 1999 (USDHHS, 2000). A large-scale investigation of 6903 Portuguese children in grades 6, 8 and 10 showed that 38.3% of them participated in physical activity 4 times or more weekly (Matos *et al.*, 2000).

A recent meta-analysis compared the results of 55 reports of the performance of children and adolescents aged 6–19 years who used the 20m shuttle run test. All data (129,882 children and adolescents) were collected in the period 1981–2000. Tomkinson *et al.*'s (2003) longitudinal comparative study confirmed that children and adolescent's aerobic fitness was declining

Both obesity and physical inactivity are the major determinants of many NCDs. Though children and young adults have very low rates of NCDs, which are leading causes of death, it is true that these diseases develop over time, and quite often begin with habits and behaviours developed earlier in life (Gilliam *et al.*, 1977). The major problem associated with child obesity is its persistence into adult life. Obese children will most likely become obese adults and carry all the extra risks for NCDs, such as heart attacks, strokes, high blood pressure, and diabetes (Wright *et al.*, 2001). In the United States, physical inactivity has contributed to the 100% increase in the prevalence of childhood obesity since 1980 and most of this increase occurred in the last 10 years (CDC, 2000). There is a worldwide trend towards inactivity. It has become increasingly clear that physical inactivity and unhealthy diets are a global public health issue (WHO, 2002a).

Earlier assessment methods of physical activity and fitness have focused on vigorous leisure time physical activity and related fitness. According to recent research, physical activity needs to be only of moderate intensity for a protective effect (Pratt, 1999). Health-enhancing physical activity (at least moderate intensity physical activity 5 or more days per week for 30 minutes or more per occasion) and health-related physical fitness are new concepts developed primarily in the 1990¥s based on research evidence on the relationship between physical activity, fitness and health (Bouchard and Shephard, 1994). So the aim of this case study was mainly designed to disclose and compare children's habitual physical activity levels (MVPA-moderate vigorous physical activity) and their health-related physical fitness between the Chinese and Portuguese children.

METHODS

Sample and Data Collection

A sample of 264 Portuguese children (boys 49.6% vs. girls 50.4%) aged between 10 and 15 were selected from the public middle schools in Braga, Portugal; a similar sample of 317 Chinese children (boy 51.1% vs. girl 48.9%) aged between 11 and 15 were selected from the public middle schools in Shanghai, China. All subjects completed the health-related physical fitness test FITNESSGRAM and answered the questionnaire during physical education classes. Survey procedures were designed to protect the children' privacy by allowing for anonymity.

Instrumentation

Assessment of health-related physical fitness (FITNESSGRAM)

The FITNESSGRAM was selected because of its ease of administration to large numbers of subjects, and in addition its choice of reliable and valid health-related physical fitness measures (Cooper Institute of Aerobics Research, 1999). Six components of health-related physical fitness were evaluated: body composition, aerobic capacity, overall flexibility, upper body strength, abdominal strength and endurance, and trunk extensive strength. Physically fit means passing all of the minimum level for health of all six items in FITNESSGRAM.

(a) Body composition (BC) was assessed by the sum of triceps and calf skinfolds. Triceps skinfold was measured at the midpoint and back of the upper right arm. Calf skinfold was measured on the side of right leg with the knee bent at a 90 degree, the skinfold being measured at the maximal girth of the calf. Three measures were taken at each skinfold site and averaged and the average of the two sites were then calculated. Body composition was determined by skinfolds according to Slaughter *et al.* (1988).

(b) Aerobic capacity (AC) was assessed by one mile run. All subjects were instructed to complete one mile in the fastest time possible by either running or walking. The mile course was completed on a 250–m track. The researchers and the PE staff counted laps, motivated the children during the test, and recorded their results. The cardiovascular fitness is depended on children's test in aerobic capacity.

(c) Overall flexibility (OF) was assessed by the test of Back-saver sit-and-reach (Patterson *et al.*, 1996). Subjects were asked to remove their shoes, with one leg fully extended and another knee bent with the sole on the floor and 5–8cm to the straight leg, children were asked to reach forward on a standardized sit-and-reach box four times and hold the position of the fourth stretch for at least one second for measuring.

(d) Upper body strength (UBS) was assessed by the right angle push-ups (cadence). Subjects were asked to complete as many push-ups as possible (at a rhythm of 20 times per minute). Researchers and PE staff counted the push-ups until the student could no longer maintain the rhythm.

(e) Abdominal strength and endurance (ASE) was assessed by sit-up (cadence). Subjects were asked to complete as many sit-ups as possible up to a maximum of 75 at a rhythm (20 times per minute). The subject lied down on a mat with the knees bent, the arms straight and parallel to the trunk, then did the sit-up with both arms across the cardboard strip (11.4cm), and back each time. The researchers and the PE teachers counted the correct push-ups until the student could no longer maintain the rhythm.

(f) Trunk extensive strength (TES) Subjects were asked to lie on the mat in a prone position and lift their upper body off the floor to allow the researcheror PE teacher to measure the trunk length.

Assessment of Overweight and Obesity

Body Mass Index (BMI) is widely used in adult populations, and a cut off point of 25 and 30 kg/m2 is recognized internationally as a definition of adult overweight and obesity respectively (WHO, 1997). The BMI in childhood changes substantially with age (Cole *et al.*, 1995). The Childhood Obesity Working Group of the International Obesity Task Force (IOTF) has developed cut-off criteria with relative (age-specific) BMI centile charts for children (2–18 yrs). The IOTF authors point out that although these cut-off points are less arbitrary, they are more internationally acceptable than others that have been used (Cole *et al.*, 2000). Height and weight were measured to an accuracy of 0.1cm and 0.1kg respectively without shoes or jumpers.

BMI was calculated as body in kilograms divided by height in meters squared ($kg/m2$).

Assessment of physical activity

The International Physical Activity Questionnaire (IPAQ) is a relatively questionnaire for the assessment of health-enhancing physical activity. Eight versions of the instrument were tested for feasibility, reliability and validity (Craig *et al.*, 2003). The short version IPAQ were selected and translated into Portuguese and Chinese. All participants completed the questionnaire during their PE classes; the researchers and PE staff explained the detail of the questionnaire. Children's physical activity levels (moderate to vigorous physical activity-MVPA) were divided into four categories (sedentary: 0–2 times/week, low: 3–4 times /week, moderate: 5–6 times/week, vigorous: 7+ times/week). To assess the instrument reliability, the two-week test-retest assessment was assessed with a random sub-sample of 28 Portuguese children. The reliability was 0.84.

Television Viewing

The amount of time spent watching television was estimated over a typical week in the questionnaire. It was expressed on a daily basis (min/day).

Statistical methods

Data were collected and analyzed by using the Statistical Package for the Social Sciences (SPSS) v. 11.0. The subject sample was described using descriptive statistics. Data are showed as means and standard deviations or percentage. Pearson Correlation Coefficients and Partial Correlation were used to describe the relationships of the variables to performance, and two-way ANOVA was performed across height, weight, BMI, the sum of skinfold thicknesses, MVPA, and TV Time to determine the effects of age and gender.
Statistical significance was set at $p<0.05$.

Results

A total of 264 Portuguese and 317 Chinese children participated in FITNESSGRAM test and questionnaire. The characters of the sample, results of FITNESSGRAM test, body composition, physical activity levels, and television viewing time of the sample, organized by gender and age, are described in the tables and figures below.

We observed that children's height, weight, and BMI generally increased with their age in both countries. But at the same age, Portuguese boys' height, weight, and BMI were higher than those of Chinese boys and Portuguese girls BMI were bigger than those of Chinese girls (see Table 1).

According to the cut-off criteria with relative (age-specific) BMI centile charts for children, we found 22.1% of the Chinese children and 27.3% of the Portuguese children suffered from being either overweight or obese, 6.0% of the Chinese children and 6.8% of the Portuguese children suffered from obesity (seeTable 2).

The results of the health-related physical fitness test (FITNESSGRAM) showed most children (Chinese: 92.7% vs. Portuguese: 82.6%) failed to meet all 6 minimum standards that would classify them as physically fit (see Table

Table 1   Characteristics of the Chinese and Portuguese middle school children

Gender	Age (yrs)	Number China/ Portugal	Height (m)		Weight(kg)		BMI(kg/m^2)	
			China	Portugal	China	Portugal	China	Portugal
Boys	10	0/9	-	1.47±0.04	-	41.1±6.7	-	18.8±2.4
	11	13/43	1.46±0.04	1.48±0.06	37.0±4.9	42.2±7.1	17.4±2.2	19.8±3.4
	12	48/18	1.54±0.08	1.57±0.10	48.3±12.7	51.3±12.3	20.2±4.4	20.6±3.7
	13	45/13	1.61±0.07	1.62±0.07	53.8±11.3	59.1±8.6	20.7±4.1	22.7±3.5
	14	30/33	1.66±0.08	1.68±0.07	57.7±15.5	58.3±9.3	20.9±5.1	20.5±2.7
	15	26/15	1.68±0.07	1.70±0.12	60.1±12.1	63.1±13.8	21.2±3.4	21.5±2.6
Girls	10	0/12	-	1.44±0.09	-	40.1±12.2	-	20.3±4.3
	11	21/40	1.50±0.06	1.49±0.07	41.5±9.1	45.4±10.9	18.3±3.4	20.3±4.3
	12	35/22	1.53±0.07	1.54±0.05	41.5±8.4	48.9±7.8	17.6±2.9	20.4±3.1
	13	41/13	1.58±0.06	1.55±0.05	47.6±7.2	48.6±8.3	19.1±2.5	20.2±3.3
	14	42/37	1.60±0.06	1.62±0.06	53.7±12.2	54.0±7.9	20.9±4.1	20.6±2.7
	15	16/9	1.59±0.05	1.61±0.07	53.3±9.5	54.9±9.9	21.2±3.3	21.3±3.6

Table 2   Children's body composition (by age-specific BMI centile charts for children)

	Chinese (M=162, F=155)	Portuguese (M=131, F=133)
Healthy weight	77.9%(M=71.0%, F=85.2%)	72.7%(M=71.2%, F=75.2%)
Overweight	22.1%(M=29.0%, F=14.8%)	27.3%(M=29.8%, F=24.8%)
Obesity	6.0%(M=8.6%, F=3.2%)	6.8%(M=6.1%, F=7.5%)

3 and Figure 1). A further breakdown of the results showed that the strongest category across all ages was in trunk strength (tested by trunk lift), where 90.9% of the Chinese children and 89.4% of the Portuguese children met the minimum standard, the weakest category across all ages was upper body strength (tested by push-ups), where only 16.1% of the Chinese children and 28.8% of the Portuguese children met the minimum standard.

Table 3: Summary of Fitness Standards Achieved (%)

Item in FITNESSGRAM	Chinese (162B/155G)	Portuguese (131B/133G)
(1) Aerobic capacity	52.1% (B: 64.2%, G: 39.4%)	83.3% (B: 87.0%, G: 79.7%)
(2) Abdominal strength and endurance	74.1% (B: 70.4%, G: 78.1%)	76.5% (B: 80.9%, G: 72.2%)
(3) Body composition (Skinfolds)	77.3% (B: 68.5%, G: 86.5%)	82.6% (B: 74.8%, G: 90.2%)
(4) Overall Flexibility	79.5% (B: 85.2%, G: 73.5%)	57.2% (B: 65.7%, G: 48.9%)
(5) Trunk extensive strength	90.9% (B: 93.2%, G: 88.4%)	89.4% (B: 90.8%, G: 88.0%)
(6) Upper body strength	15.5%(B: 29.6%, G: 0.6%)	28.8% (B: 36.6%, G: 21.1%)
Physical fit (passing all 6 items)	8.2% (B:15.4%, G: 0.6%)	17.4% (B: 22.2%, G: 12.8%)
Not physical fit (not passing all 6 items)	91.8%(B: 84.6%, G: 99.4%)	82.6% (B: 77.8%, G: 87.2%)

B: Boys, G: Girls

Figure 1: Summary of Fitness Standards Achieved (%)

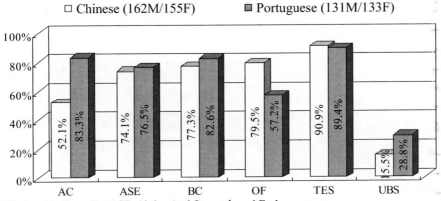

AC: Aerobic Capacity; ASE: Abdominal Strength and Endurance;
BC: Body CompositionOF: Overall Flexibility;
TES: Trunk Extensive Strength; UBS: Upper Body Strength

According to the results of the IPAQ (see Table 4 and Figure 2), we found that only 27.1% of the Chinese children and 44.4% of the Portuguese children engaged in regular basis MVPA; 15.8% of the Chinese children and 19.2% of the Portuguese children did not participate in any kind of spare-time physical activity beyond school physical education (twice a week). We found a significant difference in the children's physical activity levels (MVPA) between boys and girls in both countries, which showed that girls were less active than boys (r= -0.36 to -0.28, p< .001). Between two countries the Portuguese children were more active than Chinese children.

According to the self-report questionnaire, we found that 32.7% of the Chinese children and 67.4% of the Portuguese children watched television at least 2 hours per school day, 5.0% of the Chinese children and 23.0 % of

Table 4   Children's physical activity levels (MVPA)

Items	Chinese (B: 162, G: 155)	Portuguese (B: 131, G: 133)
More active	27.1% (B: 37.7%, G: 16.1%)	44.4%(B: 62.0%, G: 27.4%)
Not enough	57.1% (B: 51.2%, G: 63.2%)	36.4%(B: 27.7%, G: 45.0%)
No PA after SPE	15.8% (B: 11.1%, G: 20.6%)	19.2% (B: 10.3%, G: 27.6%)
PA by genders	r: — 0.28, p<0.001	r: — 0.36, p<0.001

B: Boys, G:Girls, PA:Physical Activity, SPE: School Physical Education,

Figure 2   Children's physical activity levels (MVPA)

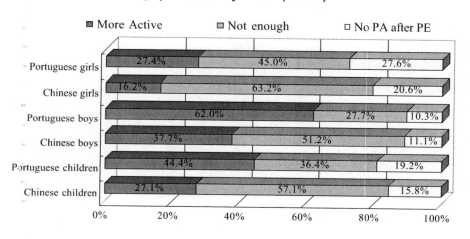

the Portuguese children even spent more than 4 hours per school day (see Table 5).

The Pearson correlation coefficients between physical activity levels (MVPA) and physical fitness of the sample are presented in Table 6. We found that the children's MVPA had a significant correlation with their physical fitness (especially among the Portuguese children; Portuguese boys: r=0.26, p<0.05; Portuguese girls: r=0.31, p<0.01), passing more fitness categories (Chinese girls: r=0.22, p<0.05; Portuguese boys: r=0.29, p<0.05; Portuguese girls: r=0.39, p<0.01) (see Table 6). Among the Chinese children the correlation was not as strong.

The Pearson correlation coefficients between body composition (overweight and obesity) and physical fitness of the sample are presented

Table 5   Children's television viewing in school day

	Chinese (B:162, G:155)	Portuguese (B:131, G:133)
X < 2h	71.0% (B:67.9%, G:74.2%)	32.6% (B:37.9%, G:27.6%)
2h ≤ X < 4h	23.6% (B:22.7%, G:24.6%)	44.4% (B:43.1%, G:45.6%)
X ≥ 4h	5.4% (B:7.4%, G:3.2%)	23.0% (B:77.8, G:87.2%)

X: Average Television viewing time in school day, B: Boys, G: Girls

Table 6   The relationship between children's physical activity levels (MVPA) and health-related physical fitness

Health-Related Physical Fitness	Physical Activity Levels (MVPA)			
	Chinese Boys	Chinese Girls	Portuguese Boys	Portuguese Girls
(1) Trunk extensive strength	NS	NS	NS	0.24**
(2) Abdominal strength & endurance	NS	NS	NS	0.31**
(3) Upper Body strength	NS	NS	0.20*	0.31**
(4) Overall flexibility	NS	NS	NS	NS
(5) Body composition	NS	NS	NS	0.18*
(6) Aerobic capacity	NS	0.21*	0.24*	NS
Passing more items	NS	0.22*	0.29*	0.39**
Physical fit (passing all 6 items)	NS	NS	0.26*	0.31**
VO$_2$ max	NS	0.17*	0.30*	0.30*

NS: not siginificant, *<0.05, **<0.01, ***<0.001,

Table 7: The relationship between weight and obesity and health-related physical fitness

	Chinese-Boys		Chinese-Girls		Portuguese-Boys		Portuguese Girls	
Health-related Physical Fitness	OW	OB	OW	OB	OW	OB	OW	OB
(1) Trunk extensive strength	-0.17*	NS	NS	NS	NS	NS	NS	NS
(2) Abdominal strength & endurance	NS	NS	NS	-0.17*	NS	-0.20*	-0.34***	-0.27**
(3) Upper Body strength	-0.20*	-0.20*	NS	NS	-0.29**	NS	-0.17*	NS
(4) Overall flexibility	NS	-0.26**	NS	NS	-0.34***	NS	.17*	NS
(5) Body composition	-	-	-	-	-	-	-	
(6) Aerobic capacity	-0.18*	-0.16*	-0.15*	-0.15*	-0.30**	-0.28**	-0.19*	NS
Passing more items	-0.38***	-0.34***	-0,26**	-0.30***	-0.48***	-0.38***	-0.27**	-0.32***
Physical fit (passing all 6 items)	NS	NS	NS	NS	-0.19*	NS	NS	NS
VO$_2$ max	-0.65***	-0.53***	-0.71***	-0.58***	-0.61***	-0.45***	-0.69***	-0.49***

in Table 7. We found that weight and obesity were negatively correlated with children with good VO2 max and who passed more FITNESSGRAM categories.

Discussion

The issue of physical fitness among children and adolescents is multi-facted. It includes documented relatively low levels of physical activity that are of great concern to health professionals. The results of numerous physical fitness studies among children and adolescents also indicate that the problem is one for public health policy, and policy related to promoting comprehensive school health education programs. The issue also calls for broad promotion of healthy lifestyles for young people.

Tomkinson *et al.* (2003) compared the results of 55 reports of the performance of 129,882 children and adolescents aged 6–19 years in the period 1981–2000. The longitudinal comparative study confirmed that the aerobic fitness of children and adolescent's is declining. In this case study, we did a transverse comparison between the Chinese and Portuguese children, which showed that few of the children (Chinese: 8.2% vs. Portuguese: 17.4%) met all six minimum standards in FITNESSGRAM that define physical fitness. We also found that the result was skewed by the fact of the lower pass rate in upper body strength (Chinese:15.5% vs. Portuguese: 28.8%) whereas the percentage that passed the other component criteria ranged from 52.1% to 90.9%. Apart form upper body stength, the children did well in other areas (Trunk Extensive Strength, Body Composition, Aerobic Capacity, Abdominal Strength and Overall Flexibility). Comparing the other results of FITNESSGRAM between children in both countries, we found that the children had similar results in the tests of Trunk Extensive Strength, Body Composition and Abdominal Strength, but Portuguese children did well in Aerobic Capacity (Portuguese: 83.3% vs. Chinese: 52.1%), while Chinese children did well in the Overall flexibility (Chinese: 79.5% vs. Portuguese: 57.2%). This may be caused by their different school PE programs, for example the Portuguese school physical education programs included more endurance training, such as long distance running and football, while the Chinese PE programs include traditional sports like martial arts, which improve flexibility. So we suggest that future school PE programs in both countries not only need to reinforce children's overall health-related physical fitness but also their weaknesses (especially in upper body strength).

A large-scale investigation of 6903 Portuguese children and adolescents in grades 6, 8 and 10 (6903 subjects) showed that 36.1% of them (boys: 25.0% vs. girls: 45.7%) were overweight in 1998. This level declined a little in 2002, when 31.9% (boys: 23.9% vs. girls: 39.5%) of the them (6131 subjects) were overweight (Matos *et al.*, 2003). Our results agreed with these results, which showed a quarter of children (Chinese: 22.1% vs. Portuguese: 27.3%) either suffered from being either overweight or obese. It seemed that more Portuguese girls (24.8%) suffered from being overwieght and obese than the Chinese girls did (11.8%). We also found that overweight and obese children had a more negative correlation with their health-related physical fitness and VO2 max (see Table 7). These results also raise serious concerns about the current and future health of these children. The major problems associated with child obesity is its persistence into adult life; it is likely that obese children will become obese adults and carry all the extra risks for NCDs (Wright *et al.*, 2001).

Lifestyle changes and technological advancement have steadily reduced physical activity levels in many developed and developing countries. It is estimated worldwide that over 60% of adults are simply not active enough to benefit their health. Among children and adolescents, physical activity declines significantly from adolescence, girls are also less active than boys (WHO, 2003).

The large-scale investigation among the Portuguese children and adolescents in grades 6, 8 and 10 (6903 subjects) found that 36.1% participated in physical activity four or more times a week in 1998. This activity level declined dramatically in all gender and age groups in 2002, when only 31.9% of the subjects (6131 children and adoelscents) of the same ages participated in physical activity four or more times a week (Matos, *et al.*, 2003). According to recent research, physical activity needs to be only of moderate intensity for a protective effect (Pratt, 1999). Health-enhancing physical activity means at least moderate intensity physical activity five or more days per week for 30 minutes or more per occasion. According to the results of the children's self-reported questionnaire, we found that less than half of the children reached recommended levels of physical activity (Chinese: 27.1% vs. Portuguese: 44.4%); nearly 20% of the children (Chinese:15.8% vs. Portuguese: 19.2%) did not participate any kind of leisure physical actvity after school physical education; girls were significantly less active than boys in both countries (r=-0.36 to -0.28, p<0.001). We found that more Chinese children (more than 50%) belonged to the category of "not enough" physical activity, while more Portuguese were "more active", and in general the Portuguese children were more active than the Chinese children.

School provides children opportunities for physical activity; additional opportunities for physical activity exist outside of school. We observed that children in both countries had their school physical education twice a week (total 135 minutes). However, there there are socioeconomic factors contributing to the lower levels of their physical activity. Many children said that their schools and communities did not have fitness rooms or equipment that they can use after school, many children (especially the girls) are required to stay indoors because their parents will not allow them to play at unsupervised areas due to safety concerns. It was found that in China, children were under extreme pressure to study and compete academically. They cited the quantity of home work they had to do after school as a constraint. The Portuguese children did not have this kind of pressure, but they spent more of their leisure time in sedentary activites such as watching television and playing video games.

There is convincing evidence that regular physical activity protects children against unhealthy weight gain whereas sedentary lifestyles, particularly sedentary occupations and inactive recreation such as watching television, promote it. Some studies indicated that the amount of time in watching television, is also associated with less physical activity, increased obesity, and lower physical fitness (Dietz and Gortmarker, 1993; Durant *et al.*, 1996). Our study confirmed that a large number of children especially the Portuguese children, spent much of their leisure time watching television for at least 2 hours per school day (Chinese: 29.0% vs. Portuguese: 77.4%). We did not find significant correlations between watching television, physical activity levels, sum of skinfolds, and BMI, but we did find that the Portuguese girls who watch television more than 4 hours per school day have a higher BMI than those Portuguese girls who watch less than 2 hours of television per school day. Stouffer and Dorman (1999) indicated that childhood obesity is a complex problem with a multifaceted aetiology. It is not merely a simple question of physical activity levels or television viewing time, but can also be associated with excess calorific intake, high fat diets, genes, parental influences, psychosocial contributors, and eating patterns; this is an area in need of further research.

Poor physical fitness levels, physical inactivity, and the rise in obesity have become a national concern in the United States. Physical inactivity is considered by health experts to be a major epidemic and a key public health challenge in the United States (NASPE, 1998). Extensive evidence, including the landmark 1996 Surgeon General's Report on Physical Activity and Health, has documented the health benefits of regular physical activity, i.e. regular moderate physical activity can substantially reduce the risk of developing chronic illnesses and improve mental health (USDHHS, 1996). Our study also showed that the children's physical activity levels (MVPA) were significantly correlated with the children's health-related physical fitness (less so with the Chinese boys).

Physical activity is a behavior, whereas physical fitness is an attribute. Inadequate physical activity is a behavior pattern that is typically established during youth, persists into a sedentary adulthood, and contributes to poor health (Morrow and Jackson, 1999). One of the most effective ways to prevent chronic diseases is to establish policies that encourage young people to develop healthy exercise habits early that they can maintain throughout their lives. Since virtually all youth attend school, school therefore is the logical place for the development of these patterns. In addition to being physically active, children need to learn fundamental motor skills and develop health related physical fitness (cardiovascular endurance, muscular strength and endurance, flexibility, and body composition). School PE is an ideal way to encourage activity and develop fitness among children and, for many children, will be their only preparation for an active lifestyle (Summerfield, 1998).

Despite a renewed emphasis on youth fitness, physical activity among youths has declined in recent years in the United States. According to statistics compiled by the Centre for Disease Control and Prevention (CDC, 2002) the percentage of adolescents who have opportunities for daily PE dropped from 42% in 1991 to 29% in 1999. Mckenzie *et al.* (2000) indicated that even in schools with daily PE classes, children were not receiving adequate amounts of physical activity. This situation is likely to be worse in many other schools, where physical education is not offered daily. A comprehensive survey in 25 European countries reveals that no European country offers a daily PE class (Armstrong and Astrand, 1997). In Portugal, before 2001, middle school children had 180 minutes PE/week, but now school PE has been reduced to 135 minutes/week. Studies also show that the quality of PE is uneven, diminishing its potential health and educational benefits. According to another study of ours among the sample of these 264 Portuguese middle school children (Wang, Pereira and Mota, 2004), we found that 7th grade Portuguese children only spent 32.0% of class time in 45–minute indoor classes and 31.0% of class time in 90–minute indoor classes exercising at recommended activity levels (50% class time in MVPA). The comparative study shows Chinese children (in Hong Kong) spent 32.4% of class time at recommended activity levels (Macfarlane and Kwong, 2003). We found that the most traditional school PE selected many competitive team sports programs rather than the health-enhancing exercise programs, children were not so active during the classes and a lot of PE time was spent changing and showering (Wang, Pereira and Mota, 2004).

Health promotion professionals have recognized the important role that school PE programs play in providing physical activity. Recommendations for increasing both the quantity and quality of school PE are included in Healthy People 2010 (USDHHS, 2000), which recommends that school PE programs need to develop comprehensive programs that promote enjoyable, lifelong physical activity (e.g., dance, strength-training, aerobics, jogging, swimming, tennis) rather than competitive team sports (Sallis *et al.*, 1992; USDHHS, 2000). In recent years school PE programs have placed a greater emphasis on health-related exercise or PE theory, focusing on the knowledge, skills and attitudes required to promote health and well-being and to encourage active lifestyles (Harris, 1994). Some appropriate school-based intervention programs increase the interest and activity levels of school children (USDHHS, 2000). In another study of ours, we found that most middle school children knew little about health-related physical fitness and health-enhacing physical activity before the intervention. After our one-year intervention, the children not only improved their knowledge, skill and attitude on health, but also improved their physical fitness and activity levels as well (Wang, Pereira, and Mota, 2004). It is argued here that school PE programs should improve children's knowledge, skills, and attitudes on health, and select some health-enhancing exercise programs. Considering the gender differences between children's habitual physical activity (girls are less active), school PE needs to provide programs that best meet the interests of all. For example, an aerobics course is likely to appeal to girls, just as football traditionally attracts boys, whereas a physical conditioning course might attract both boys and girls. There is not enough time in PE classes for children to get sufficient physical activity in most schools, so we suggest teachers at all levels should strive to encourage children to be physically active both in class and beyond the school environment. Students at all levels need to acquire the knowledge, attitudes, and skills necessary to develop patterns of daily participation in physical activity.

Conclusion

The study concludes that most of the sample of Chinese and Portuguese school children were not physically active and physically fit. Moreover, a quarter of them already suffered from being overweight and obesity. Inadequate physical activity is a behavior pattern that is typically established during youth. To help children understand, develop, and maintain a healthy lifestyle to reduce the risk of developing NCDs, government and schools need to reinforce comprehensive school health education, and to work with communites and families to maximize physical activity opportunities. Physical educators need to encourage children to live an active lifestyles and to maximize physical activity time during classes. Focused school health and PE programs should be applied to improve the knowledge, skills and attitudes of children on health and well-being, to promote enjoyable, lifelong physical activity.

References

Armstrong, N. and Åstrand, P. (1997) 'Physical education and the promotion of health and well-being in Europe', *European Journal of Physical Education* 2: pp. 158–159.

Bouchard, C. and Shephard R.J. (1994) 'Physical activity, fitness, and health: The model and key concepts', in Bouchard C., Shephard R.J. and Stephens T. (eds) *Physical activity, fitness and health*. Champaign, IL: Human Kinetics.

CDC — Centers for Disease Control and Prevention (2000) *Promoting better health for young people through physical activity and sports: A report to the President from the Secretary of Health and Human Services and the Secretary of Education*. Atlanta, GA: U.S.

--------- (2002) *Physical Activity and Good Nutrition: Essential Elements to Prevent Chronic Diseases and Obesity, At-a-Glance 2002*. Atlanta: Accessed at http://www.cnt.org/tsp/pdf/cdc obesity report 2002.pdf.

Cole, T. J., Bellizzi, M. C., Flegal, K. M. and Dietz, W. H. (2000) 'Establishing a standard definition for child overweight and obesity worldwide; international survey', *British Medical Journal* 320: pp. 1240–1243.

Cole, T. J., Freeman, J. V., Preece, M. A. (1995) 'Body mass index reference curves for UK, 1990', *Archives of Disease in Childhood* 73: pp. 25–29.

Cooper Institute for Aerobics Research (1999) *FITNESSGRAM test administration manual*. Champaign, IL: Human Kinetics.

Craig, C.L., Marshall, A.L., Sjöström, M., Bauman, A.E., Booth, M.L., Ainsworth, B.E., Pratt, M, Ekelund, U., Yngve, A., Sallis, J.F. and Oja, P. (2003) 'International Physical Activity Questionnaire: 12 country reliability and validity', *Medicine and Science in Sports and Exercise* 35: pp. 1381–1395.

Dietz, W. H. and Gortmarker, S. L. (1993) 'TV or not TV: Fat is the question', *Pediatrics* 91: pp. 499–501.

DuRant, R. H., Thompson, W. O., Johnson, M., and Baranowski, T. (1996). 'The relationship among television watching, physical activity, and body composition of 5 or 6 year-old children', *Pediatric Exercise Science* 8: pp. 15–26.

Freedson, P. S. and Rowland, T. W. (1992) 'Youth activity versus youth fitness: Let's redirect our efforts', *Research Quarterly for Exercise and Sport* 63 (2): pp. 133–136.

Gilliam, T. B., Katch, V. L., Thorland, W. and Weltman, A. L. (1977) 'Prevalence of cardiovascular disease risk factors in active children, 7 to 12 years of age', *Medicine and Science in Sports* 9: pp. 21–25.

Harris, J. (1994) 'Health-related exercise in the national curriculum: Results of a pilot study in secondary schools', *British Journal of Physical Education* 25 (2): pp. 6–11.

Martinez-Gonzalez, M.A., Varo, J.J., Santos, J.L., De Irala, J, Gibney, M., Kearney, J. and Martinez, J.A. (2001) 'Prevalence of physical activity during leisure time in the European Union', *Medicine and Science in Sports and Exercise* 33: pp. 1142–1146.

Macfarlane, D.J. and Wong, T.K. (2003) 'Children's heart rates and enjoyment levels during PE classes in Hong Kong Primary Schools', *Pediatric Exercise Science* 15: pp. 179–190.

Matos, M., Simões, C., Carvalhosa, S., Reis, C. and Canha, L. (2000) *A Saúde dos Adolescentes Portugueses*. Lisboa: FMH / PEPT-Saúde.

Matos, M. e Equipa do Projecto Aventura Social e Saúde (2003) 'A Saúde dos Adolescentes Portugueses' (Quatro Anos Depois). Edições FMH: Lisboa.

McKenzie, T. L., Marshall, S. J., Sallis, J. F. and Conway, T. L. (2000) 'Student Activity Level, Lesson Context, and Teacher Behavior During Middle School Physical Education', *Research Quarterly for Exercise and Sport* 71 (3): pp. 249–259.

Morrow, J. and Jackson, A. (1999) 'Physical Activity Promotion and School Physical Education', *The President's Council on Physical Fitness and Sports Research Digest*, September 1999, Series 3 (7).

NASPE — National Association for Sport and Physical Education. (1998) *News*. Reston, Virginia, Winter.

Patterson, P., Wiksten, D. L., Ray, L., Flanders, C., Sanphy, D. (1996) 'The validity and reliability of the back saver sit-and-reach test in middle school girls and boys', *Research Quarterly for Exercise and Sport* 67 (4): pp. 448–451.

Pratt, M. (1999) 'Benefits of lifestyle activity vs structured exercise', *Journal of American Medical Association* 281(4): pp. 375–376.

Sallis, J. F., Simons-Morton, B. G., Corbin, C. B., Epstein, L. H., Faucette, N., Iannotti, R. J., Killen, J. D., Klesges, R. C., Petray, C. K., Rowland, T. W., Stone, E. J. and Taylor, W. (1992) 'Determinants of physical activity and interventions in youth', *Medicine and Science in Sports and Exercise* 24: pp. S248–S257.

Slaughter, M. H., Lohman, T. G., Boileau, R. A., Horswill, C. A., Stillman, R. J., Van Loan, M. D. and Bemben, D. A. (1988) 'Skinfold equations for estimation of body fatness in children and youth', *Human Biology* 60 (5): pp. 709–723.

Stouffer, K. and Dorman, S. M. (1999) 'Childhood obesity: A multifaceted etiology', *International Electronic Journal of Health Education* 2: pp. 66–72.

Summerfield, L. M. (1998) 'Promoting physical activity and exercise among children', Washington, DC: ERIC Clearinghouse on Teaching and Teaching Education; retrieved 14 Dec. 2000 from ERIC database (item ED416204), http://www.ericdigests.org/19982/exercise.htm

Tomkinson, G. R., Leger, L. A., Olds, T. S. and Cazorla, G. (2003) 'Secular trends in the performance of children and adolescents (1980–2000) — An analysis of 55 studies of the 20m shuttle run test in 11 countries', *Sports Medicine* 33 (4): pp. 285–300.

USDHHS-U.S. Department of Health and Human Services. (1996) *Physical Activity and Health: A Report of the Surgeon General*. Centers for Disease Control and Prevention. Atlanta Ga.: U.S. Department of Human Services, Centers for Disease Control and Prevention, National Center for Chronic Disease Prevention and Health Promotion.

USDHHS — U.S. Department of Health and Human Services. (2000) *Health People 2010*. Washington DC, January 2000.

Wang, G. (2004) Effects of School Aerobic Exercise Intervention on Children's Health-Related Physical Fitness: A Portuguese Middle School Case Study (Unpublished Ph.D. Thesis)

Wang G. Y., Pereira, B., and Mota, J. (2004) 'Indoor physical education measured by heart rate monitor: A case study in Portugal', *The Journal of Sports Medicine and Physical Fitness* 44 [in print].

WHO-World Health Organization. (1997) *Obesity: Preventing and managing the global epidemic*. Report of a WHO consultation on obesity, Geneva.

WHO — World Health Organization. (2002a) *Reducing risks, promoting healthy life*. World Health Report 2002, Geneva.

—— (2002b) *Diet, physical activity and health*. (documents A55/16 and A55/16Corr.1). Geneva.

—— (2003) *Annual global move for health initiative: A concept paper*. WHO/NMH/NPH/PAH/03.1.

Wright, C. M., Parker, L., Lamont, D. and Craft, A. W. (2001) 'Implications of childhood obesity for adult health: Findings from thousand families cohort study', *British Medical Journal* 323: pp.1280–1284.

BEYOND PICASSO: BRINGING CONTEMPORARY MODERN ART INTO SCHOOLS AND TO YOUNG PEOPLE

Doug Sandle
Leeds Metropolitan University

In July 2004, just before the Leisure Studies Association's conference on leisure and young people, Artworks and the Clore Duffield Foundation published a major report on art education in primary and secondary schools entitled *State of the Art* (Rogers *et al.*, 2004). It contained a statement by Helen Charman, Curator Continuing Professional Development (CPD) Programme (Schools) of Tate Modern, who was a member of the discussion panel of key experts formed to provide evidence for the report. Charman, commenting on the need for continuing professional development, stated that among art and design teachers "there is a surprisingly distinct lack of passion about, or engagement with, contemporary art practice. The art teacher is becoming increasingly shaped and constricted by the institutional demands of a testing culture". She adds, "...from my professional context, the relationship between contemporary art and the art and design curriculum is also a key challenge" (p. 24). This view was also echoed at a presentation at the LSA conference when Reuben Knutson, the education coordinator for Axis, the national information service for contemporary art, asserted:

> ... although one of the key aims for art and design from an examining board's 'specification' is that students should have knowledge of art, craft and design in contemporary society ... such becomes more difficult when dealing with contemporary ideas through a lack of resources to show pupils, and also through lack of understanding, leading to diffidence on the teacher's part. (Sandle and Knutson, 2004)

175

With reference to younger children, Downing *et al.* (2003) in a survey of the arts in primary schools provided evidence from 1800 questionnaires and over 40 interviews of the extent of the squeeze on the arts curriculum. If this is the case, it follows that an interest, understanding and involvement with contemporary art among young people, both within the classroom and within cultural activity in general, will be underdeveloped, constrained and inhibited. In this paper we will be looking at one initiative that is attempting to help address this issue — the Smudgeflux project of Axis.

However, to place the project within a wider context, it is evident that in spite of Charman's assertion and its wider implications, or maybe rather because of them, there is nonetheless a growing recognition among professional agencies, stakeholders and by government itself of the need to develop an appreciation by and involvement of young people in creative culture generally, and in some cases, visual art in particular. Partly, this is a response to the recognition that with an emphasis on literacy and numeracy within the school curriculum at both primary and secondary level and with increased demands on educational resources and funding, cultural activities such as art are generally being marginalised within young people's education. The charity, Big Arts Week claims that 80% of UK headteachers report that they have to battle to find time to schedule art lessons within the national curriculum, while 90% of teachers have expressed a concern that due to various pressures the creative arts are being sidelined in schools (Big Arts Week, 2004). These concerns gain added urgency when they are aligned to the view that the arts are generally good for society, both for individual development and for the promotion and sustainment of cultural values. While this is sometimes an over-generalised and perhaps over-romanticised assertion, there is nonetheless a growing recognition that the arts can develop aesthetic and sensory discrimination, cognitive, perceptual and expressive skills, contribute to a sense of self worth, and can foster both social engagement and personal development. More pragmatically, the cultural industries are providing significant employment and career opportunities and the arts are increasingly at the centre of ambitious environmental and social regeneration programmes, particularly within the city or urban context (Evans and Shaw, 2004).

Accordingly, since the 1990s there has been an increased national imperative to develop opportunities for young people's engagement with the creative arts. While Selwood (1997) noted that we are increasingly living in an ageing society, nonetheless she observes that the need to engage young people in the arts and cultural activities generally has been the subject of a number of initiatives. In her paper, Cultural Policy and Young People's Participation in the Visual Arts, she noted that the Department of National Heritage announced in 1996 that it had "put young people at the top of its agenda" and that such was increasingly being reflected in policy documents. Accordingly, concerns to extend opportunities for children and young people to participate in the arts have been reflected in a number of initiatives fostered through various agencies. In 1996 the Arts Council of England launched its Arts for Everyone (A4E) lottery scheme and A4E was intended, in particular, to facilitate the arts experience of young people. While also recognising that the past Tory administration was also mindful of the role of the arts for young people's development, Selwood quotes Labour in 1997 as asserting that the future depends on the nation's creative talents with a recognition that "the arts and cultural activities were essential to our intellectual development, the strengthening of our communities, civic pride and economic success".

Reiss and Pringle (2003) have summarised the recent history of the key policy initiatives for young people and the arts such as The National Advisory Committee on Creative and Cultural Education (NACCCE) and its seminal report of 1999, entitled *All Our Futures: Creativity, Culture and Education*, which was published jointly by the Department for Education and Employment (DfEE) and Department for Culture, Media and Sport (DCMS). This report led to a government green paper, *Culture and Creativity: the next ten years*. Also in 1999, the report to the Cabinet Office Social Exclusion Unit by Policy Action Team 10 (PAT10) on arts and sport highlighted the contribution of both to neighbourhood renewal, improving health, employment, the prevention of crime and to individual pride. In turn the Arts Council of England (1999) responded to PAT10 with a framework document entitled Addressing Social Exclusion: a framework for action, in which it stated:

> The arts have a vital role in community development — delivering tangible social and economic benefits such as jobs, improved skills, and learning opportunities ... The value that the Arts Council will place on cultural activity aimed at addressing social exclusion and growing people and communities is founded on a profound belief in the value of the arts to inspire, challenge, empower and engage people. (ACE, 1999: p. 1)

The role of the arts in social inclusion and environmental regeneration has continued to be a central concern of the Labour government. However, such an agenda can be problematic, as there is a need for evidence-based evaluation of the effectiveness and impact of the arts, which in turn requires the development of appropriate methodologies. There is also a danger that such a requirement can neglect the creative freedom of the arts and the role of the artist to innovate, challenge and critique. However, there is no doubt such policy exhortations have led to new initiatives that theoretically should begin to provide a greater awareness of and involvement in creative culture and the arts, both among young people and within their school curriculum. Currently the DCMS regards arts and education as a priority and there is an intention to both stimulate and respond to demand for cultural activity within schools. David Fitzgerald (Head of Arts and Education at the DCMS at the time of interview) acknowledged that there was much to do on the supply side, and expressed belief the DCMS would operationalise its commitment to furthering education in the cultural sector by stimulating and matching an increased demand, while at the same time strategically building capacity through the development of quality and skills (Fitzgerald, 2004). In particular, the DCMS recognises the importance of both a national strategy and framework on the one hand, and local delivery on the other[1].

Partnerships and placements

A significant development to promote the role of the arts in education has been the establishment of partnerships and artist placements. For example, Creative Partnerships is a government-funded national initiative, established "to develop schoolchildren's potential, ambition, creativity and imagination". It states as its purpose, the development of "ambitious and adventurous programmes of creative and cultural activity, explicitly focused on learning outcomes and on the aspirations of schools and their staff "[2]. Based at Arts Council England, Creative Partnerships:

> ...helps schools to identify their individual needs and then enables
> them to develop long-term, sustainable partnerships with
> organisations and individuals including architects, theatre companies,
> museums, cinemas, historic buildings, dance studios, recording
> studios, orchestras, film-makers, website designers and many others.
> (www.artscouncil.org)

It particularly aims for such partnerships to be more than short term and to be sustainable by being embedded within a school's culture, rather than being simply an additional or extra mural activity. Creative Partnerships is also inherently tied in to the social inclusion agenda and tends to be targeted to those areas within the UK where traditional industries are in decline and to rural areas that suffer from social isolation and remoteness from established cultural infrastructures. The first 16 areas to benefit from Creative Partnerships were selected in 2000 by Government ministers from a list of the most economically and socially challenged neighbourhoods in England. From each area, up to 25 schools — a mixture of primary and secondary, special and specialist — have been working with a Creative Director to devise programmes of creative and cultural activity, which are explicitly focused on learning outcomes and on the aspirations of the schools and their staff. A further 20 areas will be designated for Creative Partnerships by 2006 with funding from both the DCMS and the Department for Education and Skills (DfES).

CAPE UK also fosters arts-schools-young people partnerships, through strategies to develop the creative capacities of children and young people across a range of curriculum subjects and activities. It facilitates artist placement across a spectrum of arts activities, particularly by using lead artists from many arts disciplines to develop teaching and learning programmes through creative activity. Its emphasis is on the national curriculum and the requirements of 16+ education and its partnerships are based within high schools in the Leeds and Manchester areas[3].

One way of raising the profile of contemporary art in schools and among young people is through an artist placement or residency. Such residencies, at primary and secondary school level can vary from a few days to a longer period and a few schools have a permanent artist as a full-time member of staff. However, such is certainly not the norm and most residencies are usually in days rather than weeks. The opportunity for artists to work with and among children is a particularly valuable way of introducing school children to contemporary art practice at first hand. Increasingly such residencies might involve artists working in new media, such as digital video, or in areas such as public art, thus extending knowledge and experience of contemporary art practice among young people. While residencies might be facilitated by the Creative Partnerships scheme, there are also a number of other organisations and initiatives that are or have been involved with promoting and facilitating artist residencies within schools and among other community organisations.

During the 1960s community arts agencies such as the UK Artist Placement Group enabled artist placement and residencies within sites such as hospitals, work places, schools and other sites for learning. Reiss and Pringle (2003) have noted, "throughout the 1970s and the 1980s there was a development and expansion of projects involving artists working within sites for learning within the UK, supported by a range of new funding initiatives". In 1996, the Visual Arts Department of the Arts Council introduced The Artist in Education grant scheme to provide funding for projects involving artists as educators. After evaluation, this was re-launched in 1997 as the Artists in Sites for Learning Scheme (AiSfL), which was designed to take account of new initiatives in both formal and informal education. Further research was commissioned by the Arts Council in 2001 to explore the role of artists and their creative and pedagogic practices within projects supported by the scheme (Pringle, 2002). Reiss and Pringle (2003) comment that one of the findings of that research was that the artists did not see themselves as teachers imparting a fixed body of knowledge but as co-learners alongside the participants taking part in a process of 'participant-centred creative enquiry'. However, they also indicate that there was some tension between this process and the potential privileging of the end product as an artistic artefact for its own sake. They stress that the creative process involved in the use of an artist in sites of learning is not like conventional knowledge transfer, but entails a dynamic relationship between process, product and context.

The report by the National Advisory Committee on Creativity and Cultural Education (1999) maintained that the UK has a leading international reputation for work by artists and other creative organisations in education and the community. Allan and Laing (2000) suggested that much of the significance of such placements is increasingly recognised and has highlighted their benefits to schools through curriculum development, staff development and pupil participation. They point to earlier assessments of the benefits of such placements and school artist partnerships such as 'the constructive use of leisure time' (Owens, 1998), 'the enhancement of a school's ability to achieve curriculum targets' (Oddie and Allen, 1998) and their reported claim by the Newcastle University Careers Service that such residencies incorporate all the key educational skills. In their own research, Allan and Laing (2000) assessed the outcomes of a residency scheme run by the Glasgow School of Art that provides placement opportunities for its own students to work in schools and sites of learning. The Student Artists in Schools project of the Glasgow School of Art commenced in 1990, engaging its students with school pupils in the nursery, primary, secondary and special school sectors. The scheme aims to give "student artists the opportunity to work with and alongside pupils of school age... in order that pupils should gain some understanding of the way in which an artist or designer thinks through and develops a piece of work" (p. 326). While the particular focus of their research was to evaluate the outcomes of this scheme for the college students, Allan and Laing also reported that the outstanding recollection for the students was of the school pupils "responding to / enjoying/ being excited by 'being into the project'". A survey of schools in Scotland, which has a more prescribed need to involve contemporary art practice within the formal curriculum, indicated that although the major reason for having artists in the classroom is for the pupils to learn new skills, teachers did not solely use residencies for that purpose. They found artists' residencies particularly useful in enhancing pupils' general experience, enhancing the curriculum and for learning about artists' work generally (Accent Marketing & Research (2004).

Artist residencies have a particular role in involving young people in contemporary practice and a survey by Axis (Potter, 2002) revealed that 51% of a sample of 563 schools had used artist residencies. The Clore Duffield report (Rogers *et al.*, 2004), *State of The Art*, indicates that in the last three years the same percentage of secondary schools had an artist in residence at one time or other. However, the duration of residencies varied considerably and Paul Brennan, Chair of The Association of Advisors in Art and Design (AAIAD) and a member of the State of the Art's discussion panel points out that growth in artist residencies is limited to a small percentage of schools. He also highlights a mixed economy, where some schools can afford such residencies and others struggle to do so (Rogers *et al.*, 2004: p. 25).

One important initiative in bringing contemporary art into schools through residencies and other activities is the Big Arts Week. Not just confined to visual art, but concerned with creative activities in general, the Big Arts Week, launched in 2002, encourages and facilitates creative artists and professionals across the whole of the arts spectrum to volunteer their services to working with young children through schools during one specified week in the year[4]. The Big Arts Week is supported by several well-known arts organisations as well as high profile organisations from media and commerce.

Art galleries and art collections are another source for developing young people's engagement with contemporary art and they are increasingly involved in educational programmes for schools, young people and for particular community groups. Many have an educational programme and designated staff developing particular activities for schools and their pupils, which are often a focus for local initiatives. Some galleries, such as the Drumcroon gallery in Wigan are funded by the local education authority with a particular educational remit involving both schools and community groups. While Selwood *et al.* (1995) were critical of poor practice and of a lack of significant involvement by galleries with young people, there have been many significant developments since their initial research[5]. For example, from 1997 the Yorkshire Sculpture Park has developed an extensive educational programme for life long learning, committed to an integrated and inclusive education programme. Anna Bowman, Head of Education, is a strong advocate of bringing school children out of school and into an art environment. She believes that for young people to develop a positive interest for contemporary art it is important that they should encounter art out of the school environment and in one that would be less associated with more formal educational pressures. Bowman (2004) maintains that for "children who, in school situations possibly don't feel comfortable enough or confident enough to contribute to what is going on in a class situation, to take them out of, what I would call a politicised space, into something that is a free space is very, very inspiring". The Tate Modern and the Tate galleries generally have developed extensive programmes targeted at young people in the 15–23 age range, and these are not confined to schools. The programme has grown substantially and during the two years 02/04 involved just over 213,000 schoolchildren and just over 6,000 young persons, the latter including 780 participating in off-site projects (Bunbury, 2005).There is also sustainable involvement in ensuring professional development for teachers and those working with young people, and the Tate is establishing a new CPD Institute (current working title) for teachers and visual culture.

The National Society for Education in Art and Design (NSEAD) takes a different approach, expanding professional development through its Artist Teacher Scheme, which provides opportunities for artist teachers and for educators working in gallery and museum programmes "to reappraise, reinforce or re-engage with their own thinking and personal development as artists by extending their awareness of the richness and complexity of contemporary fine art practice and the diversity of thinking and influences which inform it" (NSEAD, 2004).

The Visual Arts and Galleries Association (VAGA) helps to promote the sustained involvement of galleries with the school curriculum and with young people. It is particularly committed to providing a network of gallery professionals, institutions and programmes to promote the best contemporary and modern art through "exhibitions, collections, temporary projects, education and outreach programmes, biennials and artists interventions" in order to create opportunities "for learning, inspiration, enquiry and reflection" (VAGA, 2004).

"[E]ngage", the national association for gallery education specifically promotes and facilitates "access to, enjoyment and understanding of the visual arts through gallery education" and supports and develops projects and programmes, which "help schoolchildren and the wider community become confident in their understanding and enjoyment of the visual arts and galleries" (engage, 2004). One of engage's projects, Opt 4 Art, introduced 15,000 school pupils within the UK to galleries and artists and specifically encouraged them to opt for GCSE art. engage also develops networks and partnerships among schools, galleries and museums, promotes and facilitates professional development among gallery workers and teachers, facilitates action-research and has a strategic and advocacy role in the development of local and national policy for young people and the visual arts.

In 1999 the then DfEE, now the Department of Education and Skills (DfES), launched the Museums and Galleries Education Programme in response to a growing commitment within government, education and the museum sector to use museums and galleries more extensively to improve the quality of children's and young people's learning. The 65 projects of the programme during 1999–2002 covered a range of Key Stage learning from early years to post 16 across different curriculum subjects, some of which specifically involve art. For example, Dean Heritage in its educational programme focussed on the work of the contemporary artist Andy Goldsworthy to explore ways of using the natural environment to deliver innovative and stimulating work within the art curriculum. Another project involving Wolverhampton Art Gallery built on previous digital art residencies to examine how digital art could be used to enhance education within special schools. Learning Through Culture (Clarke *et al.*, 2002) provides an extensive review of the Museums and Galleries Education Programme and highlights good practice in providing a guide to developing, planning, organising and evaluating projects to ensure they address such issues as the use of new technologies, cultural and social inclusion, professional impact and sustainability.

Gallery educational and community programmes will further develop as a result of regional hubs of excellence established to promote best practice and standards for museums and galleries. The nine regional hubs, each with a network of four or five museums and galleries, are currently supported by a DCMS grant of £70 million for four years as from 2003, and among the eight priority areas identified by Re:source, the Council for Museums, Archives and Libraries, are the development of a comprehensive service to schools and the need to reach a wider community.

Many other organisations concerned with the advocacy, commissioning, hosting and development of contemporary art will often have an educational remit or programme to work with schools, community groups and children. For example, in public art many organisations and commissioning agencies such as Public Arts have an extensive educational programme and in Wales the two main public art agencies, Cywaith Cymru and CBAT run programmes that are concerned with engaging school children, young people and the wider community with contemporary art (Roberts *et al.*, 2003)[6].

The Institute of International Visual Arts, inIVA through its exhibitions, publications and multimedia and research projects aims to bring the work of artists from culturally diverse backgrounds to the attention of the widest possible public and has a particular concern for extending knowledge, debate and research on contemporary art and ideas. Its educational programme has developed cutting-edge art education projects and resources, which include residency and partnership programmes with schools bringing these to a wider audience through utilising digital resources. For example, Filter is an interactive artwork created by Mary Evans that is also a teaching resource in which a CD ROM and accompanying teachers' notes introduces pupils to Evans' work and highlights the relevance of contemporary art practice to the teaching of subjects across Key Stage 2 of the National Curriculum. DARE, Digital Art Resources for Education, is an interactive website with links to over 200 contemporary artists and many gallery and education sites worldwide. As an online education resource for contemporary international visual art, its digital format enables a broad range of educational users to access and engage with contemporary art[7].

The private sector can also contribute to the development of young persons' experience of contemporary and modern art and, for example, the law firm of Walker Morris (Solicitors) won the arts, business and corporate category in the 2004 Arts & Business Yorkshire Awards for an educational project involving contemporary art. The firm brought the Royal Academy Schools Show from London for an exhibition at Harewood House, near Leeds, and facilitated an innovative educational programme with local secondary school students, trainee arts teachers and lecturers from the University of Leeds. Within the programme a CD-Rom was produced as an aid for trainee art teachers to promote working outside the classroom and within galleries. The CD emphasises the relevance of bringing contemporary culture into young people's experience and is a useful resource for both established and trainee art teachers and for museum and gallery staff involved in educational projects.

Thus while there are real concerns about the extent to which schools and their teachers are able to bring contemporary art into both the curriculum and their pupils' experience, the above examples indicate that there is a growing infrastructure of opportunities and structures available for advocacy, guidance and support.

Axis and the Smudgeflux Initiative

Within this context it is not surprising that Axis, as a national organisation concerned with contemporary visual artists and their work, has embarked on a project to help bring visual art and contemporary practice into the school classroom. As a result of research undertaken in 1990 by Susan Jones of Artists Newsletter for the then Arts Council of Great Britain and the Gulbenkian Foundation, a national visual arts information resource was proposed to support and assist the development of visual arts, crafts, photography, performance and live art where there is a public interface, and its objectives were to serve the needs of practitioners, visual art professionals, patronage, research and education through a computerised national database and information source. Through a partnership with Leeds Polytechnic, now Leeds Metropolitan University, this proposal lead to the foundation of Axis, a company that was located within the university, but operated independently as a charity through a Board of Directors and Trustees[8]. The Axis relational database provides text and digital visual information on artists with details and examples of their work. Axis also provides an information service for anyone wanting to use contemporary artists for a wide range of work opportunities, including commissions, exhibitions and placements as well as providing a research resource. With the development of the internet, Axis has become the largest on-line collection of information about contemporary artists and makers in the UK providing details of over 4,000 contemporary UK artists and featuring over 24,000 images of their artwork.

As well as the original Axis database, programmes now include a showcase virtual space and information source for a changing selection of work by artists selected by a national network of advisors, which provides a platform for new and cutting edge art in a wide range of media. Axis also hosts the web-based version of Photostore, the Crafts Council's national database of selected makers and applied artists. More significantly for present concerns, Axis has developed a service and programme for teachers and students of art and design, particularly providing resources, advice and support for bringing contemporary art and craft into the secondary school classroom. This educational programme, initially developed under the name of Smudgeflux with resources from the National Lottery's New Opportunities Fund, is reached both through its own and the Axis website. The service incorporates a growing database of artists who have had experience of working in schools and who are subject to enhanced disclosure and police check procedures. Accordingly, both Smudgeflux and the other databases of Axis provide an additional resource for identifying and finding artists for school placement[9].

The Axis website provides detailed information about artists and their work in supporting classroom studies and also provides a 'place' through which teachers can contact artists to arrange workshops and residencies. The search function lets users look for artists under broad categories of discipline, such as painting, sculpture, etc., and/or to look for artists using more specific materials, such as glass or textiles. If searching for artists to work in schools, teachers will generally be looking for artists who live locally and hence there is also a geographical search. A free-text search enables teachers to search via themes/ideas, and it is also possible to search for an artist known by name. Search results are shown via thumbnail images so that users can either click on an image for a full-screen view, or click on the artist's name to see their details. Pages featuring artists are split into headings that feed directly into National Curriculum criteria so that: 'ideas' gives a general outline of the artist's work; 'techniques' describes the specific materials and processes the artist uses; 'inspiration' provides information about where the artist finds ideas and sources and there are also details of the artist's career path. At the bottom of the artist's page there is a link to specific projects, which can include anything from personal or commissioned work. The Axis website also provides advice regarding contacting artists for schoolwork, features example projects and illustrates good practice for schools who wish to engage artists for their teaching and learning programmes.

Within the initial Smudgeflux programme a CD-Rom was produced, which was more specifically tailored to classroom activities, grouping artists' projects under themes, which might stimulate or relate to a class project. It contains further contextual information, detailed notes about artists' projects and some video interviews with artists highlighting their working methods. The interactive CD features three main themes — Light and Shadow, Cities on the Move and Sacred Sites. For example, within Sacred Sites there are some related web links of artists working within the theme, providing a wider creative general context to the topic. More detailed information about a specific artist's projects is featured with high-resolution images, and a video-interview with the artist talking about the way they have developed the project and about the ideas and techniques they used to produce the final work. Given that the National Curriculum places emphasis on the creative act and how an artist works an idea through to a final piece of work, this aspect of the CD is designed to provide insight into such processes. For teachers the CD also contains some ideas for constructing a classroom project based on the particular artist's work.

Evaluating the Smudgeflux Initiative

During the development of the original Smudgeflux programme some preliminary research and consultation among schools and teachers highlighted a number of relevant issues. In 2002 Axis initiated a survey among secondary school art and design departments from within the UK and found that 88% of 563 respondents stated they taught contemporary art (Potter, 2002). While this would seem a positive response this varied greatly over different key stages as shown in **Table 1**, with little involvement in contemporary art at levels other than KS3 and 4.

Table 1   Axis survey on the teaching of contemporary art within secondary schools, levels at which taught (N=495)

Level	Percentage
KS3 only	1.7%
KS4 only	6.6%
KS3 & 4	32.1%
AS only	0.4%
A2 only	0.6%
AS / A2	7.9%
KS4 / AS / A2	14.3%
All levels	36.4%

Where contemporary art was not taught, lack of resources was cited as the reason by 83% of 99 respondents **(Table 2)**. When asked what kind of resources had been used or would be found useful in the teaching of contemporary art, while CD-ROMS had only been used by 28% of the sample, 58% would find such a resource helpful, suggesting at that stage a potential opportunity for the development and use of the Smudgeflux CD **(Table 3)**. Use of the web itself was around 45%, with 47% suggesting such a source would be useful. Given the rapid development of on-line galleries and catalogue sources of contemporary art the figures for web usage indicate that there is a potential and a need for user expansion. However, use of websites and CD- ROMS depend on ICT resources and expertise and several respondents indicated a lack of suitable equipment and time in schools for using the web. This situation was also highlighted by a national survey organised by Artworks and published by The Clore Duffield Foundation in 2001 that revealed that art and design teachers in both primary and secondary schools lacked training, expertise and confidence in using ICT and in choosing the best software and websites to help their pupils (Rogers

Table 2   Axis survey on the teaching of contemporary art within
secondary schools, reasons when not taught (N=99)

Reason	Percentage
Lack of resources	82.8%
Lack of staff knowledge	14.1%
Not required by curriculum	3.1%

Table 3   Axis survey on the teaching of contemporary art within
secondary schools (N=562)

Resource	% that have used resource from all respondents	% that would find resource useful from all respondents
Training course	16.2%	49.2%
Residencies	51.0%	55.2%
CD-ROM	28.2%	58.4%
Website	44.6%	47.1%
Book	60.2%	49.4%
Printed material	40.0%	55.4%

et al., 2001). The Artworks survey also indicated that much ICT equipment was out of date and that only half of school art and design departments had direct access to the Internet. Similarly, the subsequent 2004 State of The Art report indicated that only 57% of teachers consider that ICT plays a significant or highly significant role in art and design, and over half of art and design teachers (58%) were unhappy with their ICT provision. In particular, secondary school art and design teachers stated they required more equipment to facilitate the use of ICT in their lessons (Rogers *et al.*, 2004). While this might operate against the use of the Smudgeflux CD and the website resource as a way of bringing contemporary art into the classroom, it could also be argued that the development of quality inexpensive ICT provision such as Smudgeflux in itself would help provide an incentive and opportunity for the further development of ICT resources for art and design in schools. The situation would also be facilitated by a more formal requirement for contemporary art to be within the curriculum, as in Scotland for example, where a recent survey undertaken for Axis by Accent Marketing & Research (2004) more encouragingly found that 83% of schools surveyed were using websites for the teaching of contemporary visual art and 78% were using CD-ROMS.

National concerns for more contemporary art to feature in the classroom are likely to be reflected regionally and locally and to some extent this was confirmed at a Yorkshire meeting of the Royal Society of Arts, (RSA) held in Leeds in June 2004 as part of the national Big Arts Week programme. Significantly the event was entitled Pushed Out and both panel and floor speakers expressed concern that, with schools prioritising the mainstream curriculum subjects and with art teachers experiencing excessive administrative pressures, development of the creative arts was often under developed or marginalised for schoolchildren. In Leeds, the co-ordinator of the creative arts and media strand of the Aim Higher programme of Education Leeds (the body responsible for school education in Leeds) acknowledges the pressures on teachers and states that "little contemporary art gets into schools as teachers are not able to prepare and develop this area and need support to do so. Teachers don't have the time and opportunity to help them bring contemporary art into the classroom" (Hussein, 2004).

However, just as there are national initiatives to address the need for bringing contemporary art into the classroom, there are local initiatives exemplified in Leeds by the Aim Higher programme that is concerned to enhance activities and extend experience and the range of curriculum activity for the creative arts and media through such as school gallery visits, staff development and the involvement of artists. Artforms, a service grown out of the former school's advisory service also promotes partnerships between artists and educators, including resource provision for artists in schools to cover both fees and materials. Artforms has also a significant role to play in shaping the arts policy for Education Leeds. Downing (1996) gives a detailed account of the Leeds City artists in schools programme at that time and identifies the different ways artists can relate to schools and teachers.

Accordingly, while Axis and the Smudgeflux programme is very much a national UK wide initiative, a local research programme has commenced within the Education Leeds area in order to investigate attitudes and perception of contemporary and modern art among secondary school children as part of a pilot evaluation exercise on the effectiveness of Smudgeflux. Six secondary schools were initially involved with a pilot questionnaire survey among 14–15 year old Key Stage 4 pupils taking art. In the summer term of 2004 a pre-questionnaire collected data on attitudes and perception to modern art, including frequency of visits to art galleries or exhibitions. While all contemporary art is not necessarily modern, the term modern art clearly identifies art practices that are inherent among much of professional contemporary art and are the likely mode of practice of those artists featured on the Smudgeflux CD- ROM and on the Smudgeflux website.

As art galleries and exhibitions are a major source of engagement with modern and contemporary visual art, a number of questions were asked regarding the frequency and nature of visits to art galleries or exhibitions. In response to the question, "Have you visited an art gallery/ art exhibition in the last 12 months?", 59% of the 165 pupils responding to this question had done so (**Table 4**). Regarding the nature of work on show (for all visits within the last year) 11% was reported as being traditional, while 35% modern and 11% mixed. With regard to frequency of visits, in response to the question, "How often do you visit an art gallery/exhibition on average in a year?", over half (57%) replied never; 20%, once a year; 15%, 2 or 3 times a year; and 8%, 3 or 4 times a year (**Table 5**).

That just over half of a group of pupils doing art as a GCSE subject reportedly never visit an art gallery/exhibition, might seem discouraging. However, that 43% had made such a visit appears more favourable with regard to some other findings on young people's visits to art galleries. For example, Selwood (1997) reports a survey by the Arts Council in which only 20% of young people aged 15–19 claimed to visit art galleries. Selwood also reports a study by O'Brien (1966) who found that only 12 % of secondary school pupils aged 11–16 had made such visits.

Table 4   Have you visited an art gallery/ exhibition in the last 12 months? (N = 165)

	Yes	No
Boys (78)	51%	49%
Girls (87)	66%	34%
ALL	59%	41%

Table 5   How often do you visit an art gallery / exhibition on average in a year (N = 167)

	Never	Once a year	2 or 3 times	3 or 4 times
Boys (76)	65%	20%	12%	3%
Girls (91)	50%	20%	18%	12%
ALL	57%	20%	15%	8%

More recently, a survey carried out by the Social Survey Division of the Office for National Statistics reported that younger people, despite having higher levels of engagement with the arts (both as attendees and participants) were more likely than older respondents to agree that they would feel out of place in an art gallery, museum or theatre. Twenty-six percent of those aged 16–24 agreed with this statement, compared with 10% of the 45–64 age group (Skelton *et al.*, 2002). A survey by Market and Opinion Research International (MORI), conducted for the Museums and Libraries Archive in 2004, which combined museums and art galleries as a single category, found that those aged between 15 and 24 were most likely to say they did not visit museums and art galleries because there was nothing in particular that they would like to see (27%) or thought such places were boring (15%). Overall young adults (aged 15–24) with no children had the lowest average visit frequency of 2.9 over the course of the year surveyed (MORI, 2004), while a report by Harland and Kinder (1999) indicates that attendance at galleries and cultural events decreases during adolescent years.

In a sample of just over 5,000 during 1996–97, young people between the ages of 15–19 made up 7.9% of those who had visited an art gallery or art exhibition (Arts Council of England, 2000). From a local perspective it is worth noting that Leeds City Art Gallery is reported as having a strong appeal for the 16 –20 age group (Martin *et al.*, 2003). Corinne Miller (2004), Senior Curator at Leeds City Art Gallery, reports that currently young visitors are surprised and stimulated by a sound installations by international artist Bill Fontana, which does not conform to their stereotype expectations about art and galleries and that they also respond positively to work by Georgina Starr that deals with the experience of being an adolescent girl growing up in Leeds. Currently, Karen Babayan a Leeds-based artist has been working at the gallery with two groups of girls aged 11–14yrs, based at the Bangladeshi Community Centre in Harehills and also the Woodsley Centre, serving the Muslim community of Hyde Park, Leeds. Over a period of several months during Spring/Summer 2004 Babayan worked weekly with the groups using digital photography, to look at work in the exhibition as well as contemporary art from other sources. Babayan (2004) comments: "Contemporary art was the vehicle for these disenfranchised and angry young women to find a voice in a society". The work created was exhibited at Leeds City Art Gallery on the 1st December 2004. Such examples would suggest that challenging and innovative contemporary work can appeal to young people and improve a gallery's appeal for them.

However, while in the present Smudgeflux survey, a 'never' response is indicative of there not being a regular annual visit to a gallery/exhibition, some of the 'never' respondents in their response to the previous question, had in fact made one visit during the last twelve months. This would indicate that the visit they had made had been their only ever visit, which from other details requested and provided was most likely part of a school trip. Thus, of those 35% who responded as never regularly visiting an art gallery/exhibition, just over a third had in fact been just once as part of a school visit in the last twelve months, which was their first ever visit. For all respondents who had reported visiting a gallery/exhibition in the last 12 months, 62% of all the visits were part of a school trip, 21% part of a family visit, 11% with friends and 6% alone (**Table 6**). Thus, without school visits, experience of art gallery and exhibitions would be clearly much less, and for many are the source of their only art gallery experience. In this respect it is also significant and more encouraging that 63% of the sample agreed or strongly agreed to the statement, "I would like to visit and encounter more

Table 6   If you have visited an art gallery/exhibition in the last 12 months was it – (N = 140 answers)

	School visit	Family visit	With friends	Alone
Boys (57)	65%	21%	8%	6%
Girls (89)	61%	21%	12%	6%
ALL	%	21%	11%	6%

modern art". This underlines the importance of the education work of galleries and other art institutions and also the work of organisations such as engage. The particular work by Education Leeds (and other local education authorities) in providing opportunities and means for gallery visits for schoolchildren would seem essential. Without the particular visits provided, for example to the Liverpool Tate, Yorkshire Sculpture Park and Leeds City Art Gallery, the most frequently cited visits among the respondents, the scores for gallery/exhibition attendance in every respect would have been considerably lower.

A number of attitudes towards modern art were questioned and on the positive side, in response to the statement, "I do not like modern art", 68% did not agree or strongly disagreed; 72% agreed or strongly agreed that "Modern art is interesting"; and 78% disagreed or strongly disagreed with the statement, "Modern art is a load of rubbish" (**Tables 7, 8, 9**).

Table 7   I do not like modern art (N = 161)

	Strongly agree	Agree	Disagree	Strongly disagree	Positive Total
Boys (74)	16%	27%	42%	15%	57%
Girls (87)	2%	20%	61%	17%	78%
ALL	9%	23%	52%	16%	68%

Table 8   Modern art is interesting (N = 162)

	Strongly agree	Agree	Disagree	Strongly disagree	Positive Total
Boys (75)	12%	55%	20%	13%	67%
Girls (87)	17%	59%	19%	5%	76%
AALL	15%	57%	20%	8%	72%

Table 9   Modern art is a load of rubbish (N = 160)

	Strongly agree	Agree	Disagree	Strongly disagree	Positive Total
Boys (73)	21%	5%	58%	16%	74%
Girls (87)	8%	10%	52%	30%	82%
ALL	14%	8%	54%	24%	78%

Awareness of modern art's scope was reflected in **Table 10** and **Table 11**, in which 82% agreed or strongly agreed that "Modern art can be more than pictures or sculptures" and 93% agreed or strongly agreed that "Modern art can be about ideas as well as about pictures and sculptures".

For all the responses in Tables 4 to 12 (i.e. attitudes to and ideas about modern art and wanting to visit and encounter more modern art), of the total 965 responses, 76% were positive or strongly positive. However, as indicated, there was a gender difference in that 83% of responses were positive or very positive for girls compared to 67% for boys. In response to these questions, girls are notably more engaged with modern art than boys. Similarly with regard to visits to an art gallery, girls are more active than boys: for example, in the pilot questionnaire, 87% of girls compared to 78% of boys reported having visited an art gallery/exhibition in the last 12 months; 65 % of boys never regularly visit an art gallery/exhibition compared to 50% of girls; and 12% of girls visit a gallery or exhibition on average 3 or 4 times a year compared to 3% of boys[10].

Table 10   Modern art can be more than pictures and sculpture (N = 160)

	Strongly agree	Agree	Disagree	Strongly disagree	Positive Total
Boys (73)	14%	57%	21%	8%	71%
Girls (86)	22%	70%	8%	0%	92%
ALL	18%	64%	14%	4%	82%

Table 11   Modern art can be about ideas (N = 162)

	Strongly agree	Agree	Disagree	Strongly disagree	Positive Total
Boys (74)	11%	76%	9%	4%	87%
Girls (86)	22%	76%	1%	1%	98%
ALL	17%	76%	5%	2%	93%

Table 12   I would like to visit and encounter more modern art (N = 161)

	Strongly agree	Agree	Disagree	Strongly disagree	Positive Total
Boys (74)	9%	41%	32%	18%	50%
Girls (87)	19%	55%	21%	5%	74%
ALL	17%	76%	5%	2%	93%

Contemporary modern art practice extends beyond the gallery, and public art or site specific work, utilising a range of media from traditional materials to new digital technologies, increasingly provides opportunities for engaging in modern art. Adams (1997) argued that art and design teachers should encompass public art to extend the boundaries of art and design education and enable both to link with the study of the environment. Reference to the environment and artists' work does now feature within the National Curriculum, as does the work of museums and galleries, and as more teachers adopt, for example Key Stage 3 units 9c and 10 as an option, pupils experience of modern art in the public realm should develop further. Of the school pupils responding to the question, "Have you heard of the Angel of the North?", 77% answered in the affirmative (**Table 13**), with 80% of those having seen a picture of it, and 50% 'the real thing'.

While the results of the pilot questionnaire would appear encouraging with regard to the level of general overall positive engagement with modern art, given that the respondents were all doing art at Key Stage 4, there is still room for further development, especially among male pupils. For example, it is perhaps surprising that given the popularity and ubiquity of the Angel of the North image and its iconic status as cultural capital (Sandle, 2004) that a quarter of the male pupils surveyed had not heard of it. That a quarter of the boys undertaking art as a Key Stage 4 subject think that modern art is a load of rubbish, that 43% do not like modern art and a third do not find modern art interesting does not augur well for those pupils' likely engagement with contemporary art. It also confirms the need for interventions such as the Smudgeflux programme.

Although the Smudgeflux programme was enthusiastically received by many teachers where it has been demonstrated, one of aims of the pilot research was to provide a context for developing ways of evaluating the possible impact of the use of Smudgeflux in developing engagement, understanding and interest in contemporary modern art. Accordingly, as a further pilot study, some pupils experienced the Smudgeflux CD programme after the initial questionnaire, and 58% of this trial sample of 64 (mostly from one

Table 13   Have you heard of the Angel of the North (N= 166)

	Yes
Boys (74)	75%
Girls (90)	79%
All	77%

school) indicated that Smudgeflux had changed their ideas about modern art. Again however girls were more receptive to the programme with 69% indicating a change compared to 49% of boys. Indicative responses also suggested that the most likely change was in an awareness of modern art's wider use of different materials and media and of it being more than just painting and sculpture. Some typical comments included: "I thought it [modern art] was just paintings but I now know it is film, photos and ideas"; "I have seen more of it so I know what it is about and have an idea what kinds of modern art there is"; "You can use mediums I hadn't thought of to create pieces of art work — that modern art can be made from anything -- modern art can be good". A third of the post Smudgeflux respondents stated they were more likely to visit a gallery/exhibition to see modern art in the next 12 months since experiencing the Smudgeflux CD, which is encouraging[11].

Conclusions

While there are opportunities for developing young persons' engagement with contemporary modern art, it is important that there be some interaction and partnership among the various agencies and initiatives and that there be some strategic co-ordination at national, regional and local level. There is also a need for more research and evaluation, particularly to ensure that initiatives are effective and efficient in delivering strategic objectives. At the time of writing, the National Foundation for Educational Research (NFER) has just completed a research study where 54 art teachers in 18 secondary schools were interviewed; of these, 8 schools were identified as already incorporating contemporary art practice into their art curriculum. Schools engaging with contemporary art within the curriculum tended to have a much broader range of art references in their teaching, were more likely to enable pupils to work in a wider range of media and tended to have a broader range of purposes for teaching art. The potential for using websites for contemporary art reference was recognised by some of the teachers, but some concern was expressed that pupils simply copied and pasted material from internet sources without necessarily developing their knowledge and understanding of the material (Downing and Watson, 2004).

The impetus for this paper came from the concerns as expressed in the opening paragraph, which highlighted the need for a greater engagement with contemporary modern art among schoolchildren and young people generally. However there are clearly key organisations and individuals who are providing structures, processes, opportunities and the impetus for good practice and several of these have been highlighted throughout this contribution. Helen Charman, while concerned for the need for more positive engagement with contemporary art among teachers, nonetheless acknowledges that there are "very many excellent projects and awe-inspiring teachers" (Charman, 2004). There is also encouragement to be gained from research, review and evaluation and the needs for such research are being recognised and encouraged. In this respect, Hooper-Greenhill and Moussouri (2002), while acknowledging there is a need for more research in Britain, usefully identify the scope of the research agenda required to establish the processes and outcomes of museum and gallery based learning.

With regard to models of and frameworks for successful good practice, Orfali (2004) sets out a framework of quality indicators and measures that can be used to evaluate working partnerships between artists and schools. Her framework is both comprehensive and user-friendly and provides advice and guidelines to cover the requirements and indicators of quality from the perspective of the artists, schools, commissioners and pupils. ACE's publication, Partnerships for Learning: a guide to evaluating arts education projects (Arts Council England, 2004) includes reference to some case studies relevant to contemporary visual art. For example it cites the work of Fabrica, a Brighton gallery that promotes understanding of contemporary art and which has set up a multimedia residency at Cardinal Newman School. CAPE UK has conducted its own internal review (Cockett and Downing, 2000) and the NFER undertook research to establish a base-line evaluation of CAPE (Ashworth *et al.*, 1998), followed by a further second stage study in 2001. The second stage considers the nature of partnerships, their planning, the implementation of plans, partnership evaluation strategies, the assessment of continuity and an examination of any factors that may enable or inhibit the implementation of creative activities (Doherty and Harland, 2001). Pringle's extensive review of the Arts Council's Artists in Sites of Learning Scheme provides insights on the role of artists' forms of engagement within the educational sphere, and from her literature review concludes that almost all the writers she considered acknowledged that there needs to be more research in this area (Pringle 2002). At a local level, Downing's comprehensive review of the Artists in Leeds Schools' scheme of the nineties still provides salient pointers for good practice involving different art forms as well as detailed case studies of some highly effective examples of artists involving young people in the practice and appreciation of contemporary visual art (Downing, 1996).

If access to and engagement with contemporary modern art by young people is seen as worthwhile for individual, social and cultural development, there are thus some reasons to be hopeful that there is the beginnings of a culture of change that will address the issues discussed at the beginning of this paper. However, it is important to ensure that engagement and experience of contemporary modern art not only provides the benefits from the transferable skills and social processes that are implicit in cultural development, but that actual creative practice is not neglected at the expense of cultural consumption. However, we end with two comments, one from Tony Blair and one from the comedian, Jo Brand, who are both quoted on the Creative Partnerships website in support of its programme. According to the Prime Minister "we live in the most creative country in the world....But to keep that creativity alive in the future, we have to engage anew every generation, to pass on old skills and help them learn new ones". More forthrightly, Jo Brand argues that "culture is an essential part of a child's education because it anchors them to their society and enables them to see why Lucien Freud is good, for example, and Jeffrey Archer isn't".

Notes

1 Another recent government recognition of the importance of art(s) and young people was reflected in the endorsement of cultural entitlement for young people, i.e. that every young person of school age might enjoy a rich cultural life both within and beyond the curriculum. Significantly this endorsement was made jointly by the DCMS and the DfES at a special seminar in May 2004 when Estelle Morris, the Arts Minister, asserted that entitlement to a minimum level of engagement with the arts and culture would enable more effective delivery of both the national curriculum and provide for rich out of school activities, as reported on the website of the Visual Arts and Galleries Association, VAGA (2004).

2 Further information on Creative Partnerships can be found on the website of Arts Council England, htpp://www.artscouncil.org.uk.

3 Further information on CAPE can be found on the website, htpp://www.capeuk.org.

4 Further information on the Big Arts Week can be found on the website, htpp:// www.bigartsweek.com.

5 In her 1997 paper, Selwood asks what are galleries doing to attract young people and citing her own earlier research (Selwood *et al.*, 1995), her findings were not very positive. Generally it was found the schools'

projects dominated work with young persons and this made it difficult for reaching young people outside formal education, galleries rarely targeted young independent visitors and almost never mounted exhibitions for a youth market. She concluded that galleries tend to marginalize young people as the responsibility of education, community or outreach staff.

6   The Murals programme of Public Arts, for example, involves young people in Rotherham developing their ideas and computer skills to design two large images to be placed on billboards. In Huddersfield a Public Arts programme involves 10 students from Almondbury High School working with artist Norrie Harman to create large billboard displays through photography, free style drawing and computer manipulated imagery. In Market Rasen CBAT have commissioned artists to work with students from the local comprehensive school to develop public art proposals for the town. During the summer of 2004 a group of young skateboarders from the Welsh village of Talysarn developed a 6 week residency with Cywaith Cymru and artist Bryce Davies. Aged between 7 and 22, the group learned skills such as spray techniques, masking and lettering design before designing and painting their own designs on to the steel skate ramps set in the heart of Snowdonia. For further information on Public Arts see their website http://www.public-arts.co.uk. For CBAT see the website http://www.cbat.co.uk and for Cywaith Cymru see http://www.cywaithcymru.org.

7   DARE is located at http://www.dareonline.org and other educational projects and programmes produced by inIVA can be found at http://www.iniva.org/easy/education.

8   For an account of the early history of Axis see Sandle (1998). Axis and Smudgeflux can be both accessed at http:// www.axis.org.uk.

9   From January 2005, Smudgeflux was retitled Axis Learning.

10   This gender difference is well established with regard to response to the creative arts generally among secondary school pupils. For example, in researching pupils between the ages of 14 and 24 a NFER report on youth participation in the arts found that 27 per cent of females mentioned at least one arts participation compared to 10 per cent of males. (Harland *et al.*,1995).

11   For example, as well as Axis Learning and Dare there are several on-line art educational website sources, including the north west regional interactive ArtisanCam North, commissioned by Culture Online and the DCMS, (http:// www. artistCamNorth.org.uk). Along with organisa-

tions such as The Forge, an arts education agency for County Durham and Sunderland and Wigan's Drumcroon gallery, for example, liaison and sharing of good practice would be beneficial in providing a national network of resources and support.

References

Accent Marketing & Research (2004) *Smudgeflux in Scotland, art teacher research: Final analysis and recommendations.* Leeds: Axis.

Adams, E. (1997) 'Connections between public art and design education in schools', *Journal of Art and Design Education* Vol. 16, No. 3: pp. 231–239.

Allan, J., C., and Laing, A. (2000) 'Key skills enhancement for students, artists and designers through residencies in education', *Journal of Art and Design Education* Vol. 19, No. 3: pp. 325–331.

Arts Council of England (1999) *Addressing social exclusion: A framework for action.* London: Arts Council of England, p. 1 cited by Reiss and Pringle (2003).

-——— (2000) *Artstat: Digest of arts statistics and trends in the UK, 1986/87–1997/98.* London: Arts Council of England.

-——— (2004) *Partnerships for learning: A guide to evaluating arts education projects.* London: Arts Council England.

Ashworth, M., Harland, J., Haynes, J., Kinder, K. and Berger, H. (1998) *CAPE UK: Stage one evaluation report.* York: NFER.

Babayan, K. (2004) Personal communication.

Big Arts Week (2004) http:// www.bigartsweek.com [accessed July 2004].

Bowman, A. (2004) Arts Pushed Out? RSA seminar 22nd June, Leeds.

Bunbury N. (2005) Personal communication.

Charman, H. (2004) Personal communication.

Clarke, A., Dodd, J., Hooper-Greenhill, E., O'Riain, H., Swift, F. and Selfridge, L. (2002) *Learning through culture: The DFES museums and galleries education programme, a guide to good practice.* Leicester: Research Centre for Museums and Galleries (RCMA) University of Leicester.

Cockett, M. and Downing D. (2000) *CAPE UK: A review of progress 1998–2000.* Leeds: Cape.

DCMS (2001) *Culture and creativity: The next ten years.* London: HMSO.

Doherty, P. and Harland, J. (2001) *CAPE UK evaluation, phase 2 partnerships for creativity: an evaluation of implementation.* York: NFER.

Downing, D. (1996) *Artists in Leeds schools*. Leeds: Leeds Education Authority.

Downing, D., Johnston, F., and Kaur, S. (2003) Saving a place for the arts? *A survey of the arts in primary schools in England* (LGA research report 41). Slough: NFER.

Downing, D. and Watson, R. (2004) *School art — what's in it? Exploring visual art in secondary schools*. Slough: NFER.

engage (2004) http// www.engage.org [accessed November 2004].

Evans, G., and Shaw, S. (2004) *The contribution of culture to regeneration in the uk: A review of evidence — A report to the DCMS*. London: London Metropolitan University.

Fitzgerald, D. (2004) private meeting, 28th April London: DCMS.

Harland, J., and Kinder, K. (1999) *Crossing the line: Extending young persons' access to cultural venues*. London: Calouste Gulbenkian Foundation and The Arts Council of England.

Harland, J., Kinder, K. and Hartley, K. (1995) *Arts in their view: A study of youth participation in the arts, executive summary*. Slough: NFER.

Hooper-Greenhill, E. and Moussouri T. (2002) *Researching learning in museums and galleries 1990–1999: A bibliographic review*. Leicester: Research Centre for Museums and Galleries (RCMA) University of Leicester.

Hussein, A. (2004) personal communication.

Martin, A., Fraser, J. and Happs, N. (2003) *Renaissance in the regions: Museum visitor survey 2003*. Yorkshire region, London: MORI.

Miller, C. (2004) Personal communication.

MORI (2004) *Research study conducted for the museums, libraries and archives council, November 2004, revised*. London: MLAC.

National Advisory Committee on Creativity and Cultural Education (NACCCE) (1999) *All our futures: Creativity, culture and education*. London: DfEE/ DCMS.

National Society for Education in Art and Design (NSEAD) (2004) Artist teacher scheme, http:// www.nsead.org [accessed November, 2004].

O'Brien, J. (1966) *Secondary school pupils and the arts: Report of a MORI research study*. ACE Research Report No 5, London: ACE.

Oddie, D. and Allen, G. (1998) 'Artists in school: A review', Research into Arts Education, Symposium, Belfast, August, as cited in Allan and Laing (2000) and also cited in Pringle (2002) as published, London: Stationary Office.

Orfali, A. (2004) *Artists working in partnership with schools: Quality indicators and advice for planning, commissioning and delivery*. Newcastle upon Tyne: North East Arts, Arts Council, England.

Owens, P. (1998) *Creative tensions: A discussion document on arts organisations and education*. London: British Amerian Arts Association as cited in Allan and Laing (2000).

Policy Action Team 10 (1999) *The arts and sport: A report to the Social Exclusion Unit*. London: DCMS.

Pringle, E. (2002) *We did stir things up: The role of artists in sites for learning*. London: Arts Council of England.

Potter, G. (2002) *Education research report*. Leeds: Axis.

Reiss, V., and Pringle, E. (2003) 'The role of artists in sites for Learning', *The International Journal of Art and Design Educatio*, Vol. 22, No 2: pp 215–221.

Roberts, G., Ball, S., Entwistle, T., Sandle D. and Strange, I. (2003) *A review of public art in Wales 1998–2003*. Leeds: RKL / The Arts Council of Wales.

Rogers, R., Edwards, S., and Godfrey, F. (2004) *State of the art*. London: Artworks, Clore Duffield Foundation.

Rogers, R., Edwards, S. and Steers, J. (2001) *Survey of art and design resources in primary and secondary schools*. London: The Clore Duffield Foundation.

Sandle, D. (1998) 'Axis: broadening the constituency and extending the sphere of influence of visual art', *Art Libraries Journal* Vol. 23, No. 2.

––––––– (2004) 'The Brick Man versus the Angel of the North — public art as contested space', in Kennedy E. and Thornton A. (eds) *Leisure, media and visual culture: Representations and contestations*. Eastbourne: Leisure Studies Association.

Sandle, D., and Knutson, R. (2004) Beyond Picasso, bringing contemporary modern art into the school classroom: the Smudgeflux Project. Annual Conference, Leisure Studies Association, Leeds Metropolitan University, July.

Selwood, S. (1997) 'Cultural policy and young people's participation in the visual arts', *Journal of Art and Design Education* Vol. 16, No. 3: pp. 333–340.

Selwood, S., Clive, S., and Irving, D. (1995) *An enquiry into young people and arts galleries*. Arts and Society cited in Selwood (1997).

Skelton, A., Bridgwood, A., Duckworth, K., Hutton,L., Fenn, G., Creaser, C., and Babbidge A. (2002) *Arts in England: Attendance, participation and attitudes in 2001, research report 27*. London: Office for National Statistics.

VAGA (Visual Arts and Galleries Association) (2004) http://www.vaga.co.uk [accessed July 2004].

Leisure Studies Association

LSA Publications

LSA

An extensive list of publications on a wide range of leisure studies topics, produced by the Leisure Studies Association since the late 1970s, is available from LSA Publications.

Some recently published volumes are detailed on the following pages, and full information may be obtained on newer and forthcoming LSA volumes from:

LSA Publications, c/o M. McFee
email: mcfee@solutions-inc.co.uk
The Chelsea School, University of Brighton
Eastbourne BN20 7SP (UK)

Among other benefits, members of the Leisure Studies Association may purchase LSA Publications at preferential rates. Please contact LSA at the above address for information regarding membership of the Association, LSA Conferences, and LSA Newsletters.

ONLINE

Complete information about LSA Publications:

www.leisure-studies-association.info/LSAWEB/Publications.html

YOUTH SPORT AND ACTIVE LEISURE: THEORY, POLICY AND PARTICIPATION

**LSA Publication No. 87.   ISBN: 0 906337 98 4 [2005] pp. 185 + xii
eds. Anne Flintoff, Jonathan Long and Kevyn Hylton**

Contents

Editors' Introduction v

About the Contributors xi

I   Theorising youth sport and active leisure practice 1

Physical Culture, Lifelong Participation and Empowerment: Towards an
Educational Rationale for Physical Education
David Kirk 3

Indifferent, Hostile or Empowered? School PE and
Active Leisure Lifestyles for Girls and Young Women
Anne Flintoff 29

Extreme Sports and National Sport Policy in Canada
Joanne Kay 45

The Role of Sport for Young People in Community Cohesion and
Community Safety: Alienation, Policy and Provision
Phil Binks and Bob Snape 55

II   Difference, Young people and participation 69

Doing Sport, Doing Inclusion: An Analysis of Provider and Participant
Perceptions of Targeted Sport Provision for Young Muslims
James Lowrey and Tess Kay 71

The Voice of the Family: Influences on Muslim Girls' Responses to Sport
Tess Kay 89

Young People, Holiday-Taking and Cancer: The Perceived Effects
of Travel Upon Health and Wellbeing
Philippa Hunter-Jones 113

The Family Experience of Nature
Margot Edwards and Kay Thorn 129

Other Volumes from LSA Publications 153

SPORT AND ACTIVE LEISURE YOUTH CULTURES

**LSA PUBLICATIONS NO. 86. ISBN: 0 906337 97 6 [2005] pp. 238 + xxii
eds. Jayne Caudwell and Peter Bramham**

Contents

	Editors' Introduction	i
	About the Contributors	
I	**Adventure and Risk-Taking Behaviour**	1
	Cities as Playgrounds: Active Leisure for Children as a Human Right	
	Brian Simpson	3
	What Future for School Trips in a Risk Averse Society?	
	John Hunter-Jones	25
	Cool Consumption: How Do Young People Use Adventure Tourism?	
	Shelagh Ferguson and Sarah Todd	43
	Recreational Substance Use Among Lesbian, Gay, and Bisexual Youth: Frequency and Predictors	
	Arnold H. Grossman	55
II	**Gendered and Sexualised Identities**	73
	Girls, Football Participation and Gender Identity	
	Ruth Jeanes	75
	'Urban Surfers': Representations of the Skateboarding Body in Youth Leisure	
	Ian Macdonald	97
	Active Bodies for 'Real' Men: Reflecting upon the Social Constructions of Activity and Passivity for Gendered and Sexually Identified Bodies	
	Ian Wellard	115
	Making Sense of NUTS and ZOO: The Construction and Projection of Homogenised Masculinity	
	Fiona Jordan and Scott Fleming	133
III	**Youth and Social Change**	151
	Re-inventing 'The Game': Rugby League, 'Race', Gender and the Growth of Active Sports for Young People in England	
	Karl Spracklen	153
	Football Fandom, West Ham United and the 'Cockney Diaspora': from Working-class Community to Youth Post-tribe?	
	Jack Fawbert	169
	Habits of a Lifetime? Youth, Generation and Lifestyles	
	Peter Bramham	193
	Other Volumes from LSA Publications	205

LEISURE, SPACE AND VISUAL CULTURE: PRACTICES AND MEANINGS

LSA Publication No. 84. ISBN: 0 906337 95 X [2004] pp. 292+xxii
eds. Cara Aitchison and Helen Pussard

Contents

Preface: Leisure, Visual Culture and the 'Spatial Turn'
James Kneale .... *v*

Editors' Introduction: Leisure, Space and Visual Culture
Cara Aitchison and Helen Pussard .... *ix*

I   THE SPATIAL POLITICS OF VISUAL CULTURE 1

The Rules of Culture: Exhibition and the Politics of Knowledge
Tony Bennett 3

Buying Time and Space: A Critical Appraisal of Sport and Leisure
Consumption in the 'New' Belfast ....
Alan Bairner and Peter Shirlow 15

"A Relic of Bygone Days"? The Temporal Landscapes of Pleasure Grounds
Helen Pussard 41

II   MEMORY AND HERITAGE IN VISUAL CULTURE 59

Seeing Places: A Critique of the Heritage Trail as a Visual Interpretation
of Place
Nicola E. MacLeod 61

Tourist Perception of the Heritage on Show in Relation to their Own
Heritage
Yaniv Poria, Richard Butler and David Airey 79

Memory and Visual Culture: Visitors' Recollections and Repeat Visiting Intentions
Kirsten Holmes 105

III   CITYSCAPES, LEISURESCAPES AND DREAMSCAPES 123

Mass-Participation Running: Sport as Contemporary Urban Spectacle?
Jacqueline Tivers 125

Space and Leisure as Regenerative Elements of an Urban Cityscape: The Case of The
Centre for Dundee Contemporary Arts (DCA)
MariaLaura Di Domenico and Francesco Di Domenico 151

Metaphorical and Physical Leisure Spaces: Women, Pleasure
and the UK National Lottery
Emma Casey 175

IV   LEISURE AS SEEING, LEISURE AS BEING 195

The Highland Society of the Spectacle: Regulating Bodies and
Figuring the National Heritage at the Highland Games
Dan Knox 197

Visualising the Environment: Diverse Ways of 'Seeing' and
Knowing in the Outdoors
Kim Polistina 217

A Search for Idyllic Places of Leisure in the East: Recreation of the Vernacular
Culture and the Traditional Social Space in Sri Lanka
Ranjith Dayaratne 241

LEISURE, MEDIA AND VISUAL CULTURE: REPRESENTATIONS AND CONTESTATIONS

**LSA Publication No. 83. ISBN: 0 906337 94 1 [2004] pp. 282
eds. Cara Aitchison and Helen Pussard**

Contents

Editors' Introduction v

I   THEORISING THE LEISURELY GAZE 1

"Rural Glamour": Reading Fashion in the New Zealand Context
        Hilary Radner 3
Bodies Laid Bare: Sport and the Spectacle of Masculinity
        Eileen Kennedy 21
'I Know Kung Fu': The Sporting Body in Film
        Andrew Thornton 41
The Flâneur and the Stalker
        Bran Nicol 61

II TEXTS AND OBJECTS: READING THE VISUAL CULTURE
    OF LEISURE 73

Middle Class Pleasures and the 'Safe' Dangers of
    Surf Bathing on the English South Coast 1921–1937 75
        Joan Ormrod 75
Tabloid Tourists: Celebrity, Consumption and
    Performance in British Television Holiday Programmes ....
        David Dunn 113
"Is This Shirt Loud?" Semiotics and the 'Language' of
    Replica Football Shirts ....
        Jack Fawbert 131

III MAKING MEANINGS: THE CREATION AND INTERPRETATION
    OF LEISURE AUDIENCES 151

The Contribution of Reality TV in the Critique and Creation of Lifestyle Choices
        Christine Fanthome 153
It's Only A Gameshow: Evolved Intelligences And Reality Culture
        Paul Woodward and Maxine Doyle 171
The Brick Man versus the Angel of the North: Public Art as Contested Space
        Doug Sandle 187
The Socialization of Lesbian, Gay and Bisexual Youth:
    Celebrity and Personally Known Role Models
        Arnold H. Grossman and Anthony R. D'Augelli 203
Tipping the Velvet: Straight[forward] Voyeurism? Problematising the Viewing of
    Lesbianism
        Jayne Caudwell 227

Other volumes from LSA Publications 253

SPORT, LEISURE AND SOCIAL INCLUSION

LSA Publication No. 82. ISBN: 0 906337 933 [2003] pp. 296
ed. Adrian Ibbetseon, Beccy Watson and Maggie Ferguson

Contents

Editors' Introduction *Adrian Ibbetson, Beccy Watson and Maggie Ferguson* v

I   SPORT — AN INCLUSIVE COMMUNITY? 1

Modern Sports: Inalienable Common Wealth
Ken Roberts 3

Local Authority Support Networks for Sports Volunteers
AndrewAdams and John Deane 23

Setting A Standard?: Measuring Progress in Tackling Racism and
Promoting Social Inclusion in English Sport
Karl Spracklen 41

II   COMMON-WEALTH? THE USE OF MAJOR SPORTS EVENTS
FOR SOCIAL R ENEWAL 59

Major International Sports Events: Planning for Long-term Benefits
Guy Masterman 61

Can The Commonwealth Games in East Manchester Provide A Basis for
Social Renewal?
Maggie Jones and Terry Stokes 75

Developing a Cost–Benefit Structure to Analyse Sport and its Social Impacts
Charles Spring 91

III   NARRATIVES OF INVOLVEMENT: EXPLORING PARTICIPATION
AND PERCEPTION 99

In Pursuit of Excellence: Experiences of Paralympic Athletes
Ian Brittain and Barbara Humberstone 101

'Hitting 40!' The Conflict of Moral Voices Versus Concrete Sport Experiences
Lindsay King and John Lyle 119

Lifestyle and Women's Exercise Patterns: An Examination of the Constraints of
Family and Employment on Regularly Exercising Women
Iain C. Adams and Margaret Walton 141

Spirituality in Public Leisure Provision:
The Benefits of Exercise for Women in Their Middle Years
Margaret Walton and Iain C. Adams 153

Leisure Constraints and Levels of Sport Participation for Women in Iran
Mohammad Ehsani 167

IV   EXPANDING THE POSSIBILITIES: APPLYING DIFFERENT
ANALYTIC CONTEXTS 179

Social Climbing   *Linda Allin, Amanda West and Adrian Ibbetson* 181

"The Ellen Macarthur Factor" : A Study of Instructor Opinions about the
Motivations of Young Female Sailors
Michelle Moorman 197

Towards Environmentally Sustainable Lifestyles through Outdoor Leisure
Kim Polistina 213

Physical Culture in Post-communist Poland
Zofia Pawlaczek 233

ACCESS AND INCLUSION IN LEISURE AND TOURISM

LSA Publication No. 81. ISBN: 0 906337 92 5 [2003] pp. 288
eds. Bob Snape, Edwin Thwaites, Christine Williams

Contents

Editor's Introduction   *Robert Snape, Edwin Thwaites and Christine Williams* v

About the Contributors xi

I   EQUALITY AND SOCIAL INCLUSION 1

Developing the Cultural Agenda: the Socio-spatial
Dimensions of the Regional Cultural Strategies in England
Neil Ravenscroft and Alan Tomlinson 3

Local Cultural Strategies: Critiques and Challenges
Cara Aitchison 23

The Role of the Arts in Government Policies for Health and Social Exclusion
Peter Bramham 41

Taking a Part: An Evaluation of the Ability of
Cultural Activities to Promote Social Inclusion
Jonathan Long and Mel Welch 55

The Access Dilemma: Moving Towards a Coherent,
Inclusive and Sustainable Framework
Debi Hayes and Alix Slater 73

'Doing the Shopping' or 'Going Shopping'? Gender, Grocery Shopping
and the Discourse of Leisure
Cheryl Cockburn-Wootten, Nigel Morgan,
Annette Pritchard, and Eleri Jones 95

II THE VOUNTARY CONUNDRUM 117

Heritage and Leisure: Museum Volunteering As 'Serious Leisure'
Noreen Orr 119

Rambling, Socialism and the Evolution of the Countryside as a
Leisure Space
Robert Snape 141

The Role of 'The Club' in Ibadan, Nigeria from 1960 to 2000:
Exclusivity in Post-colonial Leisure and Sports Activities
Catherine Di Domenico and MariaLaura Di Domenico 155

III THE VISITOR EXPERIENCE 177

Regular and Irregular Visitors to the MillenniumGalleries, Sheffield
Kirsten Holmes 179

Access to Culture: Resolving Tourism Conflicts
through Visitor Research and Management
Terry J Brown 193

IV LEISURE MANAGEMENT 217

An investigation into the Currency of Qualifications in Relation
to Current Employment Trends within the Leisure Sector
Maggie Ferguson and Adrian Ibbetson 219

Other LSA Publications volumes 255

VOLUNTEERS IN SPORT

LSA Publication No. 80. ISBN: 0 906337 91 7 [2003] pp. 107
ed. Geoff Nichols

Contents

Volunteers in Sport — Introduction
  Geoff Nichols .... *v*

About the Contributors .... *vii*

Volunteering in English Sport: an Interim Discussion in Relation to National Governing Bodies
  of Sport
    Matthew James, Geoff Nichols and Peter Taylor 1

Modelling the Decision to become a Coach
    Brian E Wilson 19

The XVII Commonwealth Games — An Initial Overview
  of the Expectations and Experiences of Volunteers
    Rita Ralston, Paul Downward and Les Lumsdon 43

The Response of Voluntary Sports Clubs to Sport England's
  Lottery Funding: Cases of Compliance,
  Change and Resistance
    Richard Garrett 55

Other Volumes from Leisure Studies Asssociation 81

LEISURE CULTURES: INVESTIGATIONS IN SPORT, MEDIA AND TECHNOLOGY

**LSA Publication No. 79. ISBN: 0 906337 90 9 [2003] pp. 221 + xii
eds. Scott Fleming and Ian Jones**

Contents

Leisure Cultures: Investigations in Sport, Media and Technology
— Introduction   *Scott Fleming and Ian Jones* v

About the Contributors xi

Section One 1

The Gendering of Computer Gaming: Experience and Space
Jo Bryce and Jason Rutter 3

The Global, the Local and the Subcultural: Virtual Communities
and Popular Music in Singapore
Yasser Mattar 23

"These are the Voyages ...": Issues Around Interaction in
Real and Virtual Space Environments in Leisure
Lesley Lawrence 37

Section Two 55

Research with the Gloves On — An 'Insider's' Knowledge
in the Critique of Competitive Boxing in England
Alex Stewart 57

Consuming Images of Lifestyle Sports
Belinda Wheaton and Becky Beal 69

'Fair Play' in Elite Women's Field Hockey: An Ethnographic Case-study
Scott Fleming and Alison Williams 91

Section Three 105

The Culture of Market-Oriented and Televised Soccer in Israel:
A State of Anomie
Natan Uriely and Abraham Mehrez 107

Leisure and the Civilising Process: A Case Study
of the *Herts Advertiser*, 1900–2000
Ian Jones 119

Leisure Constraint Factors on the Recreational Sporting Activities
of Participants and Non-participants in Iran
Mohammad Ehsani 133

Section Four 153

Men, Sport, Body Performance and the Maintenance
of 'Exclusive Masculinity'
Ian Wellard 155

Physique, Social Comparison and Self-Conscious Emotion:
A Functional Perspective
Simon Dalley 171

PARTNERSHIPS IN LEISURE:
SPORT, TOURISM AND MANAGEMENT

LSA Publication No. 78. ISBN: 0 906337 89 5 [2002] pp. 245 + iv
eds. Graham Berridge and Graham McFee

Contents

Part One: The Very Idea of Partnership 1
    Introduction — Partnerships in Leisure: Sport, tourism
    and management
       Graham Berridge and Graham McFee 3
    "Partnering is such sweet sorrow": Some perils of partnership
       Graham McFee 11
Part Two: Paying for Partnerships 43
    'Leafy Glade' and 'City Centre' Relate: A case of marital strife
    in the voluntary sector?
       Martin Gammell and Graham Symon 27
    Support Networks for Local Volunteers:
    A case study of Athletics and Rugby Union
       Andrew Adams and John Deane 45
    The Development of East Manchester Youth Training
    Opportunities in the Run-up to the Commonwealth Games 2002
       Maggie Jones and Terry Stokes 59
    Brains and Brawn: A sporting partnership — the New Zealand
    Rugby Football Union and Massey University
       Sarah Leberman and Brendon Ratcliff 77
Part Three: Marketing Forces 93
    Market Orientation For Public Sector Sport and
    Recreation Providers
       John Beaumont-Kerridge 95
    Partnerships in Tourism: Crossing the leisure–business
    divide via cluster theory
       E. Kate Armstrong and Peter Murphy 121
    Using the Outdoors to Promote the Learning of Managerial
    Skills: Analysing the process of learning transfer
       Veronica Burke, David Collins and Mick Earle 137
    Examination of Internet Usage as an Integrated Tool for
    the Management and Marketing of Costa Rican Tourism
    Businesses: An exploratory assessment
       Sarah Guroff and Stuart Cottrell 161
Part Four: Access and Sustainability 187
    Leisure Choices — Is there a crisis in the market for
    visitor attractions in the UK?
       Angela Phelps 189
    Planning Journeys to Leisure Sites: A look at the SALSA project
       Graham Berridge 201
About the Contributors 215

LEISURE STUDIES:
TRENDS IN THEORY AND RESEARCH

LSA Publication No. 77. ISBN: 0 906337 88 7 [2001] pp. 198 + iv
eds. Stan Parker and Lesley Lawrence

Contents

Editors' Introduction
    Stan Parker and Lesley Lawrence v
About the Contributors ix

I   **Reflections** 1
    Back to the Future: Leisure Studies in Retrospect and Prospect
        Chas Critcher 3
    Which Way for Leisure?
        Stan Parker 13
    Leisure Studies: Discourses of Knowledge, Power
    and Theoretical 'Crisis'
        Cara Aitchison 19
    Leisure Studies at the Millennium: Intellectual Crisis
    or Mature Complacency?
        A. J. Veal 41
II   **Under-represented Groups** 51
    Retirement and Serious Leisure
        Jonathan Long and Sheila Scraton 53
    The Big OE: New Zealanders' Overseas Experience in Britain
        Peter Mason 67
    Transgender Youth: Challenging Traditional 'Girl-boy'
    Activities — Implications of an Exploratory Study for
    New Directions in Research
        Arnold H. Grossman, Timothy S. O'Connell and
        Anthony R. D'Augelli 83
III **Applications and Approaches** 105
    The Demand for Professional Team Sports:
    Critical Reflection on Economic Enquiry
        Paul Downward 107
    Continuity, Truth and Lies in Topical Life Histories:
    the Sport and Physical Activity Experiences of Adults
        Lindsay King 123
    Perceptions, Pedagogy and Process: An Investigation
    into the Effects on Students and Staff of the Provision
    of a Module in Leisure Studies Underpinned by Feminist Theories
        Barbara Humberstone and Laura Kirby 145
    Riding the Slipstream: An Experience with
    Multidisciplinary Working Partnerships
        Lynne M. Robinson, Laurene Rehman and Joanne MacQueen 159

SPORT TOURISM: PRINCIPLES AND PRACTICE

LSA Publication No. 76. ISBN: 0 906337 87 9 [2001] pp. 174 + xii
eds. Sean Gammin and Joseph Kurtzman

Contents

Editors' Introduction
Sean Gammon and Joseph Kurtzman v

I   **Sport Tourism Manifestations** 1

Small-Scale Event Sport Tourism: College Sport
as a Tourist Attraction
Heather J. Gibson, Cynthia Willming and Andrew Holdnak 3

Sport and Tourism Development: Avenues of Tourism
Development Associated with a Regional Sport Franchise
at an Urban Tourism Destination
James Higham and Tom Hinch 19

Football Hooligans as Undesirable Sports Tourists:
Some Meta-Analytical Speculations
Mike Weed 35

Stadia and Tourism
Geraint John 53

Fantasy, Nostalgia and the Pursuit of What Never Was
Sean Gammon 61

II   **Sport Tourism Impacts** 73

Socio-cultural Impacts of Visitors to the Network Q Rally
of Great Britain on a Rural Community in Mid-Wales
*Paul Blakey, Martin Metcalfe, John Mitchell
and Peter Weatherhead* 75

The Downhill Skier in Banff National Park: An Endangered Species
Simon Hudson 89

Sport Tourism, A Growing Sector: Issues and Perspectives in France
Charles Pigeassou 111

Sport Tourism at a Crossroad? Considerations for the Future
Heather J. Gibson 123

Other LSA Publications Volumes 141

VOLUNTEERING IN LEISURE: MARGINAL OR INCLUSIVE?

LSA Publication No. 75. ISBN: 0 906337 86 0 [2001] pp. 158+xi
eds. Margaret Graham and Malcolm Foley

Contents

Editors' Introduction
Margaret Graham and Malcolm Foley v

Volunteering — Mainstream and Marginal: Preserving the
Leisure Experience
Robert A. Stebbins 1

Research Questions for Volunteering in Leisure
Geoff Nichols and Richard Garrett 11

Volunteering, Citizenship and Action Research ....
Josephine Burden 21

Volunteerism in Sports Coaching — A Tayside Study
Christine Nash 43

The Role of Museum Volunteering in Relieving Social Isolation
Margaret Graham 57

The Strategic Responses of Voluntary Sports Clubs to
Sport England's Lottery Fund
Richard Garrett 77

The Motivation and Retention of Front-of-House
Volunteers at Museums and Heritage Attractions
Kirsten Holmes 95

Other Volumes from LSA Publications 111

LEISURE CULTURES, CONSUMPTION AND COMMODIFICATION

LSA Publication No. 74. ISBN: 0 906337 85 2 [2001] pp. 158+xi ed. John Horne

Contents

Editor's Introduction: Studying Leisure Cultures,
Consumption and Commodification
John Horne v

Part One: Diffusion, Transformation and Contestation
Anti-consumption or 'New' Consumption? Commodification,
Identity and 'New Football'
Carlton Brick 3
Football Clubs on the Stock Exchange: An Inappropriate Match?
The Case of Celtic plc
Stephen Morrow 17
Centres and Peripheries: An Historical Perspective on the
Diffusion of Leisure Practices in Rural Nineteenth Century Scotland
Lorna Jackson 41
Selling the Arts: Centre-Periphery Tensions in
Commodification Processes
Clive Gray 53
Technological Development and Changing Leisure Practices
Jo Bryce 65

Part Two: Consumption, Culture and Heritage
Brand Images of Place and New Urban Identities in Scotland:
The Case of Dundee, The City of Discovery
MariaLaura Di Domenico 81
Tourism Games and the Commodification of Tradition
Eleanor Lothian 93
Haggis and Heritage — Representing Scotland in the United States
Euan Hague 107
Visiting Places with 'Added Value': Learning from Pilgrimage
to Enhance the Visitor's Experience at Heritage Attractions
Angela Phelps 131

LEISURE AND SOCIAL INCLUSION: NEW CHALLENGES FOR POLICY AND PROVISION

LSA Publication No. 73. ISBN: 0 906337 84 4 [2001] pp. 204
eds. Gayle McPherson and Malcolm Reid

Contents

Social Exclusion and Policies for Leisure: An Introduction
    Gayle McPherson and Gavin Reid 1
The Potential of Outreach Sports Initiatives for Young People
    to Achieve Community Development and Social Inclusion
    through Leisure
        Fiona McCormack 7
Delivering Public Leisure Services: Integrating People,
    Places and Partnerships
        Francis Lobo 23
Leisure Services and Local Government in Scotland —
    Time for a Divorce?
        Ashley Pringle 39
Exercise Referral Schemes in Scotland: Is it 'Joined-up Policy'?
    Malcolm Foley, Matt Frew and Gayle McPherson 49
A Realist Approach to Evaluating the Impact of Sports
    Programmes on Crime Reduction
        Geoff Nichols 71
"... limp-wristed, Kylie Minogue-loving, football-hating,
    fashion victims ..." Gay Sports Clubs — Providing for
    Male Members, Challenging Social Exclusion?
        Lindsay King and Peter Thompson 81
Benchmarking of Public Leisure Services: A Tool for Efficiency,
    Effectiveness or Equity?
        Susan M. Ogden and David Booth 103
Home Zones for Play Space: A Community Planning Perspective
        Debbie Hinds 123
Including the Forty Percent: Social Exclusion and Tourism Policy
        Ronnie Smith 141
A Disabled Leisure Studies: Theorising Dominant Discourses
    of the Employed Body, the Able Body and the Active Body?
        Cara Aitchison 153
The Validation of Alternative Discourses in the Lifelong
    Learning Systems of Australian Appreciative Outdoor
    Recreationalists and Indigenous Peoples
        Kim Polistina 161

JUST LEISURE:
EQUITY, SOCIAL EXCLUSION AND IDENTITY

LSA Publication No 72. ISBN: 0 906337 83 6 [2000] pp. 195+xiv
Edited by Celia Brackenridge, David Howe and Fiona Jordan

Contents

Editor's Introduction
> *Celia Brackenridge, David Howe and Fiona Jordan* 3

I   **EQUITY AND SOCIAL EXCLUSION** 1

The Sexist State: Leisure, Labour and the Ideology of Welfare Policy
> *Tess Kay* 3

Equity or Exclusion? Contemporary Experiences
in Post-industrial Urban Leisure
> *Euan Hague, Chris Thomas and Stephen Williams* 17

What's the Score? Using Sport and Leisure as Diversion
> *Jonathan Long, Eddy Lloyd and Jon Dart* 35

Social Disadvantage and Leisure Access: The Case of the Unemployed
> *Francis Lobo* 49

Just sport – Sport and the Concept of
Equal Opportunities between Women and Men
> *Håkan Larsson* 69

Tied Together Through Sport? Sport and Social Cohesion
in New Housing Estates
> *Hugo van der Poel and Colette Roques* 83

II   **IDENTITY** 103

Homophobia and its Effects on the Inequitable Provision
of Health and Leisure Services for Older Gay Men and Lesbians
> *Arnold H. Grossman* 105

The "Goodness of Fit" in Norwegian Youth Sports
> *Reidar Säfvenbom* 119

Identities and Subculture in Relation to Sport: An Analysis
of Teenage Girls' Magazines
> *Claudia Cockburn* 131

Glencoe: A Case Study in Interpretation
> *Judith E. Brown* 149

Who Are These People? And What on Earth Are They Doing?!
> *Lesley Lawrence* 161

JUST LEISURE:
POLICY, ETHICS & PROFESSIONALISM

LSA Publication No 71. ISBN: 0 906337 81 X [2000] pp. 257+xiv
Edited by Celia Brackenridge, David Howe and Fiona Jordan

Contents

Editors' Introduction
Mike McNamee, Chris Jennings and Martin Reeves v

Part I   POLICY 1

Changing their Game: The Effect of Lottery Sports Funding on Voluntary
Sports Clubs
Richard Garrett 3

Issues of Legal Responsibility in Organised Sport and Outdoor Recreation
John Hunter-Jones 19

Sport and Leisure Planning: the Need for Assessment
Ari Karimäki 33

Best Value in Leisure Services: a Philosophy or a Quality System?
Christine Williams 45

Fairness and Flexibility in the Scottish Leisure Industry
*Anna MacVicar, Margaret Graham, Susan Ogden
and Bernadette Scott* 57

Part II   ETHICS

Sport, Leisure and the Ethics of Change
Alun Hardman 77

Just Leisure, Ethical Fitness, andEcophilosophical Perspectives
Karla A. Henderson 93

"Sorry Ref, I didn't see it" — The Limitations of Shields
and Bredemeier's Model of Moral Action   *Carwyn Jones* 105

The Ethos of the Game: Representations of the Good Game and the
Good Player among Junior Football Players in Sweden
Matz Franzén, Per Nilsson, Tomas Peterson 121

Ethical Leisure: The 'Dark" and the 'Deviant" Disambiguated
Heather Sheridan 131

Sport — A Moral Laboratory?
Graham McFee 153

Part III   PROFESSIONALISM

Applying the Principles of "Green Games": An Investigation into
the Green Practices of Event Organisers
Graham Berridge 171

The Professionalisation of Museum Volunteers: An Ethical Dilemma ....
Margaret Graham 185

An Examination of Coaches' Responsibilities for Premature Athletic
Disengagement of Elite Greek Gymnasts
Konstantinos Koukouris 211

The 'Hand of God'?   *Claudio M. Tamburrini* 227

WOMEN'S LEISURE EXPERIENCES: AGES, STAGES AND ROLES

LSA Publication No. 70. ISBN 0 906337 80 1 [2001]
Edited by Sharon Clough and Judy White

Contents

Editors' Introduction
   Sharon Clough and Judy White v
Leisure, Change and Social Capital: Making the Personal
   Political   *Josephine Burden* 1
Rejecting the Ghetto: The Retired Spinsteratae
   Jean Carroll 23
Sedentary and Busy: Physical Activity and
   Older Women of Color
   Karla A. Henderson and Barbara E. Ainsworth 37
Leaky Bodies or Drying Husks? Menopause, Health and
   Embodied Experience   *Eileen Green* 51
The Absent Spaces of Lone Mothers' Leisure
   Kay Standing 65
The Everyday Lives of Sportswomen: Playing Sport and
   Being a Mother   *Gertrud Pfister* 75
Using Eichler to Inform Family Leisure Research
   Laurene A. Rehman 87
Mothers on Family Activity Holidays Overseas
   Jenny Anderson 99
New Women, Same Old Leisure: The Upholding of Gender
   Stereotypes and Leisure Disadvantage in Contemporary
   Dual-earner Households
   Tess Kay 113
A Juggling Act: Women Balancing Work, Family and Leisure
   Sharon Clough 131
When Gender is Problematic: Leisure and Gender
   Negotiation for Marginalized Women
   Diane M. Samdahl, Sharon Jacobson,
   Susan Hutchinson 143
Being Cool as a Social Imperative: Young Women's Resistance
   to Health Promotion Messages about Physical Exercise
   Eleanor Peters and Diana Woodward 153
Developing Bodies: The Negotiation of Femininities and
   Physicalities by Girls in Physical Education
   Laura A. Hills 165

MASCULINITIES: LEISURE CULTURES, IDENTITIES AND CONSUMPTION

LSA Publication No. 69. ISBN: 0 906337 77 1 [2000] pp. 163

Edited by John Horne and Scott Fleming

Contents

Introdution: Masculinities and Leisure Studies
  John Horne and Scot Fleming v
Pubs and Clubs and the More Modern than Modern.
  Working-Class Man: An Exploration of the Metastasis of Masculinities beyond
  Modernity
  Tony Blackshaw 1
Teenage Kicks: A Study of the Construction and Development of Adolescent Masculine
  Identities in Organised Team Sport
  Simon David Pratt 23
Somebody to Love: The Complex Masculinities
  of 'Boy Band' Pop
  Diane Railton 39
'Bachelors in Paradise': Masculinity, Lifestyle
  and Men's Magazines in Post-war America
  Bill Osgerby 51
Mirror Men? Middle Class Young Men Discussing
  Fashion and their Bodies
  John Galilee 81
Gay Men: Body Concepts, Self Concepts and Some
  Implications For Contemporary Queer Lifestyles
  Iain Williamson 103
Gay Tourism, Sex and Sexual Health Promotion
  Stephen Clift and Simon Forrest 115

Other volumes from LSA Publications 137

GENDER ISSUES IN WORK AND LEISURE

LSA Publication No. 68.ISBN 0 906337 78 X
Edited by Jenny Anderson and Lesley Lawrence [pp. 173]

Contents

Gender Issues in Work and Leisure: Editors' Introduction
Jenny Anderson and Lesley Lawrence .... *v*

**SECTION ONE   OUT-OF-HOME LEISURE SPACES:
ISSUES OF ACCESS, EQUITY, AND RISK** 1

Gendered Leisure Spaces: A Case Study of the Young Tourist
Neil Carr 3

Social Control in the 'Big Ghetto': The Connection between
Women's Fear of Violence and Women's Leisure Experience
Fern M. Delamere 13

Gender Equity in Sport and Recreation: from Policy to Practice
(The Case of an Award-Winning Canadian City)
Aniko Varpalotai 23

Men's Leisure, Women's Work: Female Prostitutes and the Double
Standard of North-American HIV Public Health Policies
Lois A. Jackson and Colleen Deyell Hood 31

**SECTION TWO   LEISURE IN AND OUT OF HOME:
CULTURAL PERSPECTIVES** 41

Growing Up within Two Cultural Traditions: The Lives and
Leisure of Canadian South Asian Teens
Susan Tirone 43

Integration through Leisure? Leisure Time Activities and the
Integration of Turkish Families in Two Cities in the Netherlands
Jan W. te Kloeze 51

Women, Leisure and Quality of Life
Nevenka Cernigoj Sadar 63

Young People, Unemployment and Leisure: A Gender Perspective
Francis Lobo 73

Porn on the Net: What can we watch without Mother?
Sharon Clough-Todd and Hannah White-Overton 89

**SECTION THREE: WORK AND LEISURE:
THE BLURRING OF BOUNDARIES** 99

Working Around Leisure: Home-based Work, Leisure and
Confusing Male and Female Spaces
Jon Dart and Jonathan Long 101

The Gender Implications of Workplace Flexibility on Local
Government Leisure Sector Employees in Scotland
Malcolm Foley and Anna MacVicar 113

Voluntary Work, Status and Inclusion in Rural Tourist Attractions
Jenny Phillimore 125

SPORT, LEISURE IDENTITIES AND GENDERED SPACES

LSA Publication No. 67. ISBN: 0 906337 79 8 [1999] pp. 196
Edited by Sheila Scraton and Becky Watson

Contents

Editors' Introduction
  Sheila Scraton and Beccy Watson v
Identity and Gender in Sport and Media Fandom:
  An Exploratory Comparison of Fans attending
  Football Matches and Star Trek Conventions
    Ian Jones and Lesley Lawrence 1
Game, Set and Match: Gender Bias in Television Coverage of
  Wimbledon 1994
    Lesley Fishwick and Kirsty Leach 31
Are Your Kids Safe?: Media Representations of Sexual Abuse
  in Sport
    Caroline Fusco and Sandra Kirby 45
Crossing Borders: Lesbian Physical Education Students
  and the Struggles for Sexual Spaces
    Gill Clarke 75
Football in the UK: Women, Tomboys, Butches and Lesbians
    Jayne Caudwell 95
What's in a Name? That which women call softball, by the
  other name — fast pitch — would still be an
  exciting men's game
    Lynn Embrey 111
The Androgynous Athlete: Transforming Gendered Space?
    Paula Roberts 125
Women's Rugby and Subcultural Identity: A Case Study
  of an Initiation Event
    Sarah Taylorand Scott Fleming 137
Seeing and Being Seen: Body Fashion in Female
  Recreational Sport
    Kari Fasting 151
Sporting Females in Egypt: Veiling or Unveiling, an Analysis
  of the Debate
    Linda Balboul 163
About the Contributors 171

HER OUTDOORS: RISK, CHALLENGE AND ADVENTURE IN GENDERED OPEN SPACES

LSA Publication No. 66 [1999] ISBN: 0 906337 76 3; pp. 131
Edited by Barbara Humberstone

Contents

Editor's Introduction .... *Barbara Humberstone*

Women's Use and Perceptions of the Outdoors:
     A Case Study of Urban Parks .... *Tony Curson and Clare Kitts*

Recognising Women: Discourses in Outdoor Education .... *Di Collins*

Gender Issues and Women's Windsurfing .... *Val Woodward*

Women into Outdoor Education: Negotiating a Male-gendered Space — Issues of Physicality
     Linda Allin

Developing Confidence in Women Working Outdoors:
     An Exploration of Self Confidence and Competence in
     Women Employed in Adventure Recreation .... *May Carter*

Enhancing Self-esteem in Adolescent Girls: A Proposed
     Model for Adventure Education Programming
            .... *Karen Barak, Mary Anne Hendrich
            and Steven J. Albrechtsen*

Gendered 'Natural' Spaces: a Comparison of Contezmporary Women's Experiences of
     Outdoor Adventure (UK) and Friluftsliv (Norway)
            .... *Barbara Humberstone and Kirsti Pedersen*

POLICY AND PUBLICS

LSA Publication No. 65. ISBN: 0 906337 75 5 [1999] pp. 167
Edited by Peter Bramham and Wilf Murphy

Contents

Policy and Publics: Introduction

.... *Peter Bramham and Wilf Murphy*

I **Public Culture in Modernity**

The Economics of Culture in a Pluralistic Society

.... *Sylvia Harvey*

Mega-Events and Modernity: International
Expositions and the Construction
of Public Culture

.... *Maurice Roche*

II **Planning Public Sport and Leisure**

Progress towards Shaping a Safety Culture
in the Leisure Sector .... *John Hunter-Jones*

The Search for a Level Playing Field:
Planning and Sports Stadia
Development .... *Sarah McIntosh*
and Fiona Simpson

III **Leisure Capital, People and Places**

The Experience of Unemployment and the Use
of Leisure Capital .... *Francis Lobo*

Survival of Industry and the Country≠≠side, and
'Green' Leisure Development in
Post 'Resort Act 1987' Japan .... *Yohji Iwamoto*

IV **Leisure and City-Centre Regeneration**

Leisure Property as an Indicator of the Changing
Vitality and Viability of Town Centres:
A Case Study
.... *Martha Rowley and Neil Ravenscroft*
The Myth of the 24-hour City .... *John Spink and Peter Bramham*

CONSUMPTION AND PARTICIPATION: LEISURE, CULTURE AND COMMERCE

LSA Publication No. 64. ISBN: 0 906337 74 7 [2000]
Edited by Garry Whannel

Contents

Editors' Introduction .... *Malcolm Foley and Garry Whannel*

I   Public or Private Funding

Last Chance Lottery and the Millennium City .... *Graeme Evans*
The National Lottery in the UK: Sitting Pretty or Running Scared?
   The impact of having fun on developing coherent leisure
   policy in the public sector .... *Judy White*
A Cultural Enterprise? The Spread of Commercial
   Sponsorship .... *Garry Whannel and Deborah Philips*
UK Women's Attitudes to the National Lottery
   and the Implications for the Marketing of Gambling .... *Clare Brindley*

II   Commerce and Cultural Identities

The Contemporary Culture of Leisure in Japan .... *John Horne*
Consumer Sovereignty and Active Citizenship:
   An Analysis of Leisure World .... *Sharon Todd*
The Leisurization of Grocery Shopping .....
   .... *Cheryl A Cockburn-Wootten, Nigel J Morgan,*
                          Eleri Jones, Marilyn Thomas and Annette Pritchard
Dance Clubs and Disco: The Search for the Authentic Experience
   .... *Mike Lowe and Ian Atkin*
London's New Private Social Clubs: Personal Space
   in the Age of 'Hot Desking' .... *Martin Peacock*

III   Participation and Volunteering

Leisure and Culture; Consumers or Participants? .....
   Stan R. Parker
Volunteers in Uniformed Youth Organisations: A Study of the
   County of Sheffield Guide Association and the
   Sheffield City Scout Council .... *Nigel Jarvis and Lindsay King*
Volunteer Management and Satisfaction: A Case Study
   of the National Folk Festival .... *Julie Hodges*
Explanations for Declining Membership
   of the Guide Association .... *Lindsay King and Geoff Nichols*

GENDER, SPACE AND IDENTITY: LEISURE, CULTURE AND COMMERCE

LSA Publication No. 63. ISBN: 0 906337 73 9 [1998] pp. 191
Edited by Cara Aitchison and Fiona Jordan

Contents

Editors' Introduction .... *Cara Aitchison and Fiona Jordan*

I   The Construction of Gendered Space and Identity

Gender, Class and Urban Space: Public and Private
Space in Contemporary Urban Landscape .... *Liz Bondi*

Gay Tourism Destinations: Identity, Sponsorship
and Degaying .... *Annette Pritchard, Nigel J. Morgan,*
.... *Diane Sedgley and Andrew Jenkins*

Gendered (Bed)Spaces: The Culture and
Commerce of Women Only Tourism .... *Cara Aitchison*
.... *and Carole Reeves*

Shirley Valentine: Where Are You? .... *Fiona Jordan*
Sub-cultural Strategies in Patriarchal Leisure
Professional Cultures .... *Jean Yule*

II   Spaces, places, resistance and risk

Flexible Work, Disappearing Leisure? Feminist
Perspectives on Women's Leisure as Spaces for Resistance to Gender
Stereotypes .... *Eileen Green*

The Case for a Place of their Own: Queer Youth
and Urban Space .... *Arnold Grossman*

Ecofeminism, 'Risk' and Women's
Experiences of Landscape .... *Barbara Humberstone*
.... *and Di Collins*

Sex and Politics: Sites of Resistance in
Women's Football .... *Jayne Caudwell*

Gay Tourist Space and Sexual Risk Behaviour ......
.... *Simon Forrest and Stephen Clift*

THE PRODUCTION AND CONSUMPTION OF SPORT CULTURES: LEISURE, CULTURE AND COMMERCE

LSA Publication No. 62. ISBN: 0 906337 72 0 [1998] pp. 178
Edited by Udo Merkel, Gill Lines, Ian McDonald

Contents

Editors' Introduction .... *Udo Merkel, Gill Lines* .... *and Ian McDonald*

I   The Production Process

The Impact of Globalisation on Cricket
in India .... *Ian McDonald*

Modernising Tradition?: The Changing Face
of British Football ......
.... *Raymond Boyle and Richard Haynes*

Sack the Board, Sack the Board, Sack the Board:
Accountancy and Accountability
in Contemporary English Professional
Football Culture .... *Stephen Wagg*

FIFA and the Marketing of World Football ......
.... *John Sugden and Alan Tomlinson*

As Charmless as Chain-saws?:
Managing jet ski use in the UK ......
.... *Jenny Anderson and David Johnson*

II   The Consumption Process

What Happens if Nothing Happens? Staging Euro 96 ......
.... *Vincent Miller and Jeremy Valentine*

A Case Study of Adolescent Media Consumption
during the Summer of Sport 1996 .... *Gill Lines*

Read the Paper, Play the Sport: A Decade
of Gender Change ......
.... *Kay Biscomb, Kay Flatten and Hilary Matheson*

Mediawatch: Mountain Biking, the Media and the
1996 Olympics .... *Graham Berridge and Julian Kaine*

TOURISM AND VISITOR ATTRACTIONS: LEISURE, CULTURE AND COMMERCE

LSA Publication No 61. ISBN: 0 906337 71 2 [1998] pp. 211
Edited by Neil Ravenscroft, Deborah Philips and Marion Bennett

Contents

Editors' Introduction ......

.... *Neil Ravenscroft, Deborah Philips and Marion Bennett*

I   Work, Leisure and Culture

Contrasting Roles in Business Development for the
    Tourism and Leisure Industries: the case of
    Dublin and Glasgow .... *J John Lennon*

Volunteering in an Urban Museums Service:
    A Definitional Reassessment .... *Margaret Graham*
                                                                                           and Malcolm Foley

II   Identity and Commodification

The Legal Boundaries of Tourism: The State versus
    the Marketplace in Defining the Tourist ... . *Brian Simpson*

Activities, Holidays and Activity Holidays
    in Scotland .... *Malcolm Foley and Gavin Reid*

Carnival and Control: The Commodification
    of the Carnivalesque at Disneyland .... *Deborah Philips*

Re-defining the Role of Trading in a Museum Service ......

.... *Gayle McPherson, Malcolm Foley and Alastair Durie*

Leisure Consumption and the United Kingdom (UK) Zoo ......

.... *Philippa Hunter-Jones and Cheryl Hayward*

The Current Growth of Jewish Museums in Europe
    .... *David Clark*

Consuming the Countryside: Postmodern Hedonism
    or Responsible Reflexivity? ......

.... *Jim Butterfield and Jonathan Long*

Rural Recreation: Perspectives on Landholder Attitudes
    and Public Access to Private Rural Lands .... *John Jenkins*

III   Representation

Coastal Tourism as Comparative Consumption of
    Cultural Landscapes .... *Daniel O'Hare*

From 'Gayety and Diversion' to 'Developer's Lorry' — Representations of Bath
    .... *Judith E. Brown*

History as Leisure: Business and Pleasure
    at Beamish .... *Jennifer Iles*

Index

LEISURE PLANNING IN TRANSITORY SOCIETIES

LSA Publication No. 58. ISBN: 0 906337 70 4
Edited by Mike Collins; pp 218

Contents

Editor's Introduction.Time, Space and Planning; Leisure in Transitory Societies

    Mike Collins v

Leeds: Re-imaging the 24 hour European City

    John Spink and Peter Bramham 1

Historic Cities, Green Belt Planning Policy and the Provision of
    Sport and Recreation

    John Tabor 11

Leisure, Migration and the Stagnant Village

    Sean Gammon 27

Countryside Recreation Policy in England: Implications of the
    1995 Rural White Paper

    Neil Ravenscroft 37

Mountain Biking and Access to the Countryside

    Graham Berridge 51

Riding on a Wave? Water Recreation on Privatised and Public Inland Resources in England

    Michael F. Collins 69

An Analysis of a Leisure Industry Sector: Young People and Watersports

    Jenny Anderson 85

Sport and Recreation in the Tight City

    Hugo van der Poel 101

The Playground Movement in the Netherlands

    Peter Selten and Carlinde Adriaanse 117

Time-Space Research as a Tool for Management of Visitors to
    the National Park "De Hoge Veluwe" (The High Veluwe)

    Marcel Jansen, Jan W. te Kloeze

    and Han van der Voet 135

Cultural Imperialism, Globalisation and the Development of Sport in Zimbabwe

    Clare Kitts 159

Children and Land Use in the Kenyan Countryside: Turbo
    Division Case Study

    C. M. Syallow 183

Private Sector Recreation Services in Wroclaw at a Time of
    Constitutional Transformation

    Tadeusz Fak and Dorota Opoka 189

LEISURE, TIME AND SPACE: MEANINGS AND VALUES IN PEOPLE'S LIVES

LSA Publication No. 57. ISBN: 0 906337 68 2 [1998] pp. 198 + IV
Edited by Sheila Scraton

Contents

Introduction .... *Sheila Scraton*

I   ACCELERATING LEISURE? LEISURE, TIME AND SPACE IN A TRANSITORY SOCIETY

Beyond work and spend: Time, leisure and consumption
[summary] .... *Juliet Schor*

Tourist Landscapes: Accelerating transformations .... *Adri Dietvorst*

II MEANINGS AND VALUES

Ethics in leisure — an agenda for research
.... *Mike McNamee and Celia Brackenridge*

Camping and caravanning and the place of cultural meaning
in leisure practices .... *David Crouch and Jan te Kloeze*

Leisure, play and work in post-modern societies:
Liminal experiences in male adolescents ... . *Dirck van Bekkum*

Authenticity and real virtuality .... *Frans Schouten*

Half crown houses: The crisis of the country house in post-war romances .... *Deborah Philips*

III TRANSFORMATIONS OF TIME AND SPACE

Electronic manipulation of time and space in television sport
.... *Garry Whannel*

'Staying in' and 'Going out': Elderly women, leisure and the postmodern city ......*Sheila Scraton, Peter Bramham, ...* and Beccy Watson

Leisure in Bulgaria: Changes and problems .... *Maria Vodenska*

New lives for old: Young people in post-independence
Armenia and Georgia .... *Kenneth Roberts, Aahron Adibekian and Levan Tarkhnishvili*

IV LEISURE PARTICIPATION IN TIME AND SPACE

Inappropriate or inevitable? The role of the law in planning
for the illicit leisure activities of young people .... *Brian Simpson*

Play through the Lens: Children's photography of
after-school play .... *Chris Cunningham and Margaret Jones*

Participation in free-time sport recreation activities: Comparison of Gdansk Region,
Poland and Guildford, United Kingdom
.... *Barbara Marciszewska*

Leisure preferences of Polish students with disabilities ......
.... *Wieslaw Siwiński*

LEISURE, TOURISM AND ENVIRONMENT (I) SUSTAINABILITY AND ENVIRONMENTAL POLICIES

LSA Publication No. 50 Part I; ISBN 0 906337 64 X
Edited by Malcolm Foley, David McGillivray and Gayle McPherson (1999);

Contents

Editors' Introduction .... *Malcolm Foley,*
          David McGillivray and Gayle McPherson

I   ENVIRONMENT, INVESTMENT AND EDUCATION

Leisure and Green Political Thought .... *Jim Butterfield*
European Leisure and Tourism Investment Incentives: Changing
          Rationales in theUK and European Community .... *Graeme Evans*
Social Paradigms, Living Styles and Resource Policies
          .... *Thomas L. Burton and Robert Kassian*
Professional Hosts' Perceptions of Garden Festival Wales:
          A Qualitative Approach to Festival Impact Studies
          .... *Fiona Williams and David Botterill*
Greening the Curriculum: Opportunities in Teaching Tourism .... *Angela Phelps*

II   ENVIRONMENT AND POLICIES FOR SPORT

Quiet: Please: Sport in the British Countryside .... *Mike Collins*
The Hosting of International Games in Canada: Economic and Ideological Ambitions
          David Whitson and Donald Macintosh
The Social Benefit of Leisure Park Development: Environmental Economics of Fukuoka
          Dome, Japan
          Koh Sasaki and Munehiko Harada

III   ENVIRONMENT AND THE IDEA OF SUSTAINABILITY

The Nova Scotia Envirofor Process: Towards Sustainable Forest Management or
          Placation by theMultinationals? .... *Glyn Bissix*
Measuring Sustainability in Tourism: Lessons from a Study of Chepstow for Other
          Walled Towns in Europe .... *David M. Bruce and Marion J. Jackson*
Eco or Ego Tourism? Sustainable Tourism in Question .... *Brian Wheeller*
Outside In and Inside Out: Participatory Action Research with an Embryonic Social
          Movement Working for Change in Tourism .... *David Botterill*
'Sustainable Tourism' — Or More a Matter of Sustainable Societies? .... *David Leslie*

LEISURE, TOURISM AND ENVIRONMENT (II) PARTICIPATION, PERCEPTIONS AND PREFERENCES

LSA Publication No. 50 (Part II) ISBN: 0 906337 69 0; pp. 177+xii
Edited by Malcolm Foley, Matt Frew and Gayle McPherson

Contents

Editors' Introduction

I.   **MARKETING DREAMS OR NIGHTMARES**
Cultured Tourists? The Significance and Signification
of European Cultural Tourism .... *Greg Richards*
Alternative and Mass Tourists:
Will They Ever Go Away? .... *Brian Davies*
Correlations between Clusters based on the
Ragheb and Beard Leisure Motivation Scale
and the Attributes of Desired Holiday Locations .... *Chris Ryan*
The Effects of Development on the Visitor's Perception
of Unique Natural Resources
.... *Alan Jubenville and William G. Workman*

II.   **TRENDS AND TRANSITIONS**
Tourism in Our Own World: Scottish Residents' Perceptions
of Scotland as a Holiday Destination .... *Brian Hay*
Patterns of Tourist Role Preference Across the Life Course ....
.... *Heather Gibson and Andrew Yiannakis*
Dynamics in Camping Styles? The Background
of Change and/or Repetitive Behaviour
of the Camper in the Netherlands ....
.... *Erik Hout, Jan te Kloeze and Han van der Voet*

III. **DISCOURSE AND SELF-DISCOVERY**
"Provincial Paradise": Urban Tourism and City Imaging
outside the Metropolis .... *David Rowe and Deborah Stevenson*
The Influence of Wilderness Experience on
Self-Actualization .... *Won Sop Shin*
From Bushmen to Bondi Beach: The Social Construction
of 'Male≠stream' Images of Australia in Tourism Advertising*Georgia Young and Peter Brown*
The Travelog in Popular Women's Magazines ....
.... *Beverley Ann Simmons*

LEISURE: MODERNITY, POSTMODERNITY AND LIFESTYLES

LSA Publications No. 48 (LEISURE IN DIFFERENT WORLDS Volume I)
Edited by Ian Henry (1994); ISBN: 0 906337   52 6, pp. 375+

Contents

Modernity, Postmodernity and Lifestyles: Introduction
Ian Henry

I: Modernity, Postmodernity and Theory in Leisure Studies

Leisure and the Dreamworld of Modernity
>> Chris Rojek 3

Europe's Unification Project and the Ethics of Leisure Studies
>> Eric Corijn 13

Los Angeles and the Denial of Leisure in the Entertainment Capital
of the World
>> John Fiske 27

'Leisure'?According To Who?
>> Louise Bricknell 39

The Figurational Sociology of Sport and Leisure Revisited
>> David Jary and John Horne 53

II: Leisure, the City and the Nation-State

Leisure and the Postmodern City
>> Peter Bramham and John Spink 83

Same City, Different Worlds? Women's Leisure in Two
Contrasting Areas of Tyneside
>> Graham Mowl and John Towner 105

Changing Times, Changing Policies
>> Peter Bramham, Jim Butterfield,
>> Jonathan Long and Chris Wolsey 125

Cultural Activities in Greece:Tradition or Modernity?
>> Alex Deffner 135

Young People and Football in Liverpool
>> Ken Roberts 157

Leisure Systems in Europe and Their Economic and Cultural
Impact in Comparative Perspective
>> Walter Tokarski 173

III: Social Stratification and Leisure Lifestyles

Ageing and Mass Media
>> Concepción Maiztegui Oñate 181

Leisure and the Elderly: A Different World?
        Alan Clarke 189
Qualitative Assessment of Work and Leisure in the Lives of
    Retired Male Faculty Returning to Work
        Gene C. Bammel, Rebecca Hancock,
        and Lei Lane Burrus-Bammel 203
A Life Course Perspective and Sports Participation Patterns
    among Middle-aged Japanese
        Junya Fujimoto and Munehiko Harada 209
No Room for Children —The Changing Dimensions of Provision
    for Children's Play in Urban Areas
        Barbara Hendricks 217
'Having the Time of Our Lives' — Is Leisure an Appropriate
    Concept for Midlife Women?
        Myra Betschild and Eileen Green 227
An Integrated Model of Women's Leisure Constraints
        Karla A. Henderson and M. Deborah Bialeschki 243
Factors Influencing Ethnic Minority Groups' Participation in Sport
        Bob Carroll 261
Leisure Constraints, Attitudes and Behaviour of People with
    Activity Restricting Physical Disabilities
        Rick Rollins and Doug Nichols 277
Differences in Leisure Behaviour of the Poor and the Rich
    in the Netherlands
        Johan van Ophem and Kees de Hoog 291

IV: Changing Leisure Forms and Postmodernity
Collective Self-generated Consumption: Leisure, Space and Cultural
    Identity in Late Modernity
        David Crouch and Alan Tomlinson 309
Intimations of Postmodernity: the Cocktail Cult
    between the Wars
        A. V. Seaton 323
It began with the Piton. The Challenge to British Rock
    Climbing in a Post-Modernist Framework
        Dan Morgan 341
The Modularisation of Daily Life
        Hugo van der Poel 355